PSYCHOLOGY AND SOCIETY

PSYCHOLOGY AND SOCIETY

Radical Theory and Practice

Edited by

Ian Parker and Russell Spears

Pluto Press

LONDON • CHICAGO, IL.

First published 1996 by Pluto Press
345 Archway Road, London N6 5AA
and 1436 West Randolph, Chicago, Illinois 60607, USA

British Library Cataloguing in Publication Data
A catalogue record for this book is available from the British Library

ISBN 07453 0880 5 hbk

Library of Congress Cataloging in Publication Data
Psychology and society : radical theory and practice /
edited by Ian Parker and Russell Spears.
p.   cm.
Includes bibliographical references and index.
ISBN 0–7453–0880–5
1. Social psychology. I. Parker, Ian, 1956–
II. Spears, Russell.
HM251.P8334 1996
302—dc20   96–8066
                                   CIP

Designed, typeset and produced for Pluto Press by
Chase Production Services, Chipping Norton, OX7 5QR
Printed in the EC by T.J. Press, Padstow

Dedication

The original title of this edited collection was *Psychology and Marxism: Coexistence and Contradiction*. A final review was to be written by the revolutionary activist and scholar Ernest Mandel, but a serious heart attack forced him to withdraw from the project. Worse was to come, in events emblematic perhaps of the crisis of socialism in these new times, and the end of an era of struggle against capitalism, as well as the small ironies of academic life. On 20 July 1995, our publisher approached us with the suggestion of changing the title. Booksellers, it seems, now have little confidence in their abilities to sell a book with Marxism in the title. We were very sad to learn later that Mandel had died, also on the 20 July. He was an inspiration to many comrades dedicated to practical and theoretical work against oppression, and his commitment continues to provide example and hope. We dedicate this book to Ernest Mandel (1923–1995).

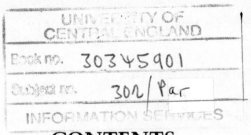
CONTENTS

CONTRIBUTORS

Kum-Kum Bhavnani is an Associate Professor at the University of California at Santa Barbara, USA, in the Department of Sociology. She is trained as a social developmental psychologist and now works in feminist and cultural studies. She is the author of *Talking Politics* (Cambridge University Press) and co-editor, with Ann Phoenix, of *Shifting Identities, Shifting Racisms* (Sage). Her academic interests now lie in cultural studies, and she is presently writing a book on 'race', gender, celebrity and class in the American popular imaginary.

Ben Bradley is a Reader in the Department of Psychology and Sociology at James Cook University of North Queensland, Australia. His main research interest is in refashioning psychological understandings of development to be means of promoting social change. To this end he is currently working with local communities to develop new practices of child and maternal care. His writings include *Visions of Infancy: A Critical Introduction to Child Psychology* (1989) and *The New Psychology* (in prep.). In 1993 he co-edited with Bill Kessen a Special Issue of the journal *Theory and Psychology* on The Future of Developmental Theory.

Mark Burton is Head of Development and Clinical Services with the Joint Learning Disability Service of Mancunian Community Health and City of Manchester Social Services Department, UK. His interests are in social and organisational change in relation to service provision for people with significant intellectual disabilities. He has used frameworks from critical theory to explore and develop theory and practice in this area.

Angela Y. Davis is a Professor of History of Consciousness at the University of California, Santa Cruz, USA. A trained philosopher, Davis studied with Herbert Marcuse at Johann Wolfgang von Goethe University in Frankfurt and at the University of California, San Diego, and now works in critical race theory and Black studies. Her essays and articles have appeared in numerous journals, both academic and popular, and she is the author of five books, including *Angela Davis, An Autobiography, Women, Race & Class*, and a forthcoming volume on Black women's music and social consciousness. Her next project will focus on the US criminal justice system.

Liam Greenslade studied psychology at the Universities of Manchester, Sussex, and Mannheim and is the author of several papers on the role of Volosinov in social psychology. For the past five years he has worked at the Institute of Irish Studies, University of Liverpool, UK, where he has researched the health and well being of Irish migrants in Britain.

Benjamin Harris is a Professor of Psychology at the University of Wisconsin, Parkside, USA, with a research interest in the political history of psychology. He is best known for his studies of myth-making in the history of behaviourism (e.g. his article 'Whatever Happened to Little Albert'). He was a founding officer of the Forum for the History of Human Science, and is a Fellow of the American Psychological Society. He is currently writing a book entitled *When Freud Met Marx*.

Grahame Hayes is a Lecturer at the University of Natal, Durban, South Africa. He was a founding editor of the anti-apartheid journal in South Africa *Psychology and Society* (PINS) in 1983, and is currently editor of PINS. He is writing a book on *Wulf Sachs and the history of psychoanalysis in South Africa*.

R.D. Hinshelwood is Clinical Director/Consultant Psychotherapist with overall responsibility for the Cassel Hospital, UK. This is a pioneering therapeutic community which applies psychoanalytic ideas to the whole organisation of the Hospital, and its parts. The Hospital treats severe personality disorders of all ages, including whole families. He has worked in or with therapeutic communities for more than 25 years, studying methods by which psychoanalytic understanding of the unconscious can be used in groups and institutions to create healthier social milieux. Much of his experience is recorded in papers, which include 'Projective Identification and Marx's concept of man' (*International Journal of Psycho-Analysis*) and 'The social possession of the individual' (in *Crises of the Self*). His current work is eventually to develop a psychoanaltyic approach to social psychology based on object-relations and Kleinian ideas and practice.

Paul Hoggett is Professor of Politics at University of West of England, Bristol, UK. Formerly a mental health worker, he was a founder editorial board member of the journal *Free Associations*. He is a group relations consultant and author of *Partisans in an Uncertain World* (Free Association Books).

Lois Holzman is on the faculty of Empire State College, State University of New York and the East Side Institute for Short Term Psychotherapy also in NYC. She directs the Institute's laboratory elementary school, the Barbara Taylor School where a Vygotskian, developmental educational approach is implemented. She is the co-author with Fred Newman of *Lev Vygotsky: Revolutionary Scientist* (Routledge, 1993) and has written numerous articles on Vygotsky's contributions to a new developmental practice in education and in psychotherapy, the most recent being 'Creating developmental learning environments: A Vygotskian practice' to appear in *School Psychology International* (1995). She is also a guest lecturer at Eureka University of Moscow which is involved in retraining teachers from the republics of the former Soviet Union and democratising education.

Bernardo Jiménez-Domínguez is a Professor of Social Psychology and a Researcher with the Centro de Estudios Urbanos at the University of Guadalajara, Mexico, where he has been head of the Department of Social Psychology. He is coordinator of the Social Psychology series for University of Guadalajara Press 'Aportes Criticos a la Psicologia en Latinoamerica', and is a member of the editorial committee for the journal *Asentamientos*. He is Professor of Urban Psychology in the Urban Design Masters programme. He was born in Colombia, and studied psychology in the National University and the University of the Andes in Bogota, where he was also a Professor of Psychology.

Carolyn Kagan is Principal Lecturer in Social Psychology at Manchester Metropolitan University, UK. Her interests are in social change in communities and organisations with a focus on vulnerable people. She has developed a model of interpersonal skills in its social context and used this in books on health care and on the social integration for people with intellectual disabilities.

Wolfgang Maiers is on the Faculty of Philosophy and Social Sciences and the Psychological Institute at the Free University of Berlin, Germany. He is on the Executive Committee of the International Society for Theoretical Psychology and on the editorial staff of *Forum Kritische Psychologie*. He was co-editor with Charles Tolman of *Critical Psychology: Toward an Historical Science of the Subject* (New York: Cambridge University Press, 1991).

Mike Michael is a lecturer at the School of Independent Studies/Centre for Science Studies and Science Policy at Lancaster University, UK. His recent publications include articles on the animal experimentation controversy, postmodernity and critical social psychology, and the public understanding of science. He has recently published a book on the construction of identity.

Ian Parker is Professor of Psychology at Bolton Institute, UK. He is author of *The Crisis in Modern Social Psychology* (1989) and *Discourse Dynamics* (1992), and co-author of *Qualitative Methods in Psychology* (1994, with P. Banister, E. Burman, M. Taylor and C. Tindall), *Carrying Out Investigations in Psychology* (1995, with J. Foster) and *Deconstructing Psychopathology* (1995, with D. Harper, E. Georgaca, T. McLaughlin and M. Stowell-Smith). He is co-editor of *Deconstructing Social Psychology* (1990, with J. Shotter) and *Discourse Analytic Research* (1993, with E. Burman).

Edward S. Reed is Associate Professor of Psychology at Franklin and Marshall College, USA. He is author of *James J. Gibson & The Psychology of Perception* (Yale: 1988), *Encountering the world: Towards an Ecological Psychology* (Oxford: 1996), and *Defending experience: A Philosophy for the Post-Modern world* (Yale: 1996).

Stephen Reicher is a Senior Lecturer in Psychology at the University of Exeter, UK. He has published widely on a series of issues relating to group processes, most notably crowd behaviour and the construction of social categories.

Martin Roiser is a Senior Lecturer in Psychology at Thames Valley University, UK, teaching on undergraduate and post-graduate courses. He studies the history of movements carrying out social and psychological research that have existed outside the academy or on the fringes, for instance; psychoanalysis, the Frankfurt Institute, the Mass-Observation movement, and the anti-psychiatry movement. He is an active trade unionist and a member of the Socialist Workers' Party.

Jane Selby is based at James Cook University, Australia. She has been seconded to train therapists for a local clinic for abused children and their families. Her current main research areas are Aboriginal and Islander health, and she is currently evaluating childcare provision in Cape York and the Torres Strait Islands. Her work integrates clinical, research and theoretical dimensions of psychology in facilitating the development and empowerment of disadvantaged individuals and groups. Amongst other things she has published in *Theory and Psychology*, and in Australian Aboriginal outlets.

Russell Spears is Professor of Psychlogy in the Department of Social Psychology at the University of Amsterdam, the Netherlands. He combines research on social stereotyping, intergroup relations and social influence processes with interests in ideology and power (especially as applied to the new communications technology), and has also contributed to debates in critical social psychology. Since 1994 he has been chief editor of the *British Journal of Social Psychology*.

Charles W. Tolman is Professor of Psychology at the University of Victoria, Canada. He teaches courses in history of psychology and psychological theory. Author of *Psychology, Society, and Subjectivity* (Routledge, 1994). Editor of *Positivism in Psychology: Historical and Contemporary Problems* (Springer-Verlag, 1992). Co-editor with Wolfgang Maiers of *Critical Psychology: Toward an Historical Science of the Subject* (Cambridge University Press, 1991). Author of the article 'Critical Social Psychology' in A.S. Manstead and M. Hewstone (eds), *The Blackwell Encyclopedia of Social Psychology* (Oxford: Blackwell, 1994).

Jerome D. Ulman is a professor in the Department of Special Education at Ball State University, USA, where he directs the doctoral program and teaches courses in the areas of behaviourological technology and behaviour disorders. His research interests include experimental methodology, the application of behaviourological technology in special education, computer technology, verbal behaviour, and the sociocultural implications of the natural science of behaviour. He is currently treasurer of The International Behaviorology Association and Associate Editor of *Behavior and Social Issues*. His recent publications include 'Experimental Analysis of Negative vs Positive Rules in the "Good Behavior Game"' (with Mary Fran Johnson and Doreen Vieitez) in *Behaviorology* (Fall 1993); 'The Ulman-Skinner Letters' in *Behaviorology* (Spring 1993); and 'Marxist Theory and Behavior Therapy', a chapter in *Theories in Behavior Therapy* edited by William O'Donohue and Leonard Krasner (in press).

Carla Willig is a Lecturer in Psychology at Middlesex University, UK. She has been working, with Martin Roiser, on a Marxist history of the Authoritarian Personality research. She has also done discourse analytic work around HIV/AIDS and condom use which has been published in the *Journal of Community and Applied Social Psychology* and elsewhere. She is currently conducting research into the meanings and practices of trust in romantic relationships.

Robert M. Young is a psychotherapist in private practice in London and Visiting Professor at the Centre for Psychotherapeutic Studies, University of Sheffield, UK. He was a founder of the *Radical Science Journal* and edits *Science as Culture* and *Free Associations*. He and Les Levidow edited *Science, Technology and the Labour Process: Marxist Studies*. His writings include *Mind, Brain and Adaptation, Darwin's Metaphor, Mental Space* and *Whatever Happened to Human Nature?*

MARXIST THESES AND PSYCHOLOGICAL THEMES

Russell Spears and Ian Parker

The relationship between Marxism and Psychology is marked by tensions that can be understood by using Psychology or by using Marxism. Were we to opt for psychological theories to understand the connections between the two domains we might focus on the appeal of Marxism as an ideology once harnessed by various totalitarian regimes, or examine the irrational attachment by some individuals to a system finally discredited, or we might describe Marxism as the hobby of misfits inside and outside the academic institutions. A host of psychological theories stand ready for deployment to assist in this enterprise, and the only thing we could be sure of is that somewhere along the line with each of them we would succeed, whether we liked it or not, in explicitly or implicitly pathologising those who adhere to Marxism as a theoretical framework. For Psychology, the political is always only personal, and a politics that sees the personal as rooted in social relations, as Marxism does, is usually seen as a personal problem.

Psychology

We work in an academic discipline which attempts to comprehend the behaviour and experience of the individual. In some formulations it is the 'science of mental life' (Miller, 1962), in others the notion of 'science' is thought unable to capture the essential nature of human action (Koch, 1964), and in others the phrase 'mental life' is thought too speculative to help further the prediction and control of behaviour (Skinner, 1971). Psychology is more than an academic discipline, however, for its theories filter out into the everyday world and its practitioners employ psychological concepts in a range of contexts from advertising to asylums. A useful term which encompasses, captures the set of theories and practices which reproduces this society from the base up, from the individual out is the 'psy-complex' (Rose, 1985).

In this chapter we will provide an overview of the tensions in that set of theories and practices from within a Marxist framework, and here the focus is on Psychology as an ideology harnessed to a multiplicity of contradictory interests (some totalitarian). We will examine the hold which the discipline has exercised on those who believe they have a scientific system to hand, and we conceive of Psychology as the activity of professional and amateur adherents of the psy-complex in Western society and those caught in its grip in other parts of the world. We are aware that two problems emerge in this first formulation of our task. The first is to do with the nature of one or other of the terms 'Marxism' and 'Psychology' as the truth (with the other as falsehood, or 'false-consciousness'); the second is to do with our own personal investment in the psy-complex (as 'psychologists'). To address the first problem: we do believe that most Psychology is false, but that Marxism is not, as Lenin once claimed, 'all powerful because it is true'.

Marxism

We see Marxism as a theoretical research programme and political movement devoted simultaneously to comprehending the historical development and dynamics of society through an attention to underlying structures of economic exploitation, and to revolutionising social relations through the praxis of the oppressed and their allies. While the central category is that of class, the architecture of capitalist society in the over-industrialised world, of the bureaucratic remnants of the Stalinist states in some countries, and of the colonised Third World, are also locked into place by structures of patriarchal and racist domination. The theoretical framework of Marxism for radical psychologists includes, as interconnected sets of analysis, an account of commodification, alienation and individualisation. This, of course, is where Psychology comes in, for it is the illusion of individuality that the discipline most thoroughly and determinedly sustains. This is also where we should address the second problem: where we are in the web of the psy-complex. We do not believe that a 'Marxist Psychology' is possible (and this, in part, is due to the continually changing 'nature' of the 'individual'), but we do believe that some varieties of Psychology are compatible with Marxism (provisionally, either as theories of change or tactically as catalysts of change).

SCIENCE AND METHOD

Questions of science and method are primary to both Marxism and Psychology, and thus promise some common ground on which problems of compatibility can be better understood. If historical materialism provides a foundation for understanding social and psychological ways of being, the next question is how we can arrive at such an understanding. A recurring issue has been the extent to which Psychology (and social science generally) can use as its model scientific investigation in the natural sciences. Bhaskar (1989) has called this the primal problem of the social sciences, and historically it has resulted in two basic camps. On the one hand there is the scientific tradition, which assumes that social behaviour is law-like, and that such regularities can be revealed by controlled observation according to positivist principles. On the other hand, the hermeneutic tradition sees radical differences between the social and natural worlds and their subject matter. On this view, the goal of social sciences is the understanding of the meaning of human action in terms of purposes and reasons, so that Psychology entails the interpretation of individual meaning. The role of intention and agency would seem to rule out the analysis and explanation of behaviour in terms of general causal laws. This philosophical divide is just as characteristic of strands in Marxist thought and is reflected in the contrast between the 'scientific' Marxism of the 'dialectical materialists' (e.g. Engels, Bukharin, Plekhanov) and the humanistic Marxism of Lukács and the Frankfurt school. Marxists such as Lukács attracted to a more humanist reading have drawn on writings of the early Marx, whereas those of the more scientific camp justify their position with reference to the later works (e.g. *Capital*). Lukács (1971) came to see science as an ally of capitalism and 'an ideological weapon of the bourgeoisie', as the ultimate expression of reification within capitalism.

The position of Lukács and others must be seen partly as a response to the orthodox Marxism of the Second International and the Stalinist diamat which followed. The effect of the positivist ('scientistic') emphasis in these strands of Marxism implied that the revolution would take its natural course as the productive forces developed, sharpening the contradictions of capitalism. Such historicism had disastrous consequences. It was used by the bureaucracies of the worker's states to prescribe approaches which paralysed class struggle and relegated agency and activity to the role of epiphenomena; sometimes characterising such activity as 'ultra-leftism' and sometimes swinging into ultra-leftism itself. In these terms, such vulgar 'Marxist' scientific underpinnings could quite genuinely be interpreted as ideological, as serving prevailing class interests. Lukács, and the writers of the Frankfurt School whom he strongly influenced, showed the dangers of an uncritical view of science and 'rationality' generally and how this can be used to reinforce rather than undermine exploitative social relations.

Increasingly, radical philosophers of science have rejected positivism and argued for a 'realist' theory of science (e.g. Bhaskar, 1989; Greenwood, 1989; Harré and Madden, 1975). Realism allows for deep explanation in terms of underlying structures and relations rather than in terms of the superficial surface regularities of positivism: in short it is wise to ideological appearance and reification, while providing a firm materialist grounding. The move to a realist position also helps to resolve the hermeneutic objections to a scientific approach to Psychology and to undermine the clear gulf between the natural and the social sciences implied by this anti-naturalist position. Nevertheless, there are dangers of elevating realism to a philosophy of science, which stands outside the world. A realist programme for Psychology could easily itself degenerate into a sort of 'deep positivism' which sought essence in the static nature of people or things, rather than in their creative activity and in historically situated social relations. This danger arguably emanates from the very split between epistemology and ontology, and we now turn to consider ways in which psychology has exploited such splits and divisions.

CONCEPTUAL SPLITS AND DISCIPLINARY BOUNDARIES

Divide and rule is maintained in Psychology by conceptual splits, dualisms and through the specification of discrete and competing domains. The splits and dualisms manifest themselves in a number of ways and even populate 'radical' and 'Marxist' analyses. The very distinctions between the expressive and the practical order (Harré), the natural and the social (Bhaskar), and epistemology and ontology, arguably serve to preserve the Kantian notion of 'two worlds', driving a wedge between the unity of theory and practice, the dialectic of theory and metatheory (Gunn, 1988). Splitting elements up for the purpose of (causal) analysis implies both the separability and primacy of particular causes, which implies in turn an external and determinist relation, requiring a transcendental explanatory position (a philosophy of science). However, relations can be seen as dialectically or internally produced, by relations of reflexivity and entailment within the concrete 'totality', without recourse or reference to an external position. Causalism, the uncritical theorising of an invariant relation of 'independent' to 'dependent' variables is deeply ingrained in Psychology. It provides security and closure, but one that describes a static and predefined world, simply waiting to be discovered by a positivist science. When we reject the external or transcendental position, and adopt internal or immanent critique, everything is up for grabs, so that which represents uncertainty and insecurity to the positivist offers the prospects of positive social change, of shaping reality, to the Marxist.

Conceptual splits service Psychology in other ways, not least through the 'individual-society' dualism. For Psychology, its object is the individual; the individual split from activity with others. An enduring problem which has affected all forms of 'radical Psychology' has been the nature of the relationship between the individual and the social. The Cartesian tradition and pervasive individualism within Psychology generate a model of the individual as pre-existing and apart from the social, whilst the social is often treated as a set of independent variables external, rather than as contained in the individual, as internal to perception and behaviour. Marxism points us from the outside in, not the reverse (which is not to deny that there is such a thing as human agency). Our starting point then is that the social does not have to be used in contrast to the individual, or a background against which individuals act, but can be seen as constituting their very being. It should be noted that certain trends within Western and Analytic Marxism are themselves not immune from Cartesian tendencies; the poststructuralist emphasis on intersubjectivity can be interpreted partly as a reaction to the individualistic elements within Western Marxism (Dews, 1987). On the other hand, structural Marxism tends to regard the individual as completely enveloped by and determined by social structure.

One alternative to viewing individuals as passive bearers of structures is to see structures themselves as collective agents which require active participation to keep them alive, and which enable social resistance and change as well as social reproduction. In other words, an understanding of the sociality of the individual should not be based on a bland social or liberal consensus, but on social division and difference. The notion that individuals can and do consititute themselves in terms of their collective agency as members of their class or group has a necessary heritage in Marxist theory and political practice, and this has been reflected, sometimes deliberately, in the psychological concept of social identity (Reicher, 1987; cf. Callinicos, 1987). This forms not only a psychological bridge between individual and collective, agent and structure, but more fundamentally, a recognition of the social dimensions of self.

The duality of structure as including agency (Giddens, 1984) has implications for method as well as theory in Marxism. Classically, Marxism has been distinguished from other forms of reductionist science in recognising the explanatory potential of social structures or groups and the relations between these (Levine, Sober and Wright, 1987). However, there has been resistance within Marxism as well as within orthodox Psychology on this issue. Analytic Marxists argue that the explanation of social and historical phenomena can be reduced to the properties of and relations between individuals ('methodological individualism'). Methodological individualism not only denies the explanatory force of social structures as a level of analysis *sui generis*, it is also ignores the characteristically social dimensions of being and behaviour which feed into it (e.g. Tajfel, 1979). Such an individualistic stance not only threatens the distinctively social cast to Marxist analysis and explanation, but also undoes much progressive critique of Psychology.

Important bridges between the individual and the social are the shared systems of meanings communicated through the language which structure our experience. Language is not simply used passively to generate consensus; class and other social divisions mean that the symbolic forms used to interpret social relations will always reflect and generate conflict, and this requires an understanding of difference, as well as of shared meaning and understandings. Whilst language and discourse may form the social medium for ideology and social reproduction, it also provides a site for resistance. A rejection of methodological individualism and, instead, attention to the social and discursive bases of being would appear to be necessary to Marxist analyses of the split between the individual and the social. We now consider the disciplinary boundaries which have institutionalised some of these analytic splits, recuperating and compartmentalising Marxism in the process.

Essence: Biologism and Humanism

The study of biology is necessary to a properly materialist understanding of the person (Timpanaro, 1976). Essentialism and humanism in both their explicit and implicit guises inform most psychological theorising, but the task of a Marxist critique would be to define the nature of human nature as a foundation for Psychology. Two fundamental questions, then, for both Psychology and Marxism are: what does it mean to be human? and what does it mean to have a human nature? Taking the human psyche as a starting point for the analysis of self or social behaviour inevitably sits uneasily with a historical materialism where economic categories and social relations have primacy. Psychology meanwhile has taken the biological and humanistic bases much more easily for granted, if not as its very building blocks.

Although Psychology appears to be characterised by such diverse essentialist approaches as biological reductionism and humanism, they are both premised to varying extents on Cartesian notions of being, as taking the subject as privileged, unitary, and preformed. The philosophical heritage in which Psychology has been embedded encourages an individualistic view of the person, abstracted from historical and social context, reifying what is found at a particular moment as the essence of people in general. In forging a break not just with these underlying philosophical traditions, but with philosophy *per se*, there is a sense in which Marxism raises fundamental questions about the viability of Psychology as a discipline. Given this basic antagonism, it is hardly surprising that many Marxists have apparently tried to write the individual, the subject, out of history altogether. Structural Marxists such as Althusser have asserted that 'history is a process without a subject', seeing individuals simply as bearers of social structures.

Marxists such as Geras (1983) and Callinicos (1987) have recently argued that Marx did posit, and more generally that Marxism entails, a conception of human nature, a philosophical anthropology. Human beings can be conceived as conscious, reflective and communicative beings who are intentional and rational agents in that they behave and act in terms of beliefs and desires. The ability to engage in communication, and to comprehend the rational beliefs and desires of others, arguably reflects shared nature or identity, and in these terms rationality can be seen as a precondition for intelligibility in the social world. It is not so much a biologically endowed feature of individuals as a socially achieved product made possible by a shared biological constitution. Thus rationality reflects simultaneously the social and biological nature of humans. Moreover, because of their ability to reflect on and give reasons for their actions, human beings are capable of second-order desires, of reflexively altering or controlling their desires and conduct. It is this flexible and reflective nature which distinguishes the activity of the 'worst of architects from the best of bees'.

Behaviour

Behaviourism is a powerful alternative and antidote, as an environmentalist framework, to conservative hereditarian explanations and justifications of class rule. The repudiation of racist theories of the inheritance of intelligence has often been made from a behaviourist position. The most powerful critiques of genetic accounts recently have been by behaviourists who are not Marxists (e.g. Kamin, 1974), and this may be precisely why they have been taken seriously.

As a theoretical system, behaviourism has offered a more optimistic view of the potential of human nature and change than biologically based accounts. In both the Soviet Union and the United States, despite the squabbles between the adherents of different behaviourist schools, and accusations by each that their counterparts were using the approach in a conformist way, behaviourism was seen by some on the left as 'radical'. Pavlov, who was himself never a Marxist nor even a materialist, and who opposed the Bolsheviks after the October Revolution, became a key figure in the development of an ostensibly materialist Psychology. The history of the development of the discipline in the Soviet Union is marked by an adherence to a supposedly socialist Psychology to which some of the most reactionary British psychologists could point when under attack as being almost identical to their own (e.g. Eysenck, 1982).

As a practical system, behaviourism seems more compatible with administration than empowerment. The problem with behaviourism's implicit split between the behaviourists, who stand apart from society to change society, and those they change is countered by some with a rather simple appeal to humanism. Some of the most influential attacks on radical behaviourism from the left, with Chomsky's (1959) critique of *Verbal Behavior* (Skinner, 1957) leading the way, have not been from a Marxist position. Chomsky, for example, appeals deliberately to objections to the idea that people are conditioned right down to their most valued properties, their speech, and his characterisation of his own politics as 'anarchist' boils down, as is often the case when this label is used by Western intellectuals, to something closer to liberalism than Marxism (Cohen and Rogers, 1991). For Marxists, the working class does not make history in conditions of its own choosing, and for some Marxists Skinnerian accounts of the structure of verbal communities describe the conditions for speech that we cannot choose but must operate within to reproduce or transform (Burton, 1979). But to do that, is there not something beyond behaviour, a cognitive ability as the condition for reflection and change?

Cognition

Behaviourism has now been largely displaced in the mainstream by Cognitive Psychology. Cognitive Psychology falls straight into the trap of what Marx calls 'contemplation', but now this is not philosophical contemplation as an alternative to 'abstract thinking', but a contemplation *of* abstract thinking, of cognition. At first glance however, cognitivism seems to offer more promise than behaviourism. As an escape from the shackles of the reinforcement schedule, a language of cognition would seem to provide the scope for insight, imagination and purpose. For such reasons Sedgwick (1974) suggested that this revolution might signal a new radical spirit, and drew parallels between the 'cybernetic model of man as an actively intervening operator' and the 'industrial, technical and practical perspective on man as a labouring species' sketched out in early Marx. If our nature rests in a general cognitive apparatus associated with our species being, as opposed to something in our genes and then our personalities, this would seem to suggest a hopeful egalitarianism, and potentially an evenly distributed 'good sense' (Palmer, 1987). Shallice (1984) also suggests that the language of cognitive Psychology may be progressive in the sense of shedding some of the ideological baggage of politically loaded concepts such as intelligence.

However, Sedgwick (1974) is quick to point out that cognitivism is just as easily put to reactionary ends, as used in the training of bomber pilots, for example. Further along this road Bowers (1990) exposes the role of cognitive science in militaristic programmes such as the Strategic Defense Initiative. The language of cognitivism here is one of hierarchy and control, which can all too easily feed back into equivalent systems of social organisation. This ideological process is facilitated by the individualistic and atomistic models of cognitivism which help to obscure social relations, reconstituting the person as a rational and detached unit for society's use. Shotter (1987) has also drawn links between cognitive Psychology and 'Taylorism'.

ALTERNATIVE TRADITIONS

Resources for Marxists in Psychology have often come from traditions which are structurally (reluctantly or deliberately) outside the discipline. In most cases, the attempt by mainstream psychologists to repress the radically different forms of knowledge they express has been their strength. They are distant and distinct from the assumptions the discipline routinely makes about the nature of the person. Conceptually, Radical personality theories, Psychoanalysis, the Soviet Developmental Psychology tradition, Feminist Psychology and Social Constructionism have been forced to tackle the theory and practice of that which Psychology normally tries to ignore or exclude from its accounts.

Personality: Sève, Work, and Theories of Liberation

The history of Marxist thought is, unfortunately, also a history of the transformation of a critical method and body of knowledge into a variety of mysticism. The development of dialectical materialism in the Soviet Union became a form both of the very scientism and of the religious mystification it claimed to displace (Lecourt, 1976). Similar processes of political policing, though, can also be identified in Western Psychology (Carey, 1977). Soviet Psychology stands as a sombre warning to those who would attempt to develop Hegelian categories into a system of thought, even if the categories are then materialist, the right way up. The problem is not that 'diamat' was wrongly appropriated by the bureaucracy and incorrectly applied to society and nature, but that the system could be applied to nature or mental life at all.

But should the rejection of a humanism in its various manifestations mean that Marxism is purged of a Psychology or a Psychology of the individual? Is 'all Psychology ... ideological for the same reason that all humanism is speculative' (Sève, 1974, p. 69)? Sève tries to get round the problem by arguing that the issues of individuality and anthropology do not necessarily disappear but that concepts like need, consumption, labour and freedom describe economic relations and individuality simultaneously; people can still be alienated because they are individuals at the same time as being bearers of economic categories. Whereas in the early Marx the human essence was the basis for social relations, this is now inverted by some so that the essence is a product of social relations. Thus Sève argues that historical materialism does not dispense with 'man' theoretically, but produces a new non-speculative concept, which at once refers to a new essence. In this way Sève asserts that *Capital* provides a scientific foundation for a theory of personality, 'scientific humanism' and others have taken up this approach for Psychology (Shames, 1981; Leonard, 1984; Burkitt, 1991). Clearly a great strength of this approach, and others like it, is its clear move against conceiving humans in terms of some sort of abstraction or essence, but rather as concrete people instantiated in specific social relations, to be seen in terms of those relations. Nevertheless, it is not clear that this formulation escapes the pitfalls of structuralism or determinism. The very employment of the concept of personality can be interpreted as a way to crystallise and compound these structuralist leanings, rather than a way out of them.

The attempts to move beyond the world of work in the West to envisage forms of exploitation and liberation in the Third World are to be found in the contribution of Fanon (1952). Psychology in the Third World is often simply a bizarre mimesis of the discipline in the old imperialist centres, and the practices and motives of colonialist Psychology in its attempts to discipline the psychology of the colonised are often clear. Alternative traditions have sometimes employed traditional survey methods, for example in the work of Martin-Baró in Latin America, but have often had to break completely from the discipline in order to understand what it was that white psychologists thought they were doing. Fanon's (1952) accounts of colonial psychology and forms of racism which operate around fantasies and projections directed to the Black as desired threat drew on psychoanalysis (Adlerian and Lacanian). The obsessive control which is exercised by the colonisers over the sexual or intellectual potential of the 'native' was described by Fanon as a process which called for the cleansing process of revolutionary violence. The violence releases the slave from internalised chains, for the colonial psychology becomes embedded in the colonised as well the colonisers. When Fanon's ideas are elaborated, it is possible to see how the mastery of the native 'other', of a disintegrating sense of 'self', of nature and of woman are closely and necessarily linked (Frosh, 1989). The theoretical and practical support which Fanon gave to national liberation struggles has resulted in a spread of his ideas from the Arab world to Africa and Latin America. In Latin America, it is the reworking of psychoanalytic theory to account for the interconnection between colonial and sexual repression which has provided a context for the reception of Fanon's work.

Psychoanalysis

'The structure of psychoanalysis is founded on repression – the repression of its own past' (Jacoby, 1983, p. 11). The same could be said of the structure of Psychology, its repression of its own history in general, and its past psychoanalytic allegiances in particular. Psychology will not remember that many of the founding fathers of the discipline were attracted to psychoanalysis precisely because it comprehended the sensuousness that other parts of Psychology could not reach. Psychoanalysis is part of academic Psychology if only as the spectre haunting the discipline, and many psychoanalytic theorists have attempted to connect sensuality with the repression necessary to class society (Kovel, 1988).

Radical political credentials for psychoanalysis cannot be read off easily from Freud's own views. The Bolsheviks were treated with suspicion by him, largely because of their attempts to rework, too dramatically and too fast, stubborn sensuous and destructive human nature, and Freud refused to side with the communists fighting on the Vienna streets in the 1930s (Gay, 1988). Those attracted to Marxism in the early years of the psychoanalytic movement had the example and then the tragic memory of Wilhelm Reich to contend with. Reich, who blended an activist understanding of class resistance to sexual oppression (in the Socialist Society for Sexual Information and Research, and in the Association for Proletarian Sexual Politics) with a misreading of Freud (replacing an emphasis on sexuality with a celebration of genital potency), was expelled from the KPD (German Communist Party), and it then seemed as if a blend of 'dialectical materialism and psychoanalysis' (Reich, 1929) was not possible. The pressures on those who connected the two traditions could only lead to madness, or it was madness to even try. Reich's books were burnt in Germany, Russia and the United States.

The repression of psychoanalysis, or at least any variety critical of conservative American adaptationist 'ego Psychology', was assisted by the medicalisation of the profession in the United States, private health care and, after the war, McCarthyism (Kovel, 1981; Jacoby, 1986). However, with the collapse of structuralist 'anti-humanism', its dissolution into the pluralism of 'post-structuralism' and dissatisfaction with the political quietism of these theoretical strands, attention has turned again to other psychoanalytic traditions. There has been a revival of interest in the Frankfurt School, though the most prominent representative now, Jürgen Habermas, is not a Marxist. There has been a development of feminist psychoanalytic theories, although influenced by Lacan or by Object Relations theory, and these are very critical of, if not hostile to, Marxism. There has also been a turn back to the roots of psychoanalytic theory, to earlier stages of infancy, and once again to pessimistic accounts of human nature, although, paradoxically, some of this Kleinian work is Marxist (e.g. Hinshelwood, 1983, 1985). There is also a Kleinian Marxist and feminist tradition running from Freud in the 1930s to Latin American liberation movements in the 1980s in the work of Marie Langer (Langer, 1989).

Soviet Developmental Psychology

Vygotsky (1962) is increasingly hailed in the West as an alternative to Piaget, but this interest functions in such a way as to depoliticise his work, and to continue the suppression of its Marxist aspects. A proper assessment of his contribution needs to come to terms with the negative, as well as the positive potential uses of Marxist theory in accounts of the relationship between psychology and culture. In a region of the world that had for many orthodox Marxists, accomplished the socialist revolution impossibly 'early', in a state which consisted of a patchwork of nations with different economic and cultural systems, there was both a temptation to, and a danger of categorising these nations according to their level of 'development'. The Marxist conception of economic 'stages' was effectively broken when the October Revolution leapt forward from pre-capitalism, but as the bureaucracy increased its grip there re-emerged a stage theory of economic and political development alongside Russian chauvinism, and this encouraged a view of minority nations in the Union as 'primitive'. The civilised centre wanted to understand and encourage these nations to 'develop', and Vygotsky was able, with this problem as the setting, to work on the intersection of culture and psychology, language and thought.

Vygotsky's work was both an expression of, and a challenge to developmentalist notions both at the level of culture and at the level of the individual. He participated in 'anthropological' work on the 'primitive' Soviet cultures (Scribner and Cole, 1981), and developed a description of intelligence which was not only rooted in the developmental stage a culture had attained, but which also always contained within it a potential for growth, for transformation. The idea of the 'zone of proximal development' is an example of a non-hereditarian account of intelligence which does not simply replace genetics with conditioning and it is, overall, a progressive Marxist theory. Both inside and outside the Soviet Union, enthusiasts for post-Pavlovian Soviet Psychology have claimed the notion as one that is authentically Marxist (e.g. Lawler, 1978). Some Marxists more sceptical of work tied to the interests of the bureaucracy have also taken up Vygotsky's work, some going so far as to claim that the degeneration into dictatorship would not have happened if Vygotsky's ideas had been taken seriously (Friedman, 1990).

Feminism and Radical Psychology

The alternative traditions in Psychology have often been glossed not as Marxist (although writers in those traditions may have characterised themselves as Marxists) but as 'humanist' or 'phenomenological' (Brown, 1973; Armistead, 1974). A term which has recently been adopted by 'radical' or 'critical' psychologists has been that they are 'feminist'. There are good reasons for this. Feminism has been able to put the traditional appeals to hard science into question more effectively than most versions of Marxism, and it has also been able to explore the motivations and effects of forms of hard Marxism which seem to be built upon fantasies of penetrating the mysteries of nature as much as is Psychology (Haraway, 1991). To put 'gender' as a key category into Marxism is to throw much Marxism into disarray. In the context of the present 'crisis' of Marxism, such a review of the masculine assumptions which have formed the bedrock of our tradition must be seen as a positive process.

In some cases, the impact of feminism in Psychology has shifted attention to the subjectivity of the 'scientists', and the ways in which the researcher constitutes her object of study (Hollway, 1989). The dangers of such a shift of attention are that radical psychologists believe that the alternative to being 'subjective' is to be 'objective', and that then because one must not be objective, one must also give up trying to provide an account which is more accurate than others. There is a risk of fleeing from science into social constructionist anti-realism.

Social Constructionism and Discourse

Social constructionism now forms a major 'radical' alternative to the mainstream within Psychology as well as providing a site for radical feminist work (e.g. Kitzinger, 1987) and 'post'- and anti-Marxist radical critique. With its roots firmly in the hermeneutic tradition, it denies that interpretations of the world are grounded in any objective reality (Gadamer, 1975). Rather, these are socially negotiated; discourse does not 'reflect' anything, but is 'an artefact of communal interchange' (Gergen, 1985). A recognition of the social and discursive bases of our representations of reality do challenge individualistic Cartesian epistemology, and they also form a basis for undermining the scientistic claims to truth within much Psychology and Marxism alike. However, social constructionism in this 'radical' form also removes any foundation for critique or change (Burman, 1990). Whereas for social constructionists representations reflect language games or stories which are their own justification, and have no claims to truth, Marxists do appeal to the material dimension, not to resolve the conflict, but to explain its very emergence, continuity and social form. To accept that many actions and practices are constructed in discourse is not to accept that they are wholly constituted by it (Greenwood, 1989).

A problem here is that representations that do not map onto class or other material interests, do not appear to reflect reality directly, and this would seem to undermine the case for a materialist foundation, strengthening the relativist hand of social constructionism. The Marxist counter here would be that the immediately available representations are often ideological representations which become real in people's experience and in their effects. Here the question becomes directed to how Marxism can allow for a theory of ideology related to material conditions without assuming that individuals are dupes of 'false consciousness' (Eagleton, 1991; Larrain, 1979; Thompson, 1984). The social constructionist position that we cannot aim for the truth but must only rely on rhetorical skills to persuade others of a version of reality necessarily ignores the differences in power and resources which may make voices more or less heard. Simply presuming an ideal speech community in which communicators are equally able (and entitled) to advance their own accounts of reality is itself inherently ideological. After all, no change is necessary if there is no basis for it in reality.

Social constructionism has also now spawned a variety of 'discourse analysis' which simultaneously appeals to the relativism of social constructionism whilst offering a method that often looks compatible with the scientific rigour demanded by mainstream Psychology (Potter and Wetherell, 1987). When discourse analysis has connected with elements of critical theory (Billig et al., 1988) or post-structuralism (Hollway, 1989; Parker, 1992) it has done so, it thinks, in order better to address questions of ideology. The development of forms of social constructionism which draw upon post-structuralism, psychoanalysis and Marxism from the journal Ideology and Consciousness (Adlam et al., 1977) to Changing the Subject (Henriques et al., 1984) has been an important influence. The dangers of social constructionism, however, continue in the more radical versions of discourse theory in Psychology, as they have outside the discipline where they have resonated with the debates over the possibility of developing a 'post-Marxism' (Laclau and Mouffe, 1985). Here, the undoubted value of Gramsci's work on hegemony is squandered on a combination of relativism and populism.

CONCLUSIONS

The philosophers have only *interpreted* the world, in various ways; the point is to *change* it. (Marx, 1845, Theses on Feuerbach).

The connections which have been made between Psychology and Marxism have, in many cases, been designed as interventions into the theory and practice of the psy-complex. The two-fold problem to which Marx's final thesis on Feuerbach draws attention is, first, the nature of the individual subject as understood by Psychology ('interpreting' the world, as if that were an optional preliminary to changing things) and, second, the nature of the psychologists as they understand themselves (interpreting the activities of the interpreting individual as if they were separate from changing what they have studied). In both aspects of this problem there is often a mistaken belief that there are activities other than those that change the world. Marxism, on the contrary, conceives of activity as 'always-already' transforming or reproducing the world (Bhaskar, 1989).

The moral/political injunction which Marx sets out then, is not one that can be simply affirmed or left to lie. The question is how we change (transform or simply reproduce) the world and how we change the Psychology that reproduces it as it is now. It is here that forms of Marxist practice have to guide theories used by psychologists who are Marxists. We should remember that Marxism itself is not a 'true' system of knowledge; rather, it is a research programme which provides a way to interpret and change the world. We want to prevent the different forms of Psychology from co-existing with one another and to force into the open the contradictions within Psychology as we open up contradictions between Marxists who contradict, in different ways, the different forms of the psy-complex.

Acknowledgement. We would like to thank John Drury and John Morss in addition to our contributors for their helpful comments on an earlier draft of this introduction.

REFERENCES

Adlam, D., Henriques, J., Rose, N., Salfield, A., Venn, C., and Walkerdine, V. (1977) 'Psychology, Ideology and the Human Subject', *Ideology and Consciousness* 1: 5–56.

Armistead, N., (ed.) (1974) *Reconstructing Social Psychology*, Harmondsworth: Pelican.

Bhaskar, R. (1989) *Reclaiming Reality: A Critical Introduction to Contemporary Philosophy*, London: Verso.

Billig, M., Condor, S., Edwards, D., Gane, M., Middleton, D. and Radley, A. (1988) *Ideological Dilemmas: A Social Psychology of Everyday Thinking*, London: Sage.

Bowers, J.M. (1990) 'All hail the Great Abstraction: Star Wars and the Politics of Cognitive Psychology', in I. Parker and J.Shotter (eds) *Deconstructing Social Psychology*, London: Routledge.

Brown, P. (ed.) (1973) *Radical Psychology*, New York: Harper Colophon.

Burkitt, I. (1991) *Social Selves: Theories of the Social Formation of Personality*, London: Sage.

Burman, E. (1990) 'Differing with Deconstruction: a Feminist Critique', in I. Parker and J. Shotter (eds) *Deconstructing Social Psychology*, London: Routledge.

Burton, M. (1979) *Skinner and Verbal Communities*, unpublished ms.

Callinicos, A. (1987) *Making History*, Oxford: Polity/Blackwell.

Carey, A. (1977) 'The Lysenko Syndrome in Western Social Science', *Australian Psychologist* 12 (1): 27–38.

Chomsky, N. (1959) 'Review of B.F. Skinner's Verbal Behavior', Language 35: 26–58.

Cohen, J. and Rogers, J. (1991) 'Knowledge, Morality and Hope: the Social Thought of Noam Chomsky', New Left Review 187: 5–27.

Dews, P. (1987). The Logics of Disintegration: Poststructuralist Thought and the Claims of Critical Theory, London: Verso.

Eagleton, T. (1991) Ideology: An Introduction, London: Verso.

Eysenck, H.J. (1982) 'The Sociology of Psychological Knowledge, the Genetic Interpretation of IQ, and Marxist-Leninist Ideology', Bulletin of the British Psychological Society 35: 449–51.

Fanon, F. (1952/1986) Black Skin, White Masks, London: Pluto Press.

Friedman, D. (1990) 'The Soviet Union in the 1920s: an Historical Laboratory', Practice 7 (3): 5–8.

Frosh, S. (1989) Between Psychology and Psychoanalysis: Minding the Gap, London: Macmillan.

Gadamer, H.-J. (1975) Truth and Method, London: Sheed and Ward.

Gay, P. (1988) Freud: A Life for Our Time, London: Dent.

Geras, N. (1983) Marx and Human Nature: Refutation of a Legend, London: Verso.

Gergen, K.J. (1985) 'The Social Constructionist Movement in Modern Psychology', American Psychologist 40: 266–75.

Giddens, A. (1984). The Constitution of Society: Outline of the theory of structuration, Cambridge: Polity Press.

Greenwood, J.D. (1989) Explanation and Experiment in Social Psychological Science: Realism and the Social Constitution of Action, New York: Springer-Verlag.

Gunn, R. (1988). Marxism and Philosophy: a Critique of Critical Realism. Capital & Class 37: 87–117.

Haraway, D.J. (1991) Simians, Cyborgs and Women, London: Free Association Books.

Harré, R. and Madden, E.H. (1975) Causal Powers, Oxford: Blackwell.

Henriques, J., Hollway, W., Urwin, C., Venn, C. and Walkerdine, V. (1984) Changing the Subject: Psychology, Social Regulation and Subjectivity, London: Methuen.

Hinshelwood, R.D. (1983) 'Projective Identification and Marx's Concept of Man', International Review of Psycho-Analysis 10: 221–6.

Hinshelwood, R.D. (1985) 'Projective Identification, Alienation and Society', Group Analysis 18 (3): 241–54.

Hollway, W. (1989) Subjectivity and Method in Psychology: Gender, Meaning and Science, London: Sage.

Jacoby, R. (1983) Social Amnesia, New York: Beacon Press.

Jacoby, R. (1986) The Repression of Psychoanalysis: Otto Fenichel and the post-Freudians, Chicago: Chicago University Press.

Kamin, L. (1974) The Science and Politics of IQ, Harmondsworth: Pelican.

Kitzinger, C. (1987) The Social Construction of Lesbianism, London: Sage.

Koch, S. (1964) 'Psychology and emerging Conceptions of Knowledge as

Unitary', in T.W. Wann (ed.) *Behaviorism and Phenomenology*, Chicago: University of Chicago Press.

Kovel, J. (1981) 'The American Mental Health Industry', in D. Ingleby (ed.) *Critical Psychiatry: The Politics of Mental Health*, Harmondsworth: Penguin.

Kovel, J. (1988) *The Radical Spirit: Essays on Psychoanalysis and Society*, London: Free Association Books.

Laclau, E. and Mouffe, C. (1985) *Hegemony and Socialist Strategy: Towards a Radical Democratic Politics*, London: Verso.

Langer, M. (1989) *From Vienna to Managua: Journey of a Psychoanalyst*, London: Free Association Books.

Larrain, J. (1979) *The Concept of Ideology*, London: Hutchinson.

Lawler, J. M. (1978) *IQ, Hereditability and Racism: A Marxist Critique of Jensenism*, London: Lawrence and Wishart.

Lecourt, D. (1976/1977) *Proletarian Science? The Case of Lysenko*, London: New Left Books.

Leonard, P. (1984) *Personality and Ideology: Towards a Materialist Understanding of the Individual*, London: Macmillan.

Levine, A., Sober, E. and Wright, E.O. (1987) 'Marxism and Methodological Individualism, *New Left Review*, **162**: 67–84.

Lukács, G. *(1971) History and Class Consciousness*, London: Merlin.

Marx, K. (1845/1975) 'Concerning Feuerbach', in *Karl Marx: Early Writings*, Harmondsworth: Pelican.

Miller, G.A. (1962/1966) *Psychology: The Science of Mental Life*, Harmondsworth: Pelican.

Palmer, A. (1987) 'Cognitivism and Computer Simulation' in A. Costall and A. Still (eds) *Cognitive Psychology in Question*, Brighton: Harvester.

Parker, I. (1992) *Discourse Dynamics: Critical Analysis for Social and Individual Psychology*, London: Routledge.

Potter, J. and Wetherell, M. (1987) *Discourse and Social Psychology: Beyond Attitudes and Behaviour*, London: Sage.

Reich, W. (1929) 'Dialectical Materialism and Psychoanalysis', in L. Baxandall (ed.) (1972) *Sex-Pol Essays 1929–1934*, New York: Random House.

Reicher, S.D. (1987) 'Crowd Behaviour as Social Action', in J.C. Turner *et al., Rediscovering the Social Group: a Self-categorization Theory*, Oxford: Blackwell.

Rose, N. (1985) *The Psychological Complex: Psychology, Politics and Society in England 1869–1939*, London: Routledge and Kegan Paul.

Roudinesco, E. (1990) *Jacques Lacan and Co.: The History of Psychoanalysis in France – 1936–1986*, London: Free Association Books.

Scribner, S. and Cole, M. (1981) *The Psychology of Literacy*, Cambridge, MA: Harvard University Press.

Sedgwick, P. (1974) 'Ideology in Modern Psychology', in N. Armistead (ed.) *Reconstructing Social Psychology*, Harmondsworth: Pelican.

Sedgwick, P. (1982) *Psychopolitics*, London: Pluto Press.

Sève, L. (1974/1978) *Man in Marxist Theory, and the Psychology of Personality*, Hassocks, Sussex: Harvester Press.

Shallice, T. (1984) 'Psychology and Social Control', *Cognition* **17**: 29–48.

Shames, C. (1981) 'The Scientific Humanism of Lucien Sève', *Science and Society* **45** (1): 1–23.

Shotter, J. (1987) 'Cognitive Psychology, "Taylorism" and the Manufacture of Unemployment', in A. Costall and A. Still (eds) *Cognitive Psychology in Question*, Brighton: Harvester.

Skinner, B.F. (1957) *Verbal Behavior*, New York: Appleton-Century-Crofts.

Skinner, B.F. (1971/1973) *Beyond Freedom and Dignity*, Harmondsworth: Pelican.

Tajfel, H. (1979) Individuals and Groups in Social Psychology, *British Journal of Social and Clinical Psychology* **18**: 183–90.

Thompson, J.B. (1984) *Studies in the Theory of Ideology*, Cambridge: Polity.

Timpanaro, S. (1976) *On Materialism*, London: Verso.

Vygotsky, L.S. (1962) *Thought and Language*, Cambridge, MA.: MIT Press.

PART ONE:

HISTORICAL MATERIAL

Conceptual problems have beset the attempt to construct a 'Marxist Psychology'. The first four chapters locate the problems in complex sets of material circumstances. Edward Reed, in Chapter 1, tackles the question of epistemology – how we come to gain knowledge about the world, social relations and ourselves – and rehearses the Marxist argument that knowledge is intimately, dialectically, bound up with labour. Psychologists are not free to make a science of human action in conditions of their own choosing, and Robert Young reminds us in Chapter 2 of the malign consequences of a distorted version of dialectical materialism, or 'diamat', which reigned in the Soviet Union. In Chapter 3, Martin Roiser and Carla Willig explore some of the forgotten byways of Marxist psychology in Germany, and how psychoanalytic speculation succeeded a strong tradition of empirical research. Benjamin Harris, in Chapter 4, reviews the ways in which Marxists in the United States tried to develop a 'socialist psychology', and how Gestaltist and Freudian notions battled with Lysenkoism and Pavlovian orthodoxy which was relayed from the Soviet Union through the Communist Party. This history is the source of grim lessons as well as pointers to progressive directions in Psychology for Marxists working in the discipline now.

1

THE CHALLENGE OF HISTORICAL MATERIALIST EPISTEMOLOGY

Edward S. Reed

The central problem of Marxist epistemology is to reconcile an adequate theory of human knowing with a materialist conception of the world. Marx's great insight was that such a reconciliation requires an historical materialism (and, hence, an historical epistemology) to succeed. This is because human activity, when it evolved into human labour, became the motive force of history. An individual's labour exists as a part of social means and relations of production, and these relations are not stable, but continually changing (Ingold, 1983, 1992; Reed, 1991; Woolfson, 1982). Specifically, each mode of production embodies modes of competition ('class struggle' being only one such mode) which transform as well as reproduce the productive relations, paving the way for historical change. Marx's pathbreaking account of history and its causes implies the need for an as yet undeveloped epistemological project. Should we not seek to characterise the historically changing modes of human knowing that evolve within and alongside the history of labour? Engels and Lenin both thought the answer to this question was a decisive 'yes' and attempted to work out historical materialist epistemologies. However, their attempts have rightly been criticised for being too mechanically materialist, for sacrificing the adequacy of their account of human knowing on the altar of their commitment to materialism.

Recently, Timpanaro (1975) has defended Engels from this charge, and initiated a defence of Lenin which was then developed into a general defence of materialism by Ruben (1979). Whether one agrees (as I mostly do) with these defenders of materialism or not, it should be recognised that they have stated the fundamental problem of Marxist epistemology in an important and revealing way. Whatever position one takes on either Marxism or materialism, Timpanaro's and Ruben's work together constitutes a *challenge*: to state epistemological principles which are adequate to both nature and history. An historical materialist epistemology should neither downplay the biological factors in knowing nor obscure the specialisations of human beings, the important and varied forces of culture and history.

Despite this chapter's concern with epistemological issues, the goal of this discussion is not purely epistemological; on the contrary, the goal is to clarify an epistemological puzzle which I believe stands in the way of the successful development of cognitive psychology. Modern cognitivism, I would argue, suffers from holding to precisely those epistemological claims that Ruben and Timpanaro have shown to be contradictory and problematic. Albeit supposedly 'scientific', a good deal of modern cognitive psychology, and almost everything which passes under the term 'cognitive science' (see Gardner, 1985, and Reed, 1986), suffers from the inverse of Lenin's problem: the adequacy of the cognitivists' account of human knowing is sacrificed on the altar of an idealist epistemology. In particular, the epistemological assumption that knowing involves the having and manipulation of mental representations (see Cummins, 1989; Fodor, 1968; Sterelny, 1990, for clear accounts) has functioned as a kind of straightjacket, preventing the free development of a theory of knowing which is appropriately materialistic and historical (Still and Costall, 1991). After reviewing Ruben's and Timpanaro's critique, extending it both epistemologically and politically, I return to the problems created for cognitive science by representationalism.

THE CHALLENGE I

Kantian Inconsistencies

Ruben states the fundamental problem for materialist epistemologists in a succinct analysis of several propositions. Timpanaro follows a more dialectical procedure, and thereby touches on a wider range of issues. I will begin with Ruben's analysis and then use Timpanaro's work to show the wide importance of the problems raised here. It turns out that the epistemological issues under discussion have important political consequences, which make them relevant beyond the narrow range of academic discussion.

Ruben (1979) succeeds in reducing the complexities of post-Kantian epistemology to the conflict between several claims, as follows. First, there is what Ruben calls *the interpretation claim* (IC). This states that to make a judgment or to claim knowledge necessarily presupposes the activity of interpretive thought. This claim is widespread in both modern science and philosophy (Reed, 1982a, 1989). For example, most students of perception would argue that the perception of an object is the result of a mental process which interprets sensory inputs caused by that object. The progressive linguist and philosopher, Chomsky (1980), has erected an entire theory of knowledge on this idea that knowing is equivalent to a rule-governed interpretation of sensory data.

As Ruben points out, IC is a claim that 'there can be no knowable uninterpreted given'. Note that IC is not incompatible with the *existence* of things independent of any knower (the traditional antimaterialist position in philosophy); however, if IC is correct, then even if such independent things exist, they cannot be known. This is Kant's argument that 'things in themselves' cannot be known, only their (interpreted) appearance. In fact, as Ruben explains, Kant very carefully stated the independence of things from knowers, which gives us Ruben's second claim, *the independence claim* IPC: 'There are objects essentially independent of thought, or of all interpretive mental activity.'

Ruben has shown that, regardless of which interpretation of IPC one follows, it is inconsistent with IC. If IC is true, then IPC cannot be known to be true; and, if IPC is known to be true, then IC cannot be true. In Ruben's terminology, the realistic epistemology implied in IPC is undermined by the idealism implied in IC. As Feuerbach explained, Kant's inconsistency is precisely in trying to hold simultaneously a (mechanical materialist) sensationalism and a form of idealism (see Lenin, 1908/1970, p. 235). Lange (1880, vol. 2, p. 158), put it even more bluntly in his *History of Materialism*, arguing that materialism cannot embrace all of science, for the science of perceptual psychology (i.e. the second interpretation described above) will then refute materialism. Neither sensationalism nor idealism is an acceptable position for a historical materialist, so Kant's contradiction must be transcended, rather than resolved one way or the other. It is from Timpanaro's politicising of the Kantian dilemma into a struggle between fatalists (mechanical materialists) and voluntarists (idealists) that the way to transcend this contradiction can be prepared.

THE CHALLENGE II

Action Must Transcend Fatalism vs Voluntarism

One of Lenin's virtues as an epistemologist was to avoid the separation of epistemology from politics. Although crude in some ways, Lenin's theory of knowledge as a 'reflection' of objective reality partly served to educate revolutionaries to bring their goals, understanding and action together. Today we must go well beyond both Lenin's politics and his epistemology, but without losing sight of the historical conditions which would exist even without our activity and interpretations. Timpanaro (1975, pp. 63–4) explains this well:

> in my opinion the value of materialism is ... cognitive, at once philosophical-scientific and cultural-political. Unless it confirms and deepens materialism ... Marxism becomes a philosophy confined to arts graduates or pure philosophers. As such it remains effective as a polemical vehicle for denouncing the myths of the welfare state, but is incapable of shedding light on the problem of the subject of the revolution and the forces which lead to the revolution itself (forces which cannot be purely voluntaristic ones).

The claim in IPC above is merely the realist's claim that *something* exists independently of interpretation. Marxism, however, is more than a form of realism, it is a materialism, and a revolutionary one at that. For Marxists like Timpanaro, one of the things which exist independently of their interpretations are the material forces of social conditions, especially forces of change. From this point of view, both IC and IPC take on a decidedly political hue. IC celebrates abstract and negative freedom of thought; thought as unconstrained by reality and, therefore, thought without empowerment to act and realise itself. This is the freedom of modern Western society, a freedom from constraint which exists only so long as one is merely thinking. The moment significant action is taken, modern society (and the state) constitutes itself as 'object without subject' and blocks any real material change from this society's norms. As Timpanaro (1975, p. 67) rightly insists, 'so-called inner freedom is a poor substitute for true freedom, which cannot exist apart from man's actual emancipation from oppressive social relationships'.

Timpanaro thus resurrects and deepens Feuerbach's account of the Kantian contradiction between sensationalism (a form of mechanical materialism) and voluntarism (a form of idealism). For Timpanaro, a materialist 'cannot ... deny or evade the element of passivity in experience: the external situation which we do not create but which imposes itself on us ...' (p. 34). 'There is, in other words, a stimulus coming from the external world which is precisely the "given" [although] the knowing process is certainly not a mere passive reception for the given' (p. 55). However, those who emphasise the interpretive activity of this non-passive knowing process seek merely 'an illusory and mystified freedom' and not true liberation. Unfortunately, Timpanaro himself cannot resolve this war between passive material sensation and active ideal interpretation; nevertheless, considered in the light of recent developments in perceptual psychology, his account of the problem offers a possible solution. The crucial concept missing from Timpanaro's work is the rejection of the concept of imposed stimuli as the basis of perception, while still maintaining the concept that awareness is of the external situation. James J. Gibson (1966, 1979) invented just such a theory of perception by distinguishing imposed from obtained stimulation, and showing how the active obtaining of stimulation was the basis of all perception of the self as situated in its environment (see Reed, 1988). In the next section Gibson's theory of non-imposed awareness will be used to complete Timpanaro's project of a non-fatalist materialism.

Many twentieth-century Marxists concerned to avoid a mechanical materialism have tried to deny that there is a 'given', and in this they are united with many non-Marxist philosophers and a whole gamut of contemporary idealists (see Ross, 1971). The emphasis of all these thinkers is on the idea that 'man makes himself' through activity or 'praxis'. But Timpanaro (1975, pp. 56-7) rightly points out that 'an unmediated identification of knowing with acting is not Marxian' because, if this identity holds, then 'to know reality is already to transform it [and therefore] one retrogresses from Marxism to idealism – i.e. to a philosophy of thought as praxis which makes action seem superfluous'. This sort of epistemology led to the deaths of many Third World revolutionaries in the past generation who accepted the *focoist* theory that the mere existence of a small cadre of fighters with revolutionary ideas could produce full-scale revolutions (compare Guevara, 1968, with Chaliand, 1978).

It is *fatalism* to accept and emphasise the given as *predetermining* the outcome of a situation, but it is merely *realism* to understand that each situation does have actually given determinants, that some situations afford change-making and others do not. Laws of nature do exist and determine human actions, but this is not to say that humans are at the mercy of such laws, or that history is predetermined by them. The successful leader of Guinea-Bissau's revolution, Amilcar Cabral (1973, p. 86), explained this well: 'I think that all kinds of struggle for liberation obey a group of laws. The application of these laws to a certain case depends on the nature of the case. Maybe all these laws are applicable, but maybe only some, maybe only one. It depends.' On the other hand, it is *voluntarism* to promote and emphasise the role of mere thought in changing situations, but it is again merely *realism* to understand that human thought itself is a powerful weapon in all struggle.

Mechanical Marxism falls easily into the error of fatalism, of an endless and passive waiting for the objective conditions to become favourable for an action which thus never materialises. Yet Marxists who emphasise praxis promote the idealist ideology that thinking in and of itself can transform reality. This may lead to a debilitating separation of intellectual labour from the many tasks of liberation at hand (as is obviously the case in most Western societies) (Sohn-Rethel, 1978). Philosophers who believe that interpreting the world is already a form of changing it will inevitably find themselves scorned by those already engaged in the struggles for liberation. 'Dialego' (1978, p. 15), a South African revolutionary, says:

This does not mean that materialists are not concerned about people's ideas. On the contrary, materialists are the only people in the world who are able to explain them properly. What materialism rejects are not ideas, or their immense importance in influencing the course of events. Rather it is the idealist theory of ideas which materialists challenge, because this treats ideas as mystical forces that somehow exist independently of material reality. (cf. Marx and Engels, 1845/1976, p. 42).

The question that emerges from the above account is straightforward but difficult. How is an historical materialism possible? That is, an historical materialism that identifies laws which determine situations, without predetermining outcomes; and, at the same time, which accounts for the very real role of intelligent human activity in promoting desirable outcomes; a science which rejects the twin notions of ideology as the result of mystical processes of will or as the inexorable and unopposable result of laws of nature. 'To have [true] ideology is to know what you want in your own condition,' says Cabral (1973, p. 88). Can we develop an epistemology consistent with the sort of struggle engaged in by Cabral for an adequate ideology combined with a realistic course of action? The history of revolutions, from Paine and America in 1775 to the revolutions of 1989–1991 suggest that revolutions are often unleashed by a mass of people who know what they want in their own situation, guided by leaders who repeatedly look elsewhere for guidance!

THE CHALLENGE III

Uniting Nature and History

Nature pulls us to emphasise IPC, to stress the givenness of the situations in which we live. Yet history reveals the force of IC, for people interpret the same situation in many different ways, and use such interpretations to guide their behaviour. Contemporary psychology recognises this conflict, but most attempts to synthesise IC and IPC are based on nothing other than brute force. The given, the stimulus, is supposed to enter consciousness only after a protracted process of transformation. This processing or interpretation of the stimulus is based on the biological, social and personal inheritance of the individual (see Neisser, 1967 for a now classical version of this theory). Yet IC and IPC are inconsistent, so merely saying that they are united is not the same as synthesising them. To put it bluntly, modern psychologists insist on holding two inconsistent hypotheses simultaneously: first, that a person can have knowledge of the world outside his/her body (a hypothesis descended from Kant's IC); and second, that such knowledge is based on interpreting the effects on the body of the world (a descendant of IPC). The physical world causes bodily sensations and the mind, *having access only to those bodily sensations*, uses a set of inborn or acquired rules to interpret or infer what the world that caused these sensations might be like (Rock, 1985).

By considering interpretive mental activity to be a mediator between sensations and awareness of the external world, modern psychologists have yet again separated humanity from nature, placing human (mental) activity totally outside the laws of nature. The disconnection between the analysis of the logical/interpretive aspects of mental activity and the biological aspects is striking, but it follows from the structure of modern psychological theories. If sensations cannot always be noticed – as most writers nowadays hold – then they must be inferred. Yet this means that psychologists are working with a theory in which *both* of the important variables, sensory inputs and rule-based interpretations, must be inferred. As mentioned above, Kohler has shown that inferring both the basis of mental states and the processes from transforming and interpreting that input is a scientific disaster: one can adjust too many variables when hypothesis and factual results do not agree. The sole source of constraint on this game is neurophysiology. This has not proved very helpful, because functional behavioural processes inevitably turn out to be served by multiple neural structures, granting sufficient room to anyone who wants to modify hypotheses about neural input or interpretation (see Luria, 1973; Reed, 1982b).

One result of this idealistic confusion is that modern human experimental psychology has been reduced to measuring a *single* parameter of behaviour in the majority of cases. Time taken from input to response (where response can be recognition, recall, adjustment of a display, choice, or a judgment) can be measured, whereas sensations and interpretation cannot (Posner, 1978; Luce, 1989). Hence, choosing among the all too abundant gamut of hypotheses about the *many* parameters of mental activity is well nigh impossible within the accepted framework because so few relevant parameters can be studied empirically.

Scientific psychology can transcend such inconsistencies only by conceptualising mental activity as falling within the realm of nature. For such a theory, mental processes would be determined (but not predetermined) by natural law. (This is not inconsistent with their being determined by historical laws as well.) This sort of psychological theory has begun to develop recently due to the influence of James J. Gibson's 'ecological approach' to psychology. The laws of action emerging from this work are not laws of purely physical nature (as in older behaviouristic psychologies), nor are they laws of so-called pure thought (as in recent cognitive psychologies) but laws of embodied and situated intentional agents. While the situations of embodied agents constrain their actions, at the same time these constraints reveal possibilities for action. The fact that the human body is subject to gravity is a very real constraint on my action in writing this sentence, but gravity also provides the field of forces within which I have evolved to be able to move pen across paper, supported at elbow, forearm and wrist, using slight oscillations of thumb and fingers.

The twin concepts underlying this theoretical breakthrough in psychology are Gibson's notions of the 'affordances' of the environment for action and his concept of the perceptual information available to specify those affordances. 'The affordances of the environment are what it offers the animal, what it provides or furnishes, either for good or for ill' (Gibson, 1979, p. 127). The relatively flat and rigid ground affords support for locomotion to terrestrial animals, whereas the buoyancy and viscosity of water affords aquatic locomotion. An affordance 'points both ways' to the environment and to the animal. What is important here is that the affordances of the environment are both subjective and objective, and neither: if something does not have the relevant properties (e.g. it is head-high) it cannot be used for the act in question (sitting) without modification. But to say that an object has some affordance is also to imply something about what it is good for and to whom. An affordance 'is equally a fact of the environment and a fact of behaviour. It is both physical and psychical, yet neither' (Gibson, 1979, p. 129).

The affordance concept forms a bridge between the evolutionary biologist's ontology of resources and the political economist's ontology of use values. Affordances are use values for any animals' behaviour, and their value is independent of the existence of any particular animal. The chair I am sitting in affords sitting and would afford sitting even if I were not here, or were dead. In general, 'the organism depends on the environment for its life, but the environment does not depend on the organism for its existence' (Gibson, 1979, p. 129). An object has a use value, or exists as a means of production simply because it has the relevant properties, and these properties need not be used at a given time. Marx (1875/1974, p. 341) understood this when he said, 'Nature is just as much the source of use values ... as labour.' In *Capital* (1867/1977, p. 278, n. 7) he noted: 'It appears paradoxical to assert that uncaught fish, for instance, are a means of production in the fishing industry. But hitherto no one has discovered the art of catching fish in water that contains none.' Nor has anyone discovered the art of walking barefoot across water. One of the great importances of the affordance concept is to call attention to the obvious by suggesting situations in which the laws of nature do *not* allow for an act to occur. The political implications of a theory that helps us to discern the *limits* of a situation should be obvious. Marx's own political work typically involved trying to apprehend such limits, and then to act so as to push to achieve as radical goals as possible, given those limits. This strategy, for example, lay behind Marx's repeated emphasis on the importance of democratic reform and the use of the vote in the United States and Great Britain.

The mere existence of an affordance, however, is no guarantee that it is something we will become aware of or use. (How much untapped oil still lies unknown in the ground, despite vast search efforts?) To become aware of affordances requires the pick-up of ecologically available information that specifies the relevant properties of the environment to the observer. Gibson's theory of the active pick-up of information in stimulation contrasts sharply with the traditional theory that stimuli cause sensory awareness. If the world imposes itself on us through stimuli, then our mental life can be free only to the extent that it resists the imposition, interpreting the given stimuli on its own terms. But if perceptual awareness is itself an activity (not of the mind or of the body, but of the whole functioning individual) then our perceptual freedom derives from what information we act so as to detect and how we use that information. Note that this is not merely the pragmatists' theory that to know the world is to change it, for the action of information detection need not change anything in the world: surveying a scene visually need not change the scene, but will enable one to detect optical information to see it. Perceptual activity is meaningful, but precedes performatory action; through perception one becomes aware of the resources surrounding one, and through performance one can utilise or change those resources. As Gibson (1966, p. 321) so well said in summing up his theory:

> Let us recognise the strength of the dead hand of habit on perception. Let us acknowledge that people – other people, of course – often perceive the word like silly sheep. But it is wrong to make a philosophy of this rather snobbish observation. The orthodox theories of perception have encouraged this fallacy and one purpose of this book has been to undermine them. This book is dedicated to all persons who want to look for themselves.

In addition to his novel theory of the active process of perceiving, Gibson radically altered our conception of what it is that people perceive. Unlike orthodox accounts of perception, which treat it as a process of becoming aware of neutral phenomena – such as colours or sounds – requiring interpretation, Gibson's theory is that through perception we gain contact with a meaningful material word around us. Whereas traditional perceptual theories claim that we perceive sensations or physical properties, such as light, space, or motion, Gibson argued that we perceive the meaningful objects, events, places, and persons surrounding us, and what they afford us. Moreover, Gibson went on to show how the terrestrial environment so structures light as to provide information adequate for humans and animals to guide themselves visually among these affordances. Gibson's work has given rise to testable hypotheses about ecological rules or laws for the steering of behaviour. These laws relate the information specifying environmental affordances to the actions and awarenesses of agents. Gibson's and his students' work has been carried on primarily at the level of more or less basic actions (e.g. locomotion), but these ideas are also highly suggestive of applications to various forms of social action, as Gibson was well aware.

There is insufficient space here to elaborate the entire conceptual scheme of ecological psychology and, besides, many of the details will surely change as the ecological develops. What is important for present purposes is the clear rejection of a separation of nature and thought without rejecting either the role of nature or the role of thought in the determination of an individual's actions. This allows us to accept the existence of objective (and meaningful) conditions constraining action without losing sight of the role of subjectivity in awareness and behaviour. The key to this successful transcendence of the dichotomy between voluntarism and fatalism is Gibson's theory of information for environmental affordances, for this theory gives us a glimpse of how to understand the situatedness of agents in a scientific manner.

PROBLEMS AND PROSPECTS

An objection might be raised to the position proposed here that an emphasis on laws produces a mechanical or vulgar historical materialism. After all, the laws I have actually discussed are primarily physical or biological laws of nature. If such laws are the primary determinants of history, then some form of technological determinism would seem to follow. One of the most powerful impetuses behind both humanistic Marxisms and certain forms of structuralist Marxism is this belief that the resolute search for laws of society and historical change leads to an exclusion of human will, effort, and culture from historical materialism (Gouldner, 1980). Yet, as Marx himself never failed to emphasise, human history is always the history of real individual human beings in determinate circumstances striving to achieve their goals.

The search for laws of history, therefore, must be a search for lawful relations which emerge from the struggles and lives of the mass of humanity. Human will, effort and culture are integral components of the processes comprising history, and cannot be excluded from historical materialism. But to include humanity in its concrete cultural aspect is not to *exclude* the laws of action (abstract capacities of evolving animals), or of labour power (abstract capacities of historical human beings). Indeed, the search for laws concerning culture is every bit as important as the search for laws concerning means of production. Cabral (1973) defines culture as the synthesis of the contradictions emerging from a society's means of production. Thus any struggle for liberation – which obviously involves revolutionising the means of production – necessarily involves a cultural struggle as an important component. For example, during revolutionary struggle in Guinea-Bissau the society's pre-existing relations between men and women were broken down as household and village modes of production became integrated into the liberation movement. As Cabral was one of the first to realise, this temporary disruption of normal cultural patterns can be an important opportunity for changing a traditional culture's patterns of oppression, in this case the oppression of women.

Psychologists will easily recognise IC as the generative idea behind many variants of cognitive theory. Mainstream American psychology teaches, for example, that when two people are interacting neither is relating directly to his or her partner; instead, each is supposedly constructing a theory of the other's behaviours, attributes, and beliefs, and acting in accordance with this theory. The solipsistic and idealistic implications of this approach to psychology are rarely developed at length, but the refusal of psychologists to acknowledge the logical implications of their thinking cannot change those implications. Hand in hand with these idealist and solipsistic tendencies is an extreme divorce from the everyday. There are literally thousands of elaborate discrimination, reaction time, and other studies concerning the perception of or reaction to artificial stimuli. In contrast, there are only a handful of studies concerned with everyday activities in the home, school, or workplace. To a large degree, at least in the USA, experimental psychologists have 'ceded rights' to the study of functioning in schools, homes, and workplaces to social workers, ergonomics researchers, developmentalists and others.

'Human activity' has thus come to mean 'mental states as measured in psychology laboratories' – and this, in turn, has come to mean little more than variations on reaction times. Psychology needs far more of Cabral's emphasis on analysing people in their own situation and far less of cognitivist and praxis theorists' empty emphasis on the 'transformative power of human action'. Cognitivism in psychology, representationalism in epistemology, and the idealistic approach to human activity in anthropology and Marxism are all major obstacles to developing an adequate psychology of the everyday because their leading assumption is that psychology is a study of things in the mind. Historical epistemology and ecological psychology could join together to emphasise the possibility of a psychology that is a study of how minds are formed within the everyday world. We make ourselves, as Marx and Engels explained, but not under conditions of our own choosing. It is about time that psychology studied the everyday processes which go into this making of selves.

CONCLUSIONS

If an historical epistemology can be developed that transcends both IC and IPC by reconciling thought and nature, by showing how law and human purpose work together in generating change, then the 'two Marxisms' which have evolved, one fatalist, the other voluntarist, can also be transcended. Fatalistic Marxism takes nature to be the motive force of history (either directly, or through technical and economic determinism), whereas voluntaristic Marxism takes human thought and volition to be the motive power behind all material change. But just as thought is a part of nature, so nature encompasses volition. History is not an amalgam of material and mental causes, but the result of combinations and divisions of human action. History is not fatalistically predetermined, nor is it voluntaristically open to change; rather, history is determined without being pre-established, and it is modified by human agency even though no one person or group can ever establish complete control over its course. History is the result of massive social competitions for resources whose end result may differ from the goals of any of the individual agents of that competition. The contribution of any one individual or group, no matter how 'revolutionary', to changing society cannot be to pre-establish the ultimate goal for all people. (The opposite is also true: even the most powerful reactionary forces cannot predetermine the outcome of situations to conform exactly with their desires.)

Marxism, like all intellectual movements (including bourgeois democratic ones) has tended to privilege a certain set of goals as being outside the above-described competition. Given the present analysis, this is unacceptable from a theoretical standpoint – and it has clearly proved to be unacceptable practically. When Lenin and Trotsky organised the Red Army to impose a certain set of goals on Russia in 1917–1919 they had the excuse of the horrible circumstances around them: Allied invasions leading to vicious civil war. But the maintenance for decades of a set of dogmatically achieved goals as outside the realm of democratic debate gradually stripped these ideals and goals of concrete meaning for the people on whom they were to be imposed. It is deeply ironic, and deeply troubling, that the present-day leaders of Russia seem hell bent on imposing an equally unpalatable set of privileged ideas about 'the market' as goals for a society which neither wants them nor has much use for them. (How many Russians will buy stocks in 'privatised' state enterprises?) The current leaders have no excuse comparable to the great civil war for this impositionist philosophy, and their goals will likely come to seem as empty as the earlier ones.

In order to change a society democratically, as many people as possible must come to see how their individual acts are combined into social forces which lead to ends of which they may or may not approve. The role of psychologists and other social scientists is to help make visible the difficult connections between personal performance and eventual outcome not only for oneself, but for others as well. The attempt to erect one set of outcomes or goals as privileged prior to allowing the majority of people into the process is a procedure which will undermine the very goals one is attempting to achieve.

The modern cognitivists and others who premise their work on IC have come to believe that no potential outcomes are real, and that all that truly exists are constructs of individual minds. Each ideal or goal can then be said to be equal (or equally valid for whomever holds the goal) but no goals can be said to have efficacy in the world. This may be a natural reaction to the inability of modern society to create the conditions in which most people can both envisage and achieve important goals. But the fact that we are prevented from achieving our ideals by forces stronger than ourselves should not be interpreted as meaning that our ideals can never be realised.

Marx understood how important it is to see human action as a unique combination of the natural and the ideal. The mechanical reduction of our actions to the patterns of motion of a predetermined nature lead to fatalistic despair; and the voluntarist's belief in the autonomous creativity of human thought is a myth, albeit a convenient one for the status quo, because it blinds us to the real forces that lead to social change – the attempt to use human action to struggle against conditions not of our own choosing. In the 'Critique of the Gotha Program' (1875/1974, p. 341) Marx explains that nature is as much the source of wealth as human labour: 'There is every good reason for the bourgeoisie to ascribe supernatural creative power to labour, for when a man has no other property than his labour power it is precisely labour's dependence on nature that forces him, in all social and cultural conditions, to be the slave of other men who have taken the objective conditions of labour into their own possession. He needs their permission to work, and hence their permission to live.' In *Capital* (1867/1977, p. 748) he was more pithy: 'If workers could live on air, it would not be possible to buy them at any price.' Those who have controlled the objective conditions of work, whether in the name of Capital or even in the name of Marx, have always tried to compel the rest of us to accept their goals as the only objectively important ones, and to see our own ideas and goals as mere subjective constructs. The ideology of IC tries to comfort us with the thought that the strength of the owners is just a veil of illusion, and that our own illusory goals within our own ivory towers are just as real as those which control the conditions of life and work. A truly liberatory psychology must try to pierce this veil to help people recognise the reality of their own ideas, and to come to understand the process whereby even the subjective conditions of our lives are dominated by conditions not of our own choosing.

REFERENCES

Berlin, I. (1969) *Four essays on liberty*, New York: Oxford University Press.

Cabral, A. (1973) *Return to the Source*, New York: Monthly Review Press.

Chaliand, G. (1978) *Revolution in the Third World*, Harmondsworth: Penguin.
Chomsky, N. (1980) *Rules and Representations*, New York: Columbia University Press.
Cummins, R. (1989) *Meaning and Mental Representation*, Cambridge, MA: M.I.T. Press.
Dialego (1978) *Philosophy and Class Struggle*, New York: Imported Publications.
Fodor, J. (1968) *Psychological Explanation*, New York: Harper-Row.
Gardner, H. (1985) *The Mind's New Science*, New York: Basic Books.

Gibson, J.J. (1966) *The Senses considered as Perceptual Systems*, Boston: Houghton-Mifflin.
Gibson, J.J. (1979) *The Ecological Approach to Visual Perception*, Boston: Houghton-Mifflin.
Gibson, J.J. (1982) 'The Concept of the Stimulus in Psychology', reprinted in E.S. Reed & R.K. Jones (eds) *Reasons for Realism: Selected Essays of James J. Gibson*, Hillsdale, NJ: Erlbaum. (First published in 1960.)
Gouldner, A. (1980) *The two Marxisms*, New York: Oxford University Press.
Guevara, E. (1968) *Guerilla Warfare*, New York: Vintage Books.
Ingold, T. (1983) 'The architect and the bee: Reflections on the work of men and animals', *Man* **18**: 1–20.
Ingold, T. (1992) 'Epilogue', in K. Gibson & T. Ingold (eds) *Tools, Language, and Cognition in Human Evolution*, New York: Cambridge University Press.
Köhler, W. (1913/1971) 'On unnoticed sensations and errors of judgment', in M. Henle (ed.) *The Selected Papers of Wolfgang Köhler*, New York: Liveright.
Lange, F.A. (1880) *The history of materialism*, 3 vols, London: Routledge & Kegan Paul.
Lee, D.N. (1980) The Optical Flow Field: the Foundation of Vision. *Philosophical Transactions of the Royal Society of London*, B, 290: 169–78.
Lenin, V.I. (1908/1970) *Materialism and Empirio-criticism*, Foreign Languages: Peking.
Luce, R.D. (1989) *Reaction Times*, New York: Oxford University Press.
Luria, A.R. (1973) *The Working Brain*, Harmondsworth: Penguin.
Marx, K. (1867/1977) *Capital*, vol 1, New York: Vintage.
Marx, K. (1875/1974) 'Critique of the Gotha Program', in K. Marx, *The First International and After*, New York: Viking.
Marx, K. & Engels, F. (1845/1976) *The German Ideology*, Moscow: Progress.
Merleau-Ponty, M. (1944/1962) *The Phenomenology of Perception*, London: Routledge & Kegan Paul.
Neisser, U. (1967) *Cognitive Psychology*, New York: Appleton-Century-Crofts.
Posner, M.I. (1978) *Chronometric Explorations of the Mind*, Hillsdale, NJ: Erlbaum.

Reed, E.S. (1982a) 'Descartes's corporeal ideas hypothesis and the origin of scientific psychology', *Review of Metaphysics* **35**, 731–52.

Reed, E.S. (1982b) 'An Outline of a Theory of Action Systems', *Journal of Motor Behavior* **14**: 98–134.

Reed, E.S. (1986) 'Review of Gardner (1985), *Isis* **77**: 530–2.

Reed, E.S. (1988) *James J. Gibson and the Psychology of Perception*, New Haven: Yale University Press.

Reed, E.S. (1989) 'Theory, Concept, and Experiment in the History of Psychology: an Old Tradition behind a "Young" Science', *History of the Human Sciences* **2**: 333–57.

Reed, E.S. (1991) 'Cognition as the Cooperative Appropriation of affordances', *Ecological Psychology* **3**: 135–58.

Rock, I. (1985) *The Logic of Perception*, Cambridge: M.I.T. Press.

Ross, J.J. (1971) *The Appeal to the Given*, London: Allen & Unwin.

Ruben, D-H. (1979) *Marxism and Materialism*, Brighton: Harvester.

Sohn-Rethel, A. (1978) *Intellectual and Manual Labor: a Critique of Epistemology*, London: Macmillan.

Sterelny, K. (1990) *The Representational Theory of Mind*, Oxford: Blackwell.

Still, A. & Costall, A. (eds) (1991) *Against Cognitivism*, Brighton: Harvester.

Timpanaro, S. (1975) *On Materialism*, London: NLB.

Vaihinger, H. (1924) *The Philosophy of 'As If'*, London: Routledge & Kegan Paul.

Williams, R. (1973) 'Base and Superstructure in Marxist Theory', *New Left Review* **82**: 3–16.

Wolf, E. (1982) *Europe and the People without a History*, Berkeley: University of California.

Woolfson, C. (1982) *The Labour Theory of Culture*, London: Routledge and Kegan Paul.

2

EVOLUTION, BIOLOGY AND PSYCHOLOGY FROM A MARXIST POINT OF VIEW

Robert M. Young

Marx and Engels admired Darwin's theory of evolution by natural selection, because it provided a unified, naturalistic, materialist account of nature, life and human nature, but they also saw it as a prime example of the penetration of ideology into knowledge. When he first read Darwin, Marx wrote to Engels in 1860 that 'although it is developed in the crude English style, this is the book which contains the basis in natural history for our view' (Marx and Engels, 1954, p. 171). He added in 1862, 'It is remarkable how Darwin recognises among beasts and plants his English society with its division of labour, competition, opening up of new markets, "inventions", and the Malthusian "struggle for existence"' (Marx and Engels, 1955, p. 128). Engels wrote, 'Darwin did not know what a bitter satire he wrote on mankind, and especially on his countrymen, when he showed that free competition, the struggle for existence, which the economists celebrate as the highest historical achievement, is the normal state of the *animal kingdom.*' He added that only 'conscious organisation of social production' could lift humankind above the animal world (Engels, 1873–86, pp. 35–6).

This ambivalence has recurred throughout the history of Marxism, so no single, unified account can be given of the Marxist approach to biology, evolution and psychology. The linking of humanity to biology through evolution is bound to be a feature of a theory which is based on the attempt to provide a unified, materialist account of all that is. However, one aspect of this account is its claim that the ruling ideas of a period are based on the ideas of the ruling class. A consequence of trying to hold both of these ideas at once is that the critique of the ideological role of knowledge reflexively threatens to undermine any settled basis for knowledge. This tension can be characterised as that between dialectical and historical materialism. It is Marxism's version of the deep, ubiquitous question of the relationship between nature and history (see e.g., Schmidt, 1972, p. 49; Ollman, 1971, p. 53).

SCIENCE AND NATURE

It is a consequence of this unresolved conundrum that it can be argued that there are two main strands in the Marxist tradition, one which stresses the penetration of ideological categories into accounts of nature and human nature, and another which asserts that nature *per se* obeys laws which are dialectical. These can be characterised as the humanistic and the diamat (for dialectical materialist) strands. There is a third strand, positivism, wherein nominally Marxist thinkers simply identified materialism with the contemporary state of natural science and technology and sought to be good at them. This approach was characteristic of the Second International, influenced communist and socialist parties well beyond 1914, and also produced the remarkable achievements of the Soviet Union in science and technology, in particular, nuclear weapons, satellites and other forms of military technology. A fourth – structuralist – strand emerged in the 1960s. It was formalistic and led eventually to deconstructionism, postmodernism (*Theory, Culture and Society*, 1988; Jameson, 1991; Docherty, 1993), extreme scepticism about grand narratives (Rorty, 1980, 1982, 1989) and cynicism about Utopian projects. This had the consequence of abandoning any serious connection between those who trod this path and a recognisably Marxist approach or project (Callinicos, 1989; Best and Kellner, 1991).

The founding document of the humanistic strand is Marx's *The Economic and Philosophical Manuscripts of 1844*, and its principal exponents were the Georg Lukács of *History and Class Consciousness* (1923) and Antonio Gramsci, who thought deeply about the concepts of matter and nature in his *Prison Notebooks*; for example, 'The idea of "objective" in metaphysical materialism would appear to me an objectivity that exists even apart from man; but when one affirms that a reality would exist even if man did not, one is either speaking metaphorically or one is falling into a form of mysticism. We know reality only in relation to man, and since man is historical becoming, knowledge and reality are also becoming and so is objectivity, etc.' (Gramsci, 1929–35, p. 446; cf. pp. 465–6). The central theses of this approach are that nature is a societal category and human nature is an ensemble of social relations (Schmidt, 1972; Berry, 1986). Lukács wrote, 'Nature is a societal category. That is to say, whatever is held to be natural at any given stage of social development, however this nature is related to man and whatever form his involvement with it takes, i.e. nature's form, its content, its range and its objectivity are all socially conditioned' (1923, p. 234). There is an ongoing debate about whether or not this approach embraces the findings of natural science as well (see Young, 1973a, esp. pp. 241–5, 1977, 1985c; RSJ Collective, 1981). Even so, there is a persistent theme in Marxist approaches to science: the close connection between theory and practice (see Bukharin, 1931).

Marxism focuses on the social determinants of human nature, so much so that many Marxists argue that there is no need for a separate discipline concerned with the individual, since the possessive individualism at the heart of bourgeois social theory is seen as a specific ideological product of the capitalist mode of production. This might lead one to think that Marxists would be very active in social psychology, but this is not the case (but see Wexler, 1983). Critics of Soviet Marxism in its Stalinist manifestations have accused it of seeking to destroy the individual with a crushing collectivist conformism (Orwell, 1949; Marcuse, 1958; Solzhenitsyn, 1973, 1975, 1978). All of this goes against the spirit of the original Marxist vision. As Marx and Engels put it in 'The Communist Manifesto', 'In place of the old bourgeois society, with its classes and class antagonisms, we shall have an association, in which the free development of each is the condition of the free development of all' (Marx and Engels, 1848, p. 87).

The concepts of alienation, commodity fetishism, reification and false consciousness recur throughout the Marxist tradition. In capitalist relations of production the worker is alienated from the means of production, the product, his or her fellow workers and species being (Ollman, 1971). The commodity form leads to a fetishism, whereby relations between people are treated as relations between things (Marx, 1967, pp. 163–77; see also 14 and 15), and human relations are thereby reified ('thingified'; Lukács, 1923, pp. 83–222). The concept of false consciousness makes the point that people's subjective sense of their motives and intentions are likely – for reasons of class location – to be a long way from an awareness of the objective, structural causes which determine their thought and action. A further characteristic of most of the literature in the Marxist tradition is that it is critique; hence, most of its views on nature and human nature are critical rather than part of a fully worked out alternative framework of ideas.

The founding document of the diamat strand is Engels' *Dialectics of Nature* (1873–86), and its central thesis is that the laws of nature are dialectical and therefore take the fundamental form of thesis, antithesis and synthesis and that, in the end, nature is what Marxists hope it is. Dialectical materialism evolved from a set of principles laid down by Marx and Engels to a formulaic set of rules which were applied to all forms of thought (Wetter, 1952; Jordan, 1967). I am presenting this approach in a caricatured form, since its most dedicated exponents involved Soviet science and technology – especially biology and agriculture – in ideological excesses which were very intellectually and economically costly. In particular, the baleful influence of T.D. Lysenko (who professed to be a disciple of the eminent breeder, I.V. Michurin and represented his ideas and policies as 'Michurinism'; see Michurin, 1949; Stoletov, 1953) in the biological sciences and on crop cultivation, precluded the Soviet Union from playing any significant part in these disciplines for decades, the very decades in which the dramatic developments in nucleotide chemistry and x-ray crystallography led to the discovery of the structure of DNA and the genetic alphabet. (It is ironic that much of it was inspired by the research and influence of the British Marxist crystallographer and polymath, J.D. Bernal, several of whose students became Nobel Laureates; see Goldsmith, 1980; Young, 1980.)

It would not be worth going into Lysenko's ideas here about how plants develop and pass on their characteristics. Although not derived from Lamarckian ideas, he stressed their affinity to the notion that acquired characteristics could be inherited, an idea completely at odds with the basic assumptions of modern genetics. Moreover, in Lysenko's writings, plants were said to struggle and cooperate and obey laws of heredity which were wholly discredited throughout the scientific world. The followers of his teachings treated seeds in special ways ('vernalisation') and planted them in large groups; most perished (for the sake of the others!) and the waste was colossal. The waste of scientific talent was too, since those who did not follow the party line – Stalin backed Lysenko, showered honours on him and made his power almost absolute in science – were sent to work camps in the Gulag Archipelago (Joravsky, 1961, 1970; Medvedev, 1969).

All of Soviet biology and medicine were, indeed, affected by this gross ideological distortion. Its assumptions appealed to the authorities because it stressed environmental influences and the malleability of nature. Michurinism claimed that 'It is possible, with man's intervention, to force any form of animal or plant to change more quickly and in a direction desirable to man. There opens up before man a broad field of activity of the greatest value to him.' By the time of Lysenko's ascendency in 1948, when Stalin endorsed his ideas, the slogan 'the transformation of nature' became the basis of a whole programme (Lysenko, 1948; Huxley, 1949; Zirkle, 1949; Graham, 1971, pp. 234, 235, 237). The claims for success of Lysenkoist procedures and ideas became fantastic, as is evidenced from the writings of the sycophantic winner (V. Safonov) of the Stalin Prize in 1949, Land in Bloom, which concludes by saying that Michurin science 'must become the pivot of all the natural sciences', that all of science was being reorganised in the wake of the 1948 congress. 'An unprecedented wave of enthusiasm swept through the ranks' of all sorts of scientists. 'Not a small group of scientists, but the entire country was promoting Michurin science, the science of man's power over the land and of the transformation of the land for the benefit of the people. It was a revolution in science' (Safonov, 1951, pp. 541–2).

Marxism has an ontology based on the concept of labour, expressed in the notion of praxis. It was being applied here in the context of massive efforts at willed change, attempting to bring a vast, fledgeling capitalist country, with a huge peasant (formerly serf) population, into a leading role among nations in a hostile international context. Stalinism tried to force nature and human nature; both turned out to be refractory. No textbooks of genetics were published from 1938 to the early 1960s; no genetics was taught to medical students in this period. Scientists in the West who supported the Soviet regime, for example, J.B.S. Haldane (1948, 1949) and J.D. Bernal (1949, 1952–3), were placed in deeply embarrassing positions (Werskey, 1978, pp. 292–304). Attempts have been made by a later generation of Marxists to salvage something from this debacle, and attempts were made to think of biology in dialectical terms (Lewontin and Levins, 1976, 1985; Lecourt, 1977; Young, 1978; S. Rose, 1982). The lesson to be learned from this episode is that, even though the ruling ideas of an epoch – including its deepest assumptions about nature – are derived from the ideas of the ruling class, if a regime seeks to dictate the categories of science with too much voluntarist precision, the result will be nonsense. The Soviet physicists stood up to the authorities and were able to deliver the knowledge, technology and weapons which made the Soviet Union a formidable adversary, although it eventually bankrupted them.

Something similar happened in Soviet psychology (Joravsky, 1989), but the consequence was, for the most part, a choice of explanatory paradigm rather than a distortion of scientific method. That is, the Soviet regime hit on the work of the distinguished experimentalist I.P. Pavlov (1927; Wells, 1956) and his concept of the conditioned reflex and made this the cornerstone of its official psychology. Once again, the focus was on changing human nature by means of habit or repeated external stimuli, paired through repetition with physiological processes. It could be said that there was no psychology *per se:* everything had to be expressed in terms of reflexes and higher nervous functions (Brazier, 1959). The result was not so much to stifle science as to ensure that all work was reported in the rhetoric of the official paradigm. In fact, Soviet studies of the nervous system and of brain function produced some subtle, classical work, e.g. that of A.R. Luria on severely brain damaged patients (Luria, 1932, 1962, 1968, 1973, 1979). Western techniques of behavioural control, e.g. F.W. Taylor's scientific management of the labour process, were eagerly taken up (Lenin, 1918, pp. 417–18). It could be argued that much of Soviet work discipline – extending from the school and factory to the use of psychiatry as a form of social control to the labour camps in the Gulag Archipelago – was a particularly coercive form of applied psychology: voluntarist rhetoric about building socialism coupled with pure fear (Medvedev and Medvedev, 1971).

In the theoretical versions of academic psychology two principles predominated: learning from habit and explanation in materialist terms. These reflected the environmentalism and belief in the plasticity of nature and human nature adopted by the Soviets, as well as the requirement that all explanations should be expressed in terms of materialist processes. The result was conditioned reflexes and explanation in terms of the functions of the nervous system. Needless to say, hypothetical constructs, such as the 'second signalling system', could proliferate here, just as they could in the West's nominally reductionist behaviourism, where 'hypothetical constructs' and 'intervening variables' filled the gaps in the reductionists' explanations (US Dept. of Health, Education and Welfare, 1950). On the other hand, after a period of some uncertainty, psychoanalysis was declared anathema and was officially dead after 1930 (Roudinesco, 1990, pp. 35–42). Among Marxists in other countries, it can in general be said that orthodox Marxists had no sympathy with psychoanalysis and considered it idealist and reactionary (Wells, 1960). Left-wing and Hegelian Marxists, on the other hand, were often sympathetic and sought to integrate or at least to relate Freud and Marx (Wolfenstein, 1993).

PSYCHOLOGY AND WESTERN MARXISM

Aside from the object lesson of Soviet science, the Marxist ideas of nature and human nature which are most interesting derive from Western Marxism, in particular from the ideas of a small number of thinkers associated with the Frankfurt School of Critical Theory and subsequent writers influenced by them (Jay, 1973). Foremost among these were Wilhelm Reich, Herbert Marcuse and Erich Fromm. One could say that they all took as their starting point the question of how the Germans could have allowed a Fascist regime to be democratically elected and establish a dictatorship. What they had in common, at least in the 1930s, was a profound belief in ideology as a material force in the deepest layers of the unconscious. All were thinking within the framework of psychoanalysis, although Marcuse was not a clinician.

Reich believed that all that stood between oppressed people and a return to a spontaneous, sexually liberated way of being was the removal of repression. He made a searching study of how mass psychology propagated authoritarianism through the generations ánd through the workplace and the family. One could say that his diagnosis was profound, but his therapy was Utopian and simplistic in the extreme. De-repression was all. He wrote a series of excellent essays and pamphlets between 1929 and 1934 (Reich, 1972), culminating in his classic, *The Mass Psychology of Fascism* (1933). Thereafter he became increasingly preoccupied with the idea that sexual energy or libido took a physical form, which he called orgone, and he set out to find it, accumulate it and increase its manifestations and benefits in people. He managed to outrage both the psychoanalytic and the communist authorities and was expelled from both organisations. (Orthodox psychoanalysis has never been tolerant of radicals and Marxists; see Jacoby, 1983.) Reich wandered about Europe for a time and ended up in the United States, where he was first a guru in an Utopian community, then was arrested and imprisoned for contravening federal regulations in the course of his research on orgone and the causes and cure of cancer. By this time he believed that he could accumulate orgone in boxes which he sold. He died in prison in an advanced state of paranoia. In spite of his tragic later life, Reich's analyses of the mediations of authoritarianism in the lives and unconscious of people remain important (I. Reich, 1969; Sharaf, 1983). On the other hand, his attempt to construe libidinal energy as a measurable and controllable material phenomenon led to nonsense.

Marcuse's most insightful writings in psychology are *Eros and Civilization: A Philosophical Enquiry into Freud* (1955) and *One Dimensional Man: Studies in the Ideology of Advanced Industrial Societies* (1964), He refined his thinking in shorter essays: *An Essay on Liberation* (1969b) and *Five Lectures* (1970). Marcuse took as his starting point the classical libido theory of Freud and accepted the dual instinct theory (which Reich rejected) of Eros and Thanatos – the struggle between loving and destructive forces in the personality. In particular, he believed that these were genuinely instinctual, which set him apart from Reich (who only ontologised libido) and Fromm (who was opposed to what he considered Marcuse's instinctual reductionism). Where Reich placed his faith in de-repression, Marcuse believed that there is a deep instinctual integrity in human nature, a fundamentally rebellious impulse which would refuse to be smashed flat by oppressive forces in capitalist societies. He called this 'the great refusal'. Marcuse applied his approach to the history of capitalism and extended it to a deep critique of advanced capitalist societies and their intellectual, scientific and social systems. In particular, he took a number of Freudian notions and historicised them. To the reality principle, which he considered to be universal, he added the historically contingent 'performance principle', an extra requirement of conformism which is specific to a given period. To the universal need for repression to ensure civilisation, he added the 'surplus repression' of authoritarian societies, with their ersatz sexual liberation in 'repressive desublimation' of girlie magazines and the like. This had a counterpart in the political realm in his idea of 'repressive tolerance', a set of liberal practices which had the deeper function of maintaining the status quo (Marcuse, 1969a). He also argued that mass society was eroding the role of the father and the Freudian superego and, increasingly, controlling the individual directly by the media and education. These ideas were very influential in the student movement of the 1960s in Europe and the United States. Marcuse's criticisms of class politics estranged him from the organised left, but his critique of the ideological construction of reality in advanced capitalist society remains fresh and trenchant.

Erich Fromm's essays in the 1930s (1971) and his most admired text, *Fear of Freedom* (1941) were, like the writings of Reich and Marcuse, helpful in illuminating the rise of Fascism and the failure of liberal democracy to stand up to it. However, after he emigrated to the United States and then to Mexico, his successive books became more and more romantic, voluntarist and open to criticism by Marxists, until Marcuse (1969b, Postscript) openly rejected his work because of its departure from the libido theory, which distanced Fromm from the biological basis of Freudianism, and others labelled it as romantic and idealist. However, Fromm's writings gained a wide audience, in particular, *The Art of Loving* (1956) and *The Anatomy of Human Destructiveness* (1974). He continued to consider himself a Marxist, but his excursions into extreme versions of Marxist humanism and romanticism took him beyond the pale as far as most Marxists were concerned.

There was a rash of Marxist psychology books and essays in the 1970s, all attempting to demonstrate how the prevailing social forces acted by structural causality to shape the thoughts and personalities of people (Ingleby, 1970; Zaretsky, 1973; Schneider, 1975; Lichtman, 1982). Two writers in this genre are of particular interest. The first, Joel Kovel, provided a history of *White Racism* (1970), followed by *The Age of Desire* (1982) and a series of increasingly sophisticated essays (1988). Reich had been an early influence, but Kovel was more and more attracted by Marcuse, with the added advantage of being a psychiatrist and psychoanalyst. He eventually came to feel that neither Marxism nor psychoanalysis reach the deepest level of human nature, the level of spirituality, which he felt should be salvaged from the Judaeo-Christian tradition, and drew on liberation theology to supply what he considered to be the missing level of human nature (1991).

Victor Wolfenstein has made contributions to the Marxist analysis of human nature which are, in my opinion, nonpareil. His biographical study of Malcolm X (1981) is a profound synthesis of the unconscious and the socio-historical influences on his mind and life, while his *Psychoanalytic-Marxism* (1993) is the most searching and clear exploration of the issues involved in treating the unconscious and the socio-economic aspects of human nature without collapsing either into the other.

In *Partisans in an Uncertain World: The Psychoanalysis of Engagement,* Paul Hoggett (1992) reflects on the problems posed by the failure of the political project of left libertarianism in the 1960s and 1970s, and returns to the writings of Klein, Bion and Winnicott to re-found socialist politics on the basis of a deeper understanding of the internal obstacles to liberation. My own *Mental Space* (1994) covers similar ground, but focuses on the problem of ways of thinking about mind in a Cartesian world view based on mind-body dualism, and explores the contributions of the Kleinian tradition in psychoanalysis and group relations and Winnicott's concept of the transitional, as compared with the reifications of neo-Freudianism. Particular attention is paid to racism and virulent nationalism. Both books seek to make explicit what we are up against in human nature – individual, group and institutional – when we seek to change the world.

EVOLUTION AND HUMAN NATURE

Turning to a broader view of ideas of evolution and human nature, the writings of Karl Figlio and Donna Haraway, along with my own, have sought to unite analyses of the concept of nature in medicine and biology with careful studies of how ideology operates as a material force in the realm of theory. Figlio (1978, 1979, 1985) has concentrated on the ideological determination of medical concepts and of disease categories. I have focused on science and ideology in general and in the history of evolutionary theory as it bears on ideas of human nature (1971, 1973a, 1973b, 1977, 1985a, 1985b, 1985c, 1992). Haraway (1989) has provided a magisterial study of the ideological determinations of primate studies, as they construct a pedigree for the concept of humanity and the family which suits the prevailing mores and current epochal forces in the history of capitalism. The greatest strength of this work lies in the care and precision with which she traces the determinations and their interrelations – ideological, economic, institutional, personal relationships, patronage, gender, government, international relations, etc. She has gone beyond this in offering a vision of a liberatory science, including feminism, cyborgs and a postmodern space which transcends current notions of scientific practice (Haraway, 1990, 1992; see also Young, 1992).

The work of Figlio, Haraway and Young falls under the rubric of 'social constructivism' in the history, philosophy and social studies of science, an approach which owes something to Marxism and something else to other, less radical, approaches to knowledge, some of which are considered to be relativist about epistemology. They have some things in common with traditional studies in these disciplines. They have other things in common with an approach which is also socially constructivist, but which concentrates on the ways in which social, economic and ideological determinations are inscribed on human subjects. There have been several phases of this approach. One which flourished in the 1970s threw up periodicals which explored the role of structural causes at work in the psychology of individuals, e.g. *Ideology and Consciousness,* and on to the publication of collections and monographs developing this approach, e.g. *Changing the Subject: Psychology, Social Regulation and Subjectivity* (Henriques *et al.,* 1984) and Nikolas Rose's *Governing the Soul: The Shaping of the Private Self* (1989). Another facet was the journal *m/f,* which was preoccupied with the interrelations among masculinity/feminism, Marx/Freud. (I make no attempt to summarise the Marxist-feminist-psychoanalytic or the related Lacanian literatures (see Mitchell, 1974; J. Rose, 1986; 1993; Soble, 1986; Brennan, 1989) or the developments from Marxism to dissident sexuality (Giddens, 1992; Squires, 1993).)

A latter phase of this tendency found itself interpreting the determinations of individuality in a deconstructionist way. In some hands, this has led to the dissolution of any abiding sense of human nature or of the subject (Barsky, 1989; Frosh, 1991; Giddens, 1990, 1992). This takes us to the heart of postmodernism and, in my opinion, to pessimism and the danger of despair (Appignanesi, 1989; Young, 1989). Much of this work has occurred under the influence of the study of language and the conceptions of the *episteme* of a period and of power which have been elaborated by Michel Foucault (Macey, 1993). Much else has been influenced by Louis Althusser in its early phase and Jacques Lacan (Macey, 1988; Roudinesco, 1990, pp. 35–58, 377–8) in its later manifestations. It has also become increasingly bound up with the discipline of cultural studies (Grossberg *et al.,* 1992; During, 1993). I am not the right person to attempt an exposition of it. Whatever else can be said of it, it is post-Marxist and therefore outside my remit. There is no doubt, however, that this is a path which has been taken by many structuralist Marxists and which has led them away from transformative politics.

CONCLUSION

Standing back and reflecting on Marxist approaches to the concepts of evolution, biology and psychology in the broadest terms, the task is to reconcile the social construction of nature and human nature as an essentially *determinist* idea based on the detailed analysis of the relevant determinations, on the one hand, with the *transformative* idea of praxis – whereby nature and human nature are seen as planned, willed, visionary projects – an essentially *voluntarist* idea of revolutionary transformation, on the other. Looking more generally at Marxist approaches to nature, science and human nature, there is much that remains to be conceptualised. As befits a tradition committed to historicity, this is the ongoing project of a number of periodicals: *Science and Society*, which began in the 1930s and still appears; *Radical Science Journal* (1974–86), renamed *Science as Culture* (1987–) which also gave birth to *Free Associations: Psychoanalysis, Groups, Politics, Culture* (1984–). The rise of ecological and environmental concerns has led to new Marxist approaches to these issues: *Capitalism, Nature, Socialism: A Journal of Socialist Ecology* (1988); *Society and Nature: The International Journal of Political Ecology* (1992).

The main features characterising Marxist approaches to biology, evolution and psychology are the interpenetration of natural and human categories, the role of the environment and of social forces and the deep embedding of prevailing ideological forces in the motivations of the human subject. The biggest problem for a Marxist psychology is how to account for the origin and sustenance of revolutionary insight and energy.

REFERENCES

Appignanesi, L. (ed.) (1989) *Postmodernism: ICA Documents*, London: Free Association Books.

Barsky, R. (ed.) (1989) *Rethinking the Subject in Discourse*, special issue of *Discours Social/Social Discourse*, vol. 2 nos 1 and 2.

Bernal, J.D. (1949) 'The Biological Controversy in the Soviet Union and its Implications', *Modern Quarterly*, 4 (Summer) pp. 203–17.

Bernal, J.D. (1952–3) 'The Abdication of Science' *Modern Quarterly* 8 (no. 1) pp. 44–50.

Berry, C. (1986) *Human Nature*, London: Macmillan.

Best, S. and Kellner, D. (1991) *Postmodern Theory: Critical Interrogations*, London: Macmillan.

Brazier, M.A.B. (ed.) (1959) *The Central Nervous System and Behavior: Transactions of the First Conference*, New York: Josia Macy, Jr. Foundation.

Brennan, T. (ed.) (1989) *Between Feminism and Psychoanalysis*, London: Routledge.

Bukharin, N.I. (1931) 'Theory and Practice from the Standpoint of Dialectical Materialism', in Bukharin *et al.* (eds), *Science at the Cross Roads: Papers Presented to the International Congress of the History of Science and Technology held in London from June 29th to July 3rd, 1931 by the Delegates of the USSR*; reprinted Cass, 1971, pp. 11–40.

Callinicos, A. (1989) *Against Postmodernism: A Marxist Critique*, Cambridge: Polity Press.

Docherty, T. (1993)
Postmodernism: A Reader, Hemel Hempstead: Harvester Wheatsheaf.

During, S. (1993) *The Cultural Studies Reader*, London: Routledge.

Engels, F. ([1873–86]1964) *The Dialectics of Nature*, 3rd edn, Moscow: Progress.

Figlio, K. (1978) 'Chlorosis and Chronic Disease in Nineteenth-century Britain: the Social Constitution of Somatic Illness in a Capitalist Society', *International Journal of Health Services* **8** pp. 589–617.

Figlio, K. (1979) 'Sinister Medicine: A Critique of Left Approaches to Medicine', *Radical Science Journal*, no. 9 pp. 14–68.

Figlio, K. (1985) 'Medical Diagnosis, Class Dynamics, Social Stability', in L. Levidow and R. M. Young (eds), *Science, Technology and the Labour Process: Marxist Studies* vol. 2, London: Free Association Books.

Fromm, E. ([1941]1956) *Fear Of Freedom*, London: Routledge.

Fromm, E. (1956) *The Art of Loving*, New York: Harper.

Fromm, E. (1971) *The Crisis of Psychoanalysis: Essays on Freud, Marx and Social Psychology*, London: Cape.

Fromm, E. (1974) *The Anatomy of Human Destructiveness*, London: Cape.

Frosh, S. (1991) *Identity Crisis: Modernity, Psychoanalysis and the Self*, London: Macmillan.

Giddens, A. (1990) *The Consequences of Modernity*, Cambridge: Polity Press.

Giddens. A. (1992) *The Transformations of Intimacy: Sexuality, Love and Eroticism in Modern Societies*, Cambridge: Polity Press.

Goldsmith, M. (1980) *Sage: A Life of J.D. Bernal*, London: Hutchinson.

Graham, L.R. (1971) *Science and Philosophy in the Soviet Union*, London: Allen Lane.

Gramsci, A. ([1929–35]1971) *Selections from the Prison Notebooks of Antonio Gramsci*, London: Lawrence and Wishart.

Grossberg, L., Nelson, C. and Treicher, P. (eds) (1992) *Cultural Studies*, London: Routledge.

Haldane, J.B.S. (1948) 'The Lysenko Controversy', *The Listener* 9 December.

Haldane, J.B.S. (1949) 'In Defence of Genetics', *Modern Quarterly* **4** (Summer) pp. 194–202.

Haraway, D. (1989) *Primate Visions: Gender, Race, and Nature in the World of Modern Science*, London: Routledge.

Haraway, D. (1990) *Simians, Cyborgs and Women: The Reinvention of Nature*, London: Free Association Books.

Haraway, D. (1992) 'The Promises of Monsters: A Regenerative Politics for Inappropriate/d Others', in Grossberg *et al.* (eds), *Cultural Studies*, pp. 295–337, London: Routledge.

Henriques, J., Hollway, W., Urwin, C., Venn, C. and Walderdine, V. (1984) *Changing the Subject: Psychology, Social Regulation and Subjectivity*, London: Methuen.

Hoggett, P. (1992) *Partisans in an Uncertain World: The Psychoanalysis of Engagement*, London: Free Association Books.

Huxley, J. (1949) *Soviet Genetics and World Science: Lysenko and the Meaning of Heredity*, London: Chatto and Windus.

Ingleby, D. (1970) 'Ideology and the Human Sciences: Some Comments on the Role of Reification in Psychology and Psychiatry', *The Human Con-*

text 2 pp. 159–87; reprinted in T. Patemen (ed.) (1972), *Counter Course: A Handbook for Course Criticism*, Harmondsworth: Penguin.

Jacoby, R. (1983) *The Repression of Psychoanalysis: Otto Fenichel and the Political Freudians*, New York: Basic.

Jameson, F. (1991) *Postmodernism: or, The Cultural Logic of Late Capitalism*, London: Verso.

Jay, M. (1973) *The Dialectical Imagination: A History of the Frankfurt School and the Institute of Social Research, 1923–1950*, New York: Little, Brown and Co.

Joravsky, D. (1961) *Soviet Marxism and Natural Science, 1917–1932*, London: Routledge.

Joravsky, D. (1970) *The Lysenko Affair*, Harvard: Harvard University Press.

Joravsky, D. (1989 *Russian Psychology: A Critical History*, Oxford: Blackwell.

Jordan, Z. A. (1967) *The Evolution of Dialectical Materialism: A Philosophical and Sociological Analysis*, London: Macmillan.

Kovel, J. (1970) *White Racism: A Psychohistory*, New York: Pantheon; reprinted Free Association Books, 1988.

Kovel, J. (1982) *The Age of Desire*, New York: Pantheon.

Kovel, J. (1988) *The Radical Spirit: Essays on Psychoanalysis and Society*, London: Free Association Books.

Kovel, J. (1991) *History and Spirit*, Boston: Beacon.

Lecourt, D. (1977) *Proletarian Science? The Case of Lysenko*, London: New Left Books.

Lenin, V.I. ([1918]1969) 'The Immediate Tasks of the Soviet Government', in *Selected Works* pp. 401–31, London: Lawrence and Wishart.

Lewontin, R. and Levins, R. (1976) 'The Problem of Lysenkoism', in H. and S. Rose (eds), *The Radicalisation of Science*, London: Macmillan.

Lewontin, R. and Levins, R. (1985) *The Dialectical Biologist*, Harvard: Harvard University Press.

Lichtman, R. (1982) *The Production of Desire: The Integration of Psychoanalysis into Marxist Theory*, London: Collier-Macmillan.

Lukács, G. ([1923]1971) *History and Class Consciousness: Studies in Marxist Dialectics*, London: Merlin.

Luria, A.R. ([1932]1960) *The Nature of Human Conflicts*, New York: Grove.

Luria, A.R. ([1962]1966) *Higher Cortical Functions in Man*, New York: Basic.

Luria, A.R. (1968) *The Mind of a Mnemonist*, New York: Basic.

Luria, A.R. (1973) *The Working Brain*, New York: Basic.

Luria, A.R. (1979) *The Making of Mind: A Personal Account of Soviet Psychology*, Cambridge, MA: Harvard.

Lysenko, T.D. (1948) *Soviet Biology: A Report to the Lenin Academy of Agricultural Sciences, Moscow, 1948*, New York: International Publishers.

Macey, D. (1988) *Lacan in Contexts*, London: Verso.

Macey, D. (1993) *The Lives of Michel Foucault*, London: Hutchinson.

Marcuse, H. (1955) *Eros and Civilization: A Philosophical Inquiry into Freud*, Boston: Beacon; 2nd edn with a new preface, London: Allen Lane, 1969.

Marcuse, H. (1958) *Soviet Marxism*, Boston, MA: Beacon.

Marcuse, H. (1964) *One Dimensional Man: Studies in the Ideology of Advanced Industrial Societies*, London: Routledge and Kegan Paul; reprinted Ark, 1986.

Marcuse, H. (1969a) 'Repressive Tolerance', in R.P. Wolff et al. (eds), *A Critique of Pure Tolerance*, London: Cape.

Marcuse, H. (1969b) *An Essay on Liberation*, Boston: Beacon.

Marcuse, H. (1970) *Five Lectures: Psychoanalysis, Politics, and Utopia*, London: Allen Lane.

Marx, K. ([1844]1961) *The Economic and Philosophical Manuscripts of 1844*, Moscow: Foreign Languages.

Marx, K. (1967) *Capital: A Critique of Political Economy*, vol. 1, Harmondsworth: Penguin.

Marx, K. and Engels, F. (1848 [1973]) 'Manifesto of the Communist Party', in *The Revolutions of 1848: Political Writings*, vol. I, Harmondsworth: Penguin.

Marx, K. and Engels, F. (1954) *Marx and Engels on Malthus*, New York: International Publishers.

Marx, K. and Engels, F. (1955/65) *Selected Correspondence*, Moscow: Progress.

Medvedev, Z.A. (1969) *The Rise and Fall of T.D. Lysenko*, Columbia; reprinted New York: Anchor, 1971.

Medvedev, Z.A. and Medvedev, R.A. (1971) *A Question of Madness*, London: Macmillan.

Michurin, I.V. (1949) *Selected Works*, Moscow: Foreign Languages.

Mitchell, J. (1974) *Psychoanalysis and Feminism*, Harmondsworth: Penguin.

Ollman, B. (1971) *Alienation: Marx's Concept of Man in Capitalist Society*, Cambridge: Cambridge University Press.

Orwell, G. ([1949]1970) *1984*, Harmondsworth: Penguin.

Pavlov, I. P. (1927) *Conditioned Reflexes: An Investigation of the Physiological Activity of the Cerebral Cortex*, Oxford; reprinted New York: Dover, n.d.

RSJ Collective (1981) 'Science, Technology, Medicine and the Socialist Movement', *Radical Science Journal* 11 pp. 3–72.

Reich, I.O. (1969) *Wilhelm Reich: A Personal Biography*, New York: Avon.

Reich, W. ([1933]1975) *The Mass Psychology of Fascism*, Harmondsworth: Penguin.

Reich, W. (1972) *Sex-Pol: Essays, 1929–1934*, New York: Vintage.

Rorty, R. (1980) *Philosophy and the Mirror of Nature*, Oxford: Blackwell.

Rorty, R. (1982) *Consequences of Pragmatism (Essays 1972–1980)*, Minneapolis: Minnesota.

Rorty, R. (1989) *Contingency, Irony, and Solidarity*, Cambridge: Cambridge University Press.

Rose, J. (1986) *Sexuality in the Field of Vision*, London: Verso.

Rose, J. (1993) *Why War? – Psychoanalysis, Politics, and the Return to Melanie Klein*, Oxford: Blackwell.

Rose, N. (1989) *Governing the Soul: The Shaping of the Private Self*, London: Routledge.

Rose, S. (ed.) (1982) *Against Biological Determinism*. The Dialectics of Biology Group, London: Alison and Busby.

Rose, S. (1982) *Towards a Liberatory Biology: The Dialectics of Biology Group*, London: Alison and Busby.

Roudinesco, E. (1990) *Jacques Lacan and Co.: A History of Psychoanalysis in France 1925–85*, London: Free Association Books.

Safonov, V. (1951) *Land in Bloom*, Moscow: Foreign Languages.

Sharaf, Myron (1983) *Fury on Earth: A Biography of Wilhelm Reich*, London: Deutsch.

Schmidt, A. (1972) *The Concept of Nature in Marx*, London: New Left Books.

Schneider, M. (1975) *Neurosis and Civilization: A Marxist/Freudian Synthesis*, New York: Seabury.

Soble, A. (1986) *Pornography: Marxism, Feminism, and the Future of Sexuality*, Yale.

Solzhenitsyn, A. (1973, 1975, 1978) *The Gulag Archipelago*, 3 vols, London: Collins/Harvill; reprinted Fontana, 1974, 1976, 1978.

Squires, J. (ed.) (1993) *Perversity*, special issue of *New Formations* **19**.

Stoletov, V.N. (1953) *The Fundamentals of Michurin Biology*, Moscow: Foreign Languages.

Theory, Culture and Society (1988) special issue on *Postmodernism* **5** (nos 2–3).

US Department of Health, Education and Welfare, Public Health Service (1950) *The Central Nervous System and Behavior: Translations from the Russian Medical Literature*. Bethesda: Russian Scientific Translation Program, National Institutes of Health.

Wells, H.K. (1956) *Ivan P. Pavlov: Toward a Scientific Psychology and Psychiatry*, New York International; reprinted London: Lawrence and Wishart.

Wells, H.K. (1960) *Sigmund Freud: A Pavlovian Critique*, London: Lawrence and Wishart.

Werskey, G. (1978) *The Visible College: A Collective Biography of British Scientists and Socialists of the 1930s*, London: Allen Lane.

Wetter, G. (1952) *Dialectical Materialism: A Historical and Systematic Study of Philosophy in the Soviet Union*; revised edn, London: Routledge, 1958.

Wexler, P. (1983) *Critical Social Psychology*, London: Routledge.

Wolfenstein, E.V. ([1981]1990) *The Victims of Democracy: Malcolm X and the Black Revolution*, London: Free Association Books.

Wolfenstein, E.V. (1993) *Psychoanalytic-Marxism (Groundwork)*, London: Free Association Books.

Young, R.M. (1971) 'Evolutionary Biology and Ideology: Then and Now', *Science Studies* **1** pp. 177–206; reprinted in W. Fuller (ed.) (1972), *The Biological Revolution: Social Good or Social Evil?* New York: Doubleday Anchor.

Young, R.M. (1973a) 'The Historiographic and Ideological Contexts of the Nineteenth-Century Debate on Man's Place in Nature', in Young, R.M. (ed.) (1985), pp. 164–248.

Young, R.M. (1973b) 'The Human Limits of Nature', in J. Benthall (ed.), *The Limits of Human Nature*, London: Allen Lane.

Young, R.M. (1977) 'Science *is* Social Relations', *Radical Science Journal* 5, pp. 65–131.

Young, R.M. (1978) 'Getting Started on Lysenkoism', *Radical Science Journal* 6/7 pp. 81–105.

Young, R.M. (1980) 'The Relevance of Bernal's Questions', *Radical Science Journal* 10, pp. 85–94.

Young, R.M. (1985a) *Darwin's Metaphor: Nature's Place in Victorian Culture*, Cambridge: Cambridge University Press.

Young, R.M. (1985b) 'Darwinism *is* Social', in D. Kohn (ed.), *The Darwinian Heritage*, Princeton: Princeton University Press.

Young, R.M. (1985c) 'Is Nature a Labour Process?', in L. Levidow and R. M. Young (eds), *Science, Technology and the Labour Process: Marxist Studies*, vol. 2, London: Free Association Books.

Young, R.M. (1989) 'Post-modernism and the Subject: Pessimism of the Will', *Free Associations* 16, pp. 81–96.

Young, R.M. (1992) 'Science, Ideology and Donna Haraway', *Science as Culture* 15, pp. 7–46.

Young, R.M. (1994) *Mental Space*, London: Process Press.

Zaretsky, E. (1973) 'Male Supremacy and the Unconscious', *Socialist Revolution* 24, pp. 7–57.

Zirkle, C. (1949) *Death of a Science in Russia: The Fate of Genetics as Described in Pravda and Elsewhere*, Philadelphia: Pennsylvania.

3

MARXISM, THE FRANKFURT SCHOOL, AND WORKING-CLASS PSYCHOLOGY

Martin Roiser and Carla Willig

There is a Marxist tradition of empirical research on the working class. Its purpose, put broadly, has been to describe the relationship between workers' conditions and their consciousness. It began in the nineteenth century with Engels' research on the English working class and Marx's questionnaire study of French workers. In the early twentieth century Adolf Levenstein, researching for the German Social Democratic Party, added a psychological dimension to his study of workers. In the late 1920s Erich Fromm and Hilde Weiss of the Frankfurt School developed the psychological aspect further, introducing the concept of authoritarianism in their workers study. Finally, in the post-war United States, Theodor Adorno, together with a team of European and American scholars, carried out the 'authoritarian personality' study, in which psychological ideas became dominant, and the concept of class largely disappeared. This chapter discusses this tradition, and its increasing focus on psychology in its attempts to explain authoritarianism in late capitalist society.

In 1844 Engels wrote *The Condition of the Working Class in England*. He used reports by factory inspectors, health officials and the like and also spoke to workers directly. He recounted that:

> I have studied the various official and non-official documents as far as I was able to get them – I have not been satisfied with this, I wanted more than a mere abstract knowledge of my subject, I wanted to see you in your own homes, to observe you in your everyday life, to chat with you on your conditions and grievances, to witness your struggles against the social and political power of your oppressors (Engels, 1969, p. 323).

Engels produced a graphic account of the degrading conditions in which workers were forced to live. In the latter part of the book he discussed their responses to this situation. He wrote:

It must be admitted, even if I had not proved it so often, that the English workers cannot feel happy in this condition ... they must strive to secure a better more human position ... and this they cannot do without attacking the interest of the bourgeoisie (Engels, 1969, p. 239).

He described their responses through machine-wrecking, secret associations, trade unions and Chartism, in short the development of class consciousness. The argument that the consciousness of workers followed from their material conditions became central to Marxist theory. But it was not argued that workers ideas arose simply from their conditions. In *The German Ideology*, Marx and Engels (1965, p. 60) wrote that, 'the ruling ideas of any era are the ideas of the ruling class'. Thus workers' attitudes combined proletarian consciousness and bourgeois ideology, but were dominated by the latter.

Marx continued this research with a questionnaire for French workers in 1880, the *Enquete Ouvriere*. It became known only when discovered by the Frankfurt School researcher Hilde Weiss in the 1920s. Its 100 items asked about the worker's occupation, size of workshop, sanitary conditions, safety of machines and so on. Most of the questions were demographic and neutrally phrased, although one asked, 'Has the employer ever paid compensation to those who have met with an accident while working to enrich him?' Another asked, 'Can they go on strike or are they only permitted to be the humble servants of their masters' (Bottomore and Rubel, 1963, p. 218).

It was hoped that by setting out before them their full conditions of life workers would be spurred into collective action. Malon's *Revue Socialiste* off-printed some 25,000 copies. Unfortunately the magazine went out of business soon after and no replies have been recovered. Both these studies may be classed as 'action research'. They differ sharply from the method and intention of, for instance, Rowntree (1901), who was concerned to classify levels of poverty, sobriety and cleanliness from the point of view of the social administrator.

WORKING-CLASS PSYCHOLOGY

In their studies of workers, Marx and Engels did not deal in any detail with psychological matters such as personality or attitude. Engels (1969, p. 239) wrote that the English working man would be 'roused to passion against the tyranny of the propertied class despite his native Northern coldness' and also that selfishness was the 'predominant trait' of the English bourgeois. But these were incidental remarks. Marx included only one attitudinal item. He asked what workers 'thought of the arbitration committees' (Bottomore and Rubel, 1963, p. 217). It was only later that German Marxists, such as Kautsky and Bernstein, systematically introduced a psychological dimension. They wished to add 'social drives' to 'economic drives', in order to explain individual actions (in Jay, 1973, p. 92).

This new psychological interest is evident in the work of Levenstein (1912). Like Marx and Engels, he asked basic demographic questions, but he added cultural and attitudinal items and attempted to fit character typologies to the responses. He asked workers about their feelings of dependency on their employers, their union and party affiliations, hopes for the future, and leisure habits such as reading or seeking solitude in the forests. Responses were classified into related groupings and four types emerged; the 'intellectual', the 'contemplative', the 'mis-educated', and the 'mass'. Levenstein's approach was part of an ongoing tradition of typological psychology, which included William James' 'tough and tender-minded types', and Freud's 'libidinal types'.

Typologies are often based on some notion of biological temperament or instinct. They thus tend to present a rigid view of individual and society. But Levenstein's typology was not biological in conception. He suggested that psychological types were influenced by a person's location in the labour process. In this respect his ideas were compatible with Marxism. Human personality would change if labour were made less monotonous. But he was not clear as to how that change would take place, nor did he suggest that it might involve a rapid break with the past. Levenstein's approach did not carry the spirit of revolutionary self-emancipation evident in Marx and Engels' work. It was conceived within the gradualist Marxism of the German Social Democratic Party. It was concerned to monitor the working class while preparing for the inevitable socialist transformation of society. Levenstein made the depressing conclusion from his work that the monotonous labour associated with modern technology led to physical and psychological degeneration. He thereby anticipated the Frankfurt School's connection between the technology of late capitalism and the deterioration of working-class consciousness.

The German Social Democratic Party's version of Marxism argued that the advent of socialism was determined by the advancement of capitalism within a particular country. Germany's industrial development was advanced, its working class huge, its trade unions well organised, and its Marxist party large and influential. But the First World War and the party's role in its outbreak was to shatter this version of Marxism. In 1914, Social Democratic deputies in the Reichstag voted for war credits, an act of class treachery that plunged millions of workers across Europe into war against one another. After the war, German Social Democracy, still nominally Marxist, was responsible for the reconstruction of capitalism and the violent suppression of revolutionary forces, including the murders of Karl Liebknecht and Rosa Luxemburg. In contrast the Bolsheviks, in economically backward Russia, opposed the war and led a workers' revolution.

This diametrical contradiction of expectations threw Marxist theorists into confusion, to 'a searching re-examination of the very foundations of Marxist theory, with the hope of explaining past errors and preparing for future action' (Jay, 1973, p. 3), and to the creation of the Frankfurt School and to further research on the working class.

THE FOUNDATION OF THE FRANKFURT SCHOOL

The School began informally with a Marxist workshop in Summer 1922. The participants hoped to arrive at a 'true' Marxism through discussion among different trends. Felix Weil used his substantial inheritance to found the 'Institute for Social Research'. It was independent of political party, and largely independent of the university system. Early appointments included the social philosopher Max Horkheimer and the economist Friedrich Pollock. Carl Grunberg was appointed as director. He was editor of the 'Archive for the History of Socialism' which assisted the school's examination of the roots of Marxism and became its official journal until 1930. The archival research brought to light much early Marxist writing. But it was only with Grunberg's departure that the School developed the dialectical and critical approach for which it is now famous. Horkheimer became director in 1929 and founded the *Zeitschrift fur Sozialforschung*. In the same period it began to integrate psychology and later psychoanalysis into its theoretical approach.

The Frankfurt School gathered an extraordinarily talented group; Max Horkheimer, Theodor Adorno, Erich Fromm, Franz Neuman, Friedrich Pollock, Walter Benjamin, Hilde Weiss, Herbert Marcuse, Felix Weil, and many others. They carried out theoretical and empirical work in areas of philosophy, sociology, psychology and cultural criticism. Their initial intent was to explain the failure of German Social Democracy. To this end they developed a major Marxist theoretical critique. As the events of the 1920s and 1930s unfolded they attempted to explain the nature and culture of the mass society of late capitalism. They studied its authoritarian tendencies at the levels of both political economy and psychology and, in particular, the rise of Fascism.

The scope and development of their work may be summarised under four headings:

1 Archival research and philosophical writings which sought to re-establish an authentic Marxism and in particular to restore the dialectic to the mechanical Marxism of Kautsky. This work brought about what is now known as 'critical theory'. It dealt with issues of truth, dialectics and phenomenology.

2 An analysis of political economy which argued that late capitalism had taken on a new form, namely that of state monopoly capitalism, relatively undescribed in the works of Marx and Engels. It dealt with economics and politics; for instance Pollock (1940) on 'State Capitalism; its possibilities and limitations' and Horkheimer (1940) on 'The Authoritarian State'.

3 A study of the socio-cultural characteristics of this new society such as Marcuse on the social implications of modern technology, Adorno on

the fetish character in music, and Benjamin's 'Art in the age of mechanical reproduction'.

4 An examination of the social psychology of this form of society and its impact on the individual. This included studies of authority and the family, of anti-semitic prejudice, and of the authoritarian personality, cultivated under late capitalism. This involved work by Fromm in Weimar Germany and by Adorno and others in the United States. It is this group of studies that developed the psychological aspect of their work.

Our subsequent discussion will concentrate on this work. Central to it is the concept of authoritarianism. Although this was increasingly seen in psychological terms it initially had a basis in political economy.

In their theory of neo-capitalism, the Frankfurt School extended the argument of classical Marxism that, as capitalism developed, capital would become increasingly concentrated. As a political consequence the state would play a growing role in regulating the relationships between the gathering accumulations of capital.

Horkheimer (1940) argued that the authoritarian state negated the market economy but was also subversive of working-class organisation. He blamed, among other things, the media;

> the art of authoritarian rule must be systematically furthered by all media of communication – newspapers, radio, and movies, to isolate individuals from one another. They should listen to everyone, from the Fuhrer to the local boss, but not to one another (in Arato and Gebhardt, 1988, p. 103).

They did not argue that Marx and Engels were wrong, rather that society had developed in an unexpected manner. The latest phase of capitalism was a new form in which cultural and psychological factors were increasingly important. They were thus able to turn the expectations of German Marxism upside down, thereby offering an explanation for its disconfirmation in the First World War. Developments in late capitalism did not move the revolution closer, they made it more difficult, because the psychological effects of mass society debilitated working-class resistance. The authoritarian state exercised control over the economic base of society and over its superstructure of political and cultural institutions, such as the media. These ideas were present in Marx and Engels, but the Frankfurt School extended the argument considerably. Following their analysis of mass society under late capitalism they argued that irrationality was not merely a feature of the economics of capitalism and its political institutions. It now entered the individual psyche. There it recruited a deeper, more psychological, irrationality which was slow to change and obstructed the road to emancipation. Late capitalism created an authoritarian state, an authoritarian culture and an authoritarian personality.

Such theoretical arguments could not be substantiated without empirical investigation of the sociology and psychology of the working class. Erich Fromm set out to do this with his study of blue- and white-collar workers in Weimar Germany. In turn this led to studies on authority and the family, anti-semitic prejudice, and the authoritarian personality. These were central to the school's critique of late capitalism and their analysis of Fascism.

In 1929 Fromm and Weiss conducted their study of workers in Weimar Germany. It used a 271-item questionnaire which contained demographic questions, together with attitudinal and cultural items. They asked, for instance, 'How in your opinion can a new war be prevented?' and 'Who, in your view, has the real power in the State today?', 'Do you like jazz?', 'Do you like present day women's fashions?', 'What books do you read?', 'Do you think you can bring up children entirely without corporal punishment?' (Fromm, 1984, p. 268).

The study borrowed from Marx's *Enquete Ouvriere* which Weiss had found in the archives of the Social Democratic Party. They also recognised merit in Levenstein's work;

> [his] social psychological enquiry of 1912 into the workers question is the only study which like our own used a questionnaire to capture social attitudes and behaviour outside the work situation. Nevertheless one does miss a theoretical interpretation of the data in Levenstein's work ... (Fromm, 1984, p. 41).

Fromm sought to provide a theoretical interpretation of his data.

The responses were content-analysed and subjected to descriptive and interpretative classification. Fromm argued that, 'the replies must amount to more than a number of independent statements about this or that problem, they represent a unity in which every single detail is related to the responding personality' (Fromm, 1984, p. 205). The analysis went further to 'allow for certain insights into the personality structure of individual respondents' (Fromm, 1984, p. 207). The researchers selected three sets (or complexes) of questions, concerned with politics (e.g. 'How can a war be prevented'), authority (e.g. 'Can children be brought up without corporal punishment'), and attitudes to fellows (e.g. 'Do you lend money to friends'). Responses were classified as 'Radical/Revolutionary', 'Authoritarian', 'Compromise' and 'Neutral'. Individuals were then identified according to their syndrome, from RRR, the most radical, through to AAA, the most authoritarian, on the basis of their responses. Thus one respondent, typed as a radical, said that war could be prevented 'through the actions of the workers', believed that one 'achieved more with words than blows' in dealing with children. On the other hand a typical authoritarian said 'one can never prevent a war' and that corporal punishment 'was necessary' for children. The two individuals had different reading preferences, the radical liking Maxim Gorki, Jack London and Upton Sinclair, while the authoritarian preferred the Kaiser's memoirs and the Bible.

Fromm argued that some of the systematic divergences from which the typologies were derived, 'represented the contrasting programmes of the Left and the Right'. He argued that, 'the psychic structure of a class is an aspect of its objective situation' (Fromm, 1984, p. 207). He then outlined an argument which became central to the Frankfurt School and important in its move away from classical Marxism and towards psychology. He wrote, 'psychic change is slower than economic change ... class members can be very advanced in their political views, but very reactionary in their emotional attitudes' (Fromm, 1984, p. 209). Thus some respondents were politically radical, but personally authoritarian, for instance wishing to submit to a strong leader.

Despite these mentions of 'psychic change' and 'emotional attitudes' the Weimar study owed more to Marx than to Freud, indeed it did not mention psychoanalysis. Although Fromm's typology was to open the way to a psychoanalytic interpretation, his use of character typology stemmed from Levenstein and predated Freud's 'libidinal types'. Authoritarianism was not explained in Freudian terms as the product of a strict childhood, as it was to be in the post-war California study. The integration of psychoanalysis into the work of the Frankfurt School, for which Fromm was largely responsible, came after the Weimar study. In 1932 he published 'On the method and function of an analytic social psychology'. Here he criticised the view that Marxism relied on an 'economic psychology', that people's ideas rose directly from their financial circumstances. Fromm argued that Marx and Engels had a more complex view of the relationship between economic base and the ideological superstructure of society. But he went on to say that, in practice, there was a 'gap in Marxism', 'Lacking a satisfactory psychology, Marx and Engels could not explain how the material base was reflected in man's head and heart' (in Arato and Gebhardt, 1988, p. 488). But it was not until 1940 that the full statement of this argument appeared, in the well-known *Fear of Freedom* (Fromm, 1955). Here he argued that the characteristics of possessiveness and puritanism, typical of the early bourgeoisie, had persisted into late capitalism. The psychoanalyst recognised these in the obsessive orderliness of the anal character type, beset with guilt and with tendencies to sado-masochism. Such characteristics were especially evident in the psychology of the petit bourgeois, but were also present in some members of the working class. This was the psychological basis of authoritarianism. In times of social and economic crisis, he argued, such characteristics could become manifest, widespread, and of serious political consequence.

The evidence on which this was based came from the Weimar workers study, which had been published in brief in German in 1936 (Horkheimer *et al.*, 1936). The whole study remained unprocessed and unpublished for many years, which greatly diminished its impact, but it is of great importance. It 'was integrally related to the programme of the Frankfurt Institute, sometimes even described as a central work' (Bonss, 1984, p. 3). Fromm said later in life that Horkheimer delayed publication because he thought it 'too Marxist' and could endanger the Institute. Of course Horkheimer had a point, but if the study had been published at the time its impact would have been great. It might even have exercised some restraining influence on the increasingly psychological direction of subsequent research.

PREJUDICE AND AUTHORITARIANISM IN AMERICA

When the Nazis came to power they closed the Institute on the ground of anti-state activities. Its members fled, but not all escaped. Karl Landauer died in the gas chambers and Walter Benjamin was driven to suicide when on the point of escape from occupied France. The School was re-established in the United States. Renamed the 'New Institute for Social Research' it continued work. Though they were now far from Nazi Germany, the new location was not inappropriate for research purposes. The United States was an advanced industrial society and many of the social and cultural features of neo-capitalism were to be found there. Thus they carried out a project on anti-semitism among American workers, funded by the Jewish Labor Committee. A disguised interview technique was used. Assistants working in factories memorised a set of questions which they asked when the Jewish question was raised, for instance: 'Do you think there is a Jewish problem?' 'How do Jews behave at work?' 'What about the alleged Jewish industriousness?' 'Are they aggressive, clannish, too smart etc?' (Adorno et al., 1950, p. 606). Some 500 interviews were conducted and results categorised according to features such as union membership and ethnic background. About half the workers surveyed showed some form of anti-semitic bias (Jay, 1973, p. 225). Horkheimer feared public reaction and the report was never published. The purpose of the study was to isolate and examine anti-semitism. Its attention was still on the working class, but there was not the sense of opposing world views so prominent in the Weimar study. The focus now shifted towards the prejudiced individual.

The 'Authoritarian Personality' research continued this trend. It was a large-scale project whose authors included European exiles and established American academics. It used a series of Likert-style attitude scales concerning Anti-Semitism, Ethnocentrism, Political and Economic Conservatism, and Implicit Anti-Democratic Trends (or potentiality for Fascism). Respondents were asked to indicate levels of agreement with items such as: 'The trouble with letting Jews into a nice neighbourhood is that they gradually give it a typical Jewish atmosphere' (AS) and 'Negroes have their own rights but it is best to keep them in their own districts and schools to prevent too much contact with whites' (EC) and 'The only way to provide adequate medical care for the entire population is through some program of socialised medicine' (PEC-ve) and 'Obedience and respect for authority are the most important virtues children must learn' (F) (Adorno et al., 1950). High scores on the attitude scales and on the F-scale indicated an authoritarian personality type with a potentiality for Fascism. They also used interviews and the Thematic Apperception Test. These last two techniques were used to look inwards into the personalities and family backgrounds of high and low ethnocentric individuals for correlates of their attitudes. It contrasts with the Weimar study which looked outwards for correspondence with political affiliation. It found that there was a minority of authoritarian personality types. While the Weimar study looked to political world views for its typology this study focused on child-rearing practices. In part this reflected the absence of political affiliations in the American sample, in part it reflected the changed outlook of the researchers. The conclusion was that there was a potentiality for Fascism in American society despite its democratic institutions and lack of any significant Fascist movement.

The 900-page work *The Authoritarian Personality* was published in 1950 to considerable acclaim. It was widely read and the scales were used in subsequent research. Its appeals for the reduction of prejudice and anti-semitism and the encouragement of tolerance through milder child-rearing and educational methods were well-received by liberal America. Roger Brown wrote: '"The Authoritarian Personality" has affected American life, the theory of prejudice it propounded has become a part of popular culture and a force against racial discrimination' (Brown, 1970, p. 479). But the study also attracted criticism, both methodological and ideological.

The concept of typology was under critical attack. Anne Anastasi, the leading personality psychologist, argued that traits were generally normally distributed, not clustered into types. Adorno accepted this and endeavoured, with considerable skill, to extricate himself from these criticisms by saying that,

> Ours is a critical typology in the sense that it comprehends the typification of men itself as a social function. The more rigid a type the more deeply does he show the hallmarks of social rubber stamps. This is in accordance with the characterisation of our high scorers by traits such as rigidity and stereotypical thinking (Adorno *et al.*, 1950, p. 749).

Thus authoritarianism was due to rigid thinking of the type and not of the typologist. However, this psychological typology, as distinct from the political typology of the Weimar study, had an important corollary. While the narrow-minded authoritarians 'thought themselves' into distinct categories, the broader-minded democrats did not. They were thus less distinctive as a type and indeed tended to fade away. In comparison, Fromm's radical type was quite distinctive and in sharp conflict with the authoritarian.

But the rigidity of the authoritarian personality concept was not the main reason for its critical reception. Anastasi's critique was essentially liberal. The main attack came from the Right. The ideologists of the Cold War insisted that extremism of the Right was symmetrically matched by that of the Left. There thus had to be left-wing authoritarians and a search was launched for this sub-type. It was difficult to look in America where few would admit to being communists, and impossible to research in the Eastern bloc. Eysenck claimed to have found left authoritarians in Britain, but his interpretation of his findings was vigorously disputed (see Brown,

1970, p. 526). In Australia, Ray (1972) redesigned the scales but still could not convincingly locate the left authoritarian. More recently the demise of the communist parties has removed the impulse for this search.

The authoritarian personality has thus survived reasonably intact as a creature of the Right; racist, disciplinarian and conservative. The remaining problem for our discussion concerns not so much the description of the phenomenon, nor even its origins, but whether it can sustain the considerable role given it by the Frankfurt School. Individual authoritarianism was advanced as the inevitable human product of the culture of late capitalism and as a potential cause of authoritarian and Fascist government. An important test of this idea is whether it helps explain what has happened politically during the period of late capitalism.

In the societies of the 1930s the association between late capitalism and authoritarian government was actually very uneven. Germany was the obvious confirming example, showing both features. The findings of the Weimar study would have been rightly seen as predictive had they been published in 1931. But Fascism also triumphed in relatively backward Spain and Portugal, and failed to make headway in advanced Britain and the United States, which maintained more or less liberal democracies. In the post-war United States the findings of The Authoritarian Personality seemed ominous against the backdrop of McCarthyism and the Cold War. They warned of the possible resurgence of Fascism. But Adorno himself was cautious:

> the present study deals with dynamic potentials rather than overt behaviour. We may be able to say something about the readiness of an individual to break out into violence, but we are pretty much in the dark as to the remaining necessary conditions under which an outbreak would occur. There is, in other words, still plenty of room for action research ... Outbreaks into action must be considered the result of both internal potentialities and a set of eliciting factors in the environment (Adorno et al., 1950, p. 972).

In the event his caution was prudent. Contrary to the generally negative warnings drawn from the book the following 20 years witnessed the growth of the civil rights movement, the anti-Vietnam war movement and the women's liberation movement. These challenged the ethnocentric, patriotic and sexist attitudes upon which the research had focused. They indicated shifts in the opposite direction to those expected, combined with a polarisation and politicisation of American society.

The authoritarian personality thesis thus fails to provide a reliable explanatory intermediary between the economics and politics of advanced capitalism. The argument that psychological factors become more important in late capitalism is hard to sustain. Hyman and Sheatsley (1954, p. 108) identified this weakness in saying that the authoritarian personality served to, 'take the irrationality out of the social order and impute it to the respondent'. Of course, none of this denies the existence of individual authoritarianism nor its tendency to increase in periods of crisis, but it serves as a warning to social psychologists who turn their attention to this area to be cautious in making generalisations between individual personality characteristics and socio-political events.

THE FRANKFURT SCHOOL
AND WORKING-CLASS PSYCHOLOGY

We have directed considerable criticism at the studies by the Frankfurt School and its American successor. They came to neglect their Marxist roots, and to focus increasingly on individual psychology, adopting a pessimistic view of the vulnerability of human personality to authoritarianism under late capitalism. Nonetheless we would argue that the school made important contributions to both Marxism and psychology. Thorough reading reveals an unexpected connection between the studies of Marx and Engels and later research on the social psychology of attitude and personality. There is a link between classical Marxist studies of the 'conditions' of the working class and later more psychological studies of the 'conditioning' of workers.

Fromm's and Weiss's study of Weimar workers produced fascinating portraits of the authoritarians and revolutionaries of Weimar Germany and their cultural surroundings. This work should be accorded a proper place both in Marxism and social psychology. The contribution of the authoritarian personality research should also be recognised. It was a serious and sustained attempt to investigate the nature and dynamics of reactionary attitudes. It studied people's world views against the background of their real lives in a manner now quite lost to attitude and opinion poll research. It should be defended from its right-wing critics who sought to subvert it with the search for the 'left-wing authoritarian'. But we have to conclude that the Frankfurt school's continued interest in typological psychology, and its incorporation of psychoanalysis resulted in an approach that proved complex, cumbersome and of limited relevance in understanding the ideological dynamics of the working class under late capitalism.

Finally it should be added that the Frankfurt School were among a small number of Marxists, including Lukács, Gramsci and Trotsky, who retained an independence from the destructive influences of social democracy and Stalinism. They each offered their own explanations for the failures of socialism and the rise of Fascism in the 1920s and 1930s. For instance Lukács' concept of false consciousness and Gramsci's notion of ideological hegemony offered complementary insights to those of the Frankfurt School. Of this short list, Trotsky remained the closest to classical Marxism and the most optimistic about the future. From exile he wrote extensively on the rise of the Nazis (Trotsky, 1989). His account contains many references of a psychological kind about the mentality of the petit bourgeoisie and the basis of Fascism's mass appeal. He had a sympathetic interest in psychoanalytic theory but was also cautious of projecting theories of individual psychology onto the stage of history. He would therefore have been critical of Fromm's *Fear of Freedom* and of the *The Authoritarian Personality*. He made his psychological observations within a class and historical framework, and maintained an optimism in the future self-emancipation of humanity.

THE PSYCHOLOGY OF FASCISM REVISITED

It is understandable that the study of authoritarianism declined during the 1950s and 1960s. It was diverted by a wild-goose chase in search of left-authoritarianism, and in a real sense authoritarianism was in decline. But during the 1970s organisations of the far right began to re-emerge in Europe and the United States. In Britain, for instance, a small core of convinced Nazis regrouped under the name of the National Front. Billig (1978) studied the social psychology of this organisation. He began with a review of *The Authoritarian Personality* which he saw as, 'a major landmark in the history of psychology, as well as being the single most important contribution to the psychology of fascism' (Billig, 1978, p. 36). Because of the different circumstances of his study, Billig used interviews to construct detailed portraits of a small number of committed National Front members and a content-analysis of their publications. It showed that its members included 'classic authoritarians' and 'men of violence' and that its publications expressed authentic Fascist values. This research was valuable because the National Front sought to hide these characteristics.

Their strategy was to conceal their Nazi origins and play on the racist views of potential supporters. To this end they presented themselves to the public as patriotic Britons concerned about immigration, hence the importance of Billig's study in exposing their real nature. But what his study did not address was the operation of their strategy as the Front attempted, initially with some success, to gain electoral support of a wider periphery who had some sympathy with their racist views but were not in other respects Fascist. This process was not academically researched. It would have been extremely difficult, requiring detailed opinion polling of National Front voters who were often reluctant to admit either their voting intention or their other attitudes. However the experience of the Anti-Nazi League campaign tells us something of this process. The League sought to reduce the electoral support of the National Front by widely publicising their Nazi affiliations and policies to potential supporters. It was hoped that this would separate the periphery of voters from the hard-core Nazis.

As might be expected, the range of policies proposed by the National Front and the ideas expressed in their publications were quite similar to the attitudes contained in the scales of *The Authoritarian Personality*. They were ethno centric, anti-semitic, politically and economically conservative and implicitly anti-democratic (indeed sometimes explicitly). However these attitudes did not prove to form such a cohesive syndrome as *The Authoritarian Personality* suggested. The elements could be prised apart and disaggregated. The 'potential Fascists' could be persuaded to disagree strongly with some items of the neo-Nazi programme. This did not necessarily turn potential supporters into liberals or socialists, but it served to separate those who could have become the rank and file from their would-be leaders. Between 1978 and 1981 the electoral base of the National Front was destroyed.

The recent resurgence of neo-Nazi groups in France and Germany has been far more extensive than that in Britain of the 1970s. For the first time since the Second World War a Fascist organisation, the French National Front, has gained a serious electoral foothold, and for the first time national socialism has re-appeared in Germany. Social psychologists should once more give their attention to the critical study of these phenomena. There is a tradition to learn from, and a serious problem to confront. We can hope to make a contribution to understanding the resurgence of Nazism in Europe. But it is not sufficient merely to understand. In the 'Theses on Feuerbach' Marx wrote: 'The philosophers have only interpreted the world in various ways. The point, however, is to change it.' The criticism applies with equal force to psychologists.

REFERENCES

Adorno, T.W., Fraenkel-Brunswick, H., Levinson, D. and Sanford, R.N. (1950) *The Authoritarian Personality*, New York: Harper Row/Norton.

Arato, A. and Gebhardt, E. (eds) (1988) *The Essential Frankfurt School Reader*, New York: Continuum.

Benjamin, W. (1940) 'Art in the Age of Mechanical Reproduction', in Nelson, C. and Grossberg, L. (eds) (1988) *Marxism and the interpretation of Culture*, Basingstoke: Macmillan.

Billig, M. (1978) *Fascists, a Social Psychological View of the National Front*, London: Harcourt, Brace and Jovanovich.

Bonss, W. (1984) 'Critical Theory and Empirical Social Research', Introduction to Fromm, E. (1984), *The Working Class in Weimar Germany*, Warwick: Berg.

Bottomore, T.B. and Rubel, M. (eds) (1963) *Karl Marx, Selected Writings in Sociology and Social Philosophy*, Harmondsworth: Penguin.

Brown, R. (1970) *Social Psychology*, London: Macmillan.

Engels, F. (1969) *The Condition of the Working Class in England*, London: Panther.

Freud, S. ([1931]1985) 'Libidinal Types', in *Pelican Freud Library vol. 7*, Harmondsworth: Penguin.

Fromm, E. (1955) *The Fear of Freedom*, London: Routledge and Kegan Paul.

Fromm, E. (1932) 'On the Method and Function of an Analytical Social Psychology', in Arato, A. and Gebhardt, E. (eds) *The Essential Frankfurt School Reader*, New York: Continuum.

Fromm, E. (1984) *The Working Class in Weimar Germany*, Warwick: Berg.

Horkheimer, M., Fromm, E. and Marcuse, H. (1936) *Studien über Autorität und Familie*, Paris: Felix Alcan.

Horkheimer, M. (1940) 'The Authoritarian State', in Arato, A. and Gebhardt, E. (eds) *The Essential Frankfurt School Reader*, New York: Continuum.

Hyman, H.H. and Sheatsley, P.B. (1954) 'The Authoritarian Personality a Methodological Critique', in R. Christie and M. Jahoda (eds) *Studies in the Scope and Method of the Authoritarian Personality*, Illinois: Glencoe.

Jay, M. (1973) *The Dialectical Imagination*, Boston: Little Brown.

Levenstein, A. (1912) *Die Arbeiterfrage*, Munchen: Reinhardt.

Marx, K. and Engels, F. (1965) *The German Ideology*, London: Lawrence and Wishart.

Marx, K. and Engels, F. (1975) *The Communist Manifesto*, Peking: Foreign Languages Press.

Pollock, F. (1940) 'State Capitalism; Its Possibilities and Limitations', in Arato, A. and Gebhardt, E. (eds) *The Essential Frankfurt School Reader*, New York: Continuum.

Ray, J.J. (1972) 'Non-ethnocentric authoritarianism', *Australian and New Zealand Journal of Sociology* 8, pp. 96–102.

Rowntree, B.S. (1901) *Poverty, a Study of Town Life*, London: Macmillan.

Trotsky, L. (1989) *Fascism, Stalinism and the United Front*, London: Bookmarks.

Weiss, H. (1936) 'Die Enquete Ouvriere von Karl Marx', *Zeitschrift fur Sozialforschung*, vol. VI, pp. 76–98.

4

PSYCHOLOGY AND MARXIST POLITICS IN THE UNITED STATES

Benjamin Harris

In 1951 a soon-to-be blacklisted screenwriter named Abraham Lincoln Polonsky published *The World Above*, a fictional account of a psychiatrist struggling to develop a Marxist understanding of human psychology. Toward the end of that novel, the character Dr Carl Meyers successfully establishes a hospital that uses a new, revolutionary therapy to 'help undo the misery of history', rather than 'accept[ing] the general conditions of social life as normal, healthy, ordinary' (Polonsky, 1951, p. 361). Soon, however, the word leaks out that a radical approach to human suffering is being supported by Federal funds, and a reactionary southern Congressman forces Meyers to choose between continuing his career or holding onto the truth of his new psychosocial therapy. In the climax of Polonsky's novel, the crusading Dr Meyers defies the Congressman and his McCarthyite committee, and prepares to be sent to prison for his convictions. Although Meyers' new therapy is never actually described, Polonsky implies that it is worth the sacrifice of a career.

Examining the history of Marxist psychology in the US is similar to reading Polonsky's *The World Above* and watching the character of Carl Meyers fight for his ideals. If one looks carefully enough, one can find scientists, activists, and philosophers who reject traditional psychological theories and develop Marxist critiques of the status quo that are cogent, stylish, and influential. Like the fictional Dr Meyers, one finds these historical figures full of optimism that a new revolutionary science of man can be developed, and one sees them dedicate years of work to that effort.

Finally, however, no theory is developed to successfully compete with behaviourism, neo-Freudianism, humanistic psychology and the myriad of other approaches that have co-existed throughout this century. Instead, we are left with a record of the struggle between Marxist critics and their non-Marxist colleagues – as well as with each other – rather than with a successfully articulated theory. To the historian of science, that lack of theoretical success is no more disappointing than the climax of *The World Above* was to admirers of Abraham Polonsky's writing. It's the struggle that is the real story.

This chapter surveys a century of struggles by Marxist activists in the United States to make sense of psychology and psychological issues. By specifying 'Marxist *activists*', I indicate a focus on those individuals who believed that theoretical work must be accompanied by political activity – whether it be teaching medicine at a labour college or organising a chapter of Psychologists for a Democratic Society. Rather than apply my own judgment as to who deserves the label 'Marxist', I equate 'Marxist activists' with members and supporters of the many political organisations which have represented themselves as Marxist, most notably the Socialist and Communist Parties. This means that my survey is a more institutional and social history than an intellectual history of Marxism. Rather than write another account of the Frankfurt School in the United States, I survey the work of people similar to Polonsky's Dr Meyers: activist-scholars and activist-clinicians. Although thousands of such individuals existed, their world is largely *terra incognita* to historians of science and to historians of labour and the political Left.

In this chapter I follow Spears and Parker's (introduction) broad use of the term 'psychology' to include theories and practices traditionally associated with clinical and academic psychology, psychoanalysis and psychiatry. Further, I am interested in everything that self-described political Marxists have made of psychology, whether or not their understandings or applications of psychology would be called 'Marxist' today. By grounding my survey in the activities of socialists and communists, I allow the examination of processes by which institutional, national, and political forces shape the psychological beliefs of activists – even if the results stray from what one might consider Marxist psychology. A benefit of this approach is that it admits that philosophically non-Marxist versions of psychology may have been used as part of Marxist political programmes. Conversely, my historical approach allows for the possibility that seemingly Marxist theories of psychology (e.g. Newman, 1991) have been developed as a cover for *practices* which are anti-humanist and authoritarian (Harris, 1993a, 1993c).

PSYCHOLOGY AND THE SOCIALIST PARTY

In the early decades of the twentieth century, psychology was one of the sciences from which socialists hoped to fashion a new vision of human motivation and social change. Throughout the history of the Socialist Party (SP), rhetorical uses of science were shaped as much by the needs of Party factions as by socialists' shared desire for effective anti-capitalist arguments (Pittenger, 1993). For each tendency, psychological theories were helpful in addressing two central problems: the somnolence of the working class and the SP's lack of success.

On the extreme right, psychological extensions of Herbert Spencer's social-evolutionism were used to prove the futility of socialist agitation. Thus, Ernest Untermann (1927) explained that the masses were not sufficiently evolved to attain class consciousness, but they could at least acquire socialist 'habits of mind' by participating in a democratically-run workers' movement. Closer to the centre, opponents of political abstentionism accused the Old Guard of adopting a crudely mechanistic psychology which saw physical deprivation as the only stimulus for anti-capitalist revolt. As an alternative, Harry Laidler described workers' pro-social instincts (e.g. creativity, affiliation), to which the Party could appeal in its propaganda (Laidler, 1927). On the Left, writers for the *Masses* and *New Review* polemicised against 'Victorian evolutionary pessimis[m]' and embraced the liberating force of 'the primitive' – which they found in new trends in psychology, art, and anthropology (Pittenger, 1993, p. 227). Although their pragmatism would eventually lead literary bohemians like Max Eastman and Floyd Dell to reject Marxism, before the First World War they admired the 'new psychology' of Freud, Jung and James for its modernism and experimentalism – qualities also attributed to Lenin and the Bolsheviks.

In the early 1920s, socialist psychology began to be professionalised, as a few individuals with graduate training began contributing to SP publications and teaching at socialist schools. Their most visible contributions were regular psychology articles in *Labor Age*, the monthly journal of a Left/militant grouping around A.J. Muste. There, the most frequent writer on psychology was Prynce (aka Prince) Hopkins, a 'Red millionaire' who helped found the magazine, served on its board, and kept it afloat financially (Santa Barbara Public Library, n.d.; Hopkins, 1962). Typical of the period, Hopkins was a free spirit who had dabbled in various approaches to psychology, went to Europe to be psychoanalysed and attend graduate school, and returned with enhanced authority. In Hopkins' writing, Freudian theory provided not only a guide for directing the positive instincts of the masses toward activism, but also for pointing out the unconscious complexes of militants whose anger at the ruling class Hopkins judged excessive (Hopkins, 1927).

For the cohort of socialists who shared Hopkins' desire to fashion a politically useful psychology, analysing phenomena on both the collective and the individual levels was difficult, but necessary for practical as well as theoretical reasons. Those teaching at socialist and labour schools found, for example, that such balance was demanded by working-class students who wanted a psychology just as personalised as that offered to wealthy students by elite universities (Daniels, 1923, 1925). Psychoanalysis offered one solution to this dilemma by describing the suppression of the instinctual drives of entire social classes, with each person then finding his own substitute gratification – through religion or charity work or psychosomatic illness (Hopkins, 1922, 1923). Behaviourism, by contrast, seemed to be a throwback to the mechanistic thinking of old-style socialism. Rejecting its cynicism and authoritarian potential, the SP's *New Leader* lampooned Watsonianism as a 'rat's eye view of the universe', and 'an excellent creed for a machine-made man ... whose mind is [the size] of a pin's head' (Grenden, 1928, p. 5).

In the early 1930s, psychologists with more traditional training and university employment largely replaced amateurs such as Hopkins within the socialist movement. At the same time, academic psychology abandoned the instinct-based motivational theories which centrists had earlier used to support their Kropotkinesque predictions of social change through mutual aid. The results were rationalist and Gestaltist explanations of how socialism would replace capitalism, advanced by a new generation of Christian Socialist and Social Democratic psychologists who embraced psychology for its promise to help engineer social reform (Harris and Nicholson, in press; Hilgard, 1986). Although radical in their opposition to unbridled capitalism, these academics did not grant special authority to the working classes; nor did they doubt that the same psychology taught to the sons of wealth at Harvard could be used to advance the socialist cause.

One of the most innovative of these socialist psychologists was George W. Hartmann, who studied political attitudes to find support for the programmes of his faction in the SP and for the progressive education movement. While a candidate for Congress in 1934, Hartmann learned that rural Pennsylvania voters agreed with various Socialist reforms, such as the public ownership of utilities, *if* they were dissociated from the Party's name (Hartmann, 1936a). Encouraged by this finding of latent socialist values, the following year he tested the effects of two different campaign leaflets upon voters, in what is often considered the first self-conscious *experiment* in political psychology. Validating the political strategy of the Norman Thomas wing of the SP, Hartmann found that an emotional, personalised message elicited more votes than did the dispassionate, impersonal appeals of the Socialist Old Guard (1936b). Although he never won any of the elections in which he ran, Hartmann cited Gestalt principles to predict that eventually the populace would experience a political figure-ground reversal of the sort that evokes an 'aha' in psychology undergraduates, and that would forever change how people perceived capitalist society (Hartmann, 1939, 1941).

PSYCHOLOGY AND THE COMMUNIST MOVEMENT

From the mid-1930s until the 1950s, most attempts to integrate Marxism and psychology were the work of members or sympathisers of the Communist Party (CP). During the period of the Popular Front, communists joined with socialists to pursue theoretical work and political activism in anti-Fascist caucuses in psychology, social work and medicine. In the Psychologists League, clinicians and academics with graduate degrees but uncertain job prospects developed 'historical materialist' critiques of the dominant schools of psychology; simultaneously they agitated for social reforms on the job and in the American Psychological Association (Finison, 1976; 'Little Psychologist', 1936).

In addition to this work within individual professions, academics close to the CP founded the journal *Science and Society* to apply Marxist theory throughout the social and natural sciences. From the start psychology received more attention than other disciplines, and psychologists played key roles in the journal's creation and early management. In both submissions and published articles, psychological writing for *Science and Society* was eclectic, with Pavlovians, Freudians, and Gestaltists all analysing their orientations as compatible in essence with Marxist philosophy and sociology.

From the launching of the Popular Front until the end of the Second World War, books by two American authors dominated discussions of psychology in *Science and Society* and other venues associated with the CP. Typical of innovations in the history of science, both came from the periphery, i.e., were written by figures operating on the professional and geographic boundaries of their professions. First was *Psychology and the Social Order*, an application of the Gestaltist psychology of Kurt Lewin to relations between social classes, written by a thirty-four-year-old communist sympathiser and Associate Professor at the University of Kansas, Junius F. Brown (1936, n.d.). In Brown's theory the atomistic reductionism of behaviourism was replaced by a psychological equivalent of nuclear physicists' field theory. Situating the individual in a 'psychological field', Brown incorporated forces such as social class and political leadership into a discussion of subjective experience (Schanck, 1936–37). Using topological mathematics and formal logic he derived the superiority of socialism over Fascism, and reached conclusions such as: 'Communism represents the attempt at realisation of the avowed aims of liberal democracy through restructuring of [its] class alignments' (Brown, 1936–37, p. 410).

The other influential book of the period was *Sigmund Freud: A Marxian Essay* by Francis H. Bartlett (1938), a twenty-five-year-old Dartmouth College graduate who had taught himself psychoanalytic theory while working as a labour organiser in Vermont, Hawaii, and New York. Intended as a rebuttal to Rubin Osborn's *Freud and Marx*, Bartlett's book had the same publisher (The Left Book Club) but was written for a smaller audience: those who knew the basics of both Freudian theory and Marxist philosophy, and were interested in whether Freudian theory was consistent with dialectical-materialism – as Osborn had claimed. Where Osborn presented a simplified primer of Freudian and Marxist basics, Bartlett gave his readers long passages from Marx, Engels, and Freud, which he examined for their compatibility. He also conducted a historical study of Freud, modelled upon classical Marxist examinations of eighteenth- and nineteenth-century political figures and events. Bartlett's verdict was a variation of that which Wilhelm Reich had pronounced in Europe a decade earlier: psychoanalysis had a revolutionary essence that transcended its author's bourgeois outlook (Harris and Brock, 1992).

Although many in the CP *nomenklatura* were hostile to all forms of psychoanalysis, members in the arts, universities, and professions often embraced a psychodynamic view of the individual. In the late 1930s their dissent from the Party's occasional anti-Freud polemics was encouraged by the editors of the *New Masses* (a literary weekly loyal to the CP) as part of a sympathetic treatment of Freudian-Marxist discussions (Sharnoff, 1937). Typical of this openness, when Freud died the *New Masses* printed an obituary by Francis Bartlett (1939) that praised Freud's 'brilliant insights', and the magazine editorialised that Freud had provided 'a scientific psychological basis for many of the postulates of progressive social movements'. Beginning in 1941, such evaluations of psychology and psychoanalysis occurred in the context of the CP's attempt to downplay its revolutionary programme and present itself as the embodiment of 'twentieth-century Americanism.' As the Party's schools recruited sympathetic liberals to their faculties, curricula in psychology drew closer to that found in traditional universities, and enrolments soared in courses such as Abnormal Psychology, The Pre-School Child, and Everyday Problems of Family Life (Harris, 1993b).

At the same time that the Party was forming multi-class alliances, members in psychiatry and related fields continued to work toward the development a Marxist psychology. At the end of the Second World War, New York psychiatrists in the CP and its periphery founded the Benjamin Rush Society to promote discussions of Marxist personality theory, and to recruit some of the thousands of young clinicians who were re-establishing their careers following military service (Harris, in press). Co-existing within the Society were three viewpoints that competed for hegemony at public forums, at the CP's schools, and in the *New Masses* and *Science and Society*. On the extreme left, organicist Freudophobes condemned all psychologically-based therapy as idealist and polemicised against the intrusion of liberal, social psychiatry into everyday life. A second tendency agreed with Francis Bartlett that key Freudian notions must either be revolutionised or abandoned, and formed study groups dedicated to such work. A third group, which included leading students and teachers in New York psychoanalytic institutes, maintained that 'psychoanalysis ... reduced to its *basic concepts* is fully in accord with the principles of modern materialism' (Marmor, 1949, pp. 317–18).

As the Cold War began, the anti-psychotherapeutic faction drew strength from anti-Freudian developments within the French and Soviet CPs. It gained control of the *Benjamin Rush Bulletin*, turning it into a reprint service for crude Lysenkoist and Pavlovian polemics from the USSR. Simultaneously, the CPUSA launched a campaign to purge itself of what it identified as the subversive influence of Freudianism. Metaphorically linking psychoanalysis with dirt and disease, one national officer of the Party announced to the membership:

A more resolute fight must be made for the Party line against opportunistic deviations in all spheres, including the reactionary above-class ideology of Freudianism and psychoanalysis which like a pest has made serious inroads, particularly in the white collar and middle class strata of the Party (Weinstone, 1950, p.7).

Citing concerns over internal security and ideological decay, Party officials prohibited members from undergoing psychotherapy of any sort and banished non-Pavlovian psychology from the CP's schools and press. Echoing the Catholic Church's recent condemnation of psychoanalytic values (Sheen, 1982), the Sunday *Worker* explained that 'Freudianism in the US is not a medical question. It is one of the most formidable enemies of the Marxist-Leninist philosophy of life' (Howard, 1950, p. 9).

For the next six years the CP campaigned against psychotherapy and non-Soviet psychology in its newspapers and theoretical journals. Despite this, many clinicians and academics remained loyal to both the communist movement and to the project of developing a revolutionary, post-Freudian human science. Some quarrelled in *Science and Society* over which Freudian concepts should be retained (Wilson and Cooper, 1952–53), some vainly submitted defences of psychotherapy to the Party's press (Freedberg, 1984), and the majority quietly pursued research programmes informed by dialectical materialism (Chess, 1948; Schneirla, 1949). One group, led by the psychoanalyst Bernard Robbins, even established a psychiatric day hospital to apply Marxist ideas to the treatment of seriously disturbed patients (Robbins Institute, 1955).

Others, however, resented the promotion of ultra-environmentalism in the name of 'proletarian science', left the CP and its orbit, and devoted themselves to careers in traditional empirical research or as psychotherapists (Hansberg, 1982). Meanwhile, a few anti-Stalinist Marxists spent the postwar years attempting to link psychoanalysis to political change and social issues. Paul Goodman, for example, praised the revolutionary essence of both Freud and Reich to the readers of *Politics* (1945), while critiquing the Freud's political naivety and Reich's 'Rousseauian' faith in the unfettered instinctual life.

DENOUEMENT: PSYCHOLOGY AND THE LEFT AFTER 1956

Following the Khrushchev revelations in 1956, there was a brief period in which the CPUSA allowed internal dissent to be voiced publicly. During that brief ideological thaw, the rank and file criticised the anti-Freud campaign for its sectarianism and denial of the reality of neurotic suffering (Cohen *et al.*, 1956–57; Levine and Robertson, 1956). Soon, however, the status quo ante was restored and neither the methods nor the effects of the Party's anti-Freud campaign could be discussed further. More significant to the history of Marxist psychology, mass resignations of CP members in 1956 ended whatever vestigial influence the Party had on professionals and intellectuals. In New York, for example, its one remaining school was forced to close not by McCarthyite repression, but by the 'very serious decline in the [school's] ideological prestige and authority' ('Memorandum', 1956).

In the four decades following the 20th Congress of the Soviet Communist Party, the Old Left in the United States contracted, expanded, and finally shrank to a minuscule, fragmented residue of a political movement. What remains are a few, self-styled Marxist parties, almost all of which are organised around the teachings of a single, allegedly infallible leader. Due to this atomisation of the organised left, the project of a Marxist psychology has recently been the province of those operating independently of formal political organisations (e.g. as described in later chapters in this volume).

Within the leftovers of the political left, psychology has taken on new meanings. In a few Marxist sects, the distinction between psychological theory and political practice has been intentionally breached, as socialising and controlling the membership have become explicitly *psychopolitical* procedures. The best known example of an allegedly Marxist psychology used to control activists was developed in the mid-1970s in Lyndon LaRouche's National Caucus of Labor Committees (NCLC). Reminiscent of the extreme anti-Freudian wing of the CP, LaRouche claimed that the popularity of psychoanalysis and social psychiatry was the result of a Rockefeller-funded plot to disarm the working class with an anti-humanist, sexually-permissive philosophy. Thanks to the 'rock-drug-sex counterculture ... unleashed by Margaret Mead *et al.* during 1963', LaRouche charged, the New Left had become a cabal of prostitutes and psychotics whose campus protests resembled 'an insurrectionary takeover of a lunatic asylum' by the patients (1987, pp. 155; 159).

To keep his own cadre free of moral pollution, LaRouche applied techniques of psychological coercion usually associated with religious cults and modern police states. By isolating the individual and having him undergo intense criticism in a small group, LaRouche would 'strip away' the bourgeois 'aspects of the [individual's] persona', inducing 'a growing depression' – the feeling of being 'a degraded thing, intrinsically unlovable' (Marcus, 1973, p. 39). Then, the person would be 'reconstructed': offered a new, LaRouchite identity that promised to bring social approval from the only remaining reference group: the NCLC. Although filtered through the jargon of the NCLC's bizarre, post-Freudian Marxism, this use of psychology to maintain the loyalty of cadre was openly admitted by LaRouche and his disciples (e.g. Newman, 1974). In contrast to the liberatory psychological projects of the 1930s and 1940s, LaRouche offered: 'Socialist organizing ... directed to the mobilization of workers around a new sense of social identity ... replacing the "little me" [with] a new sense of identity which the propagandist and organizer must *synthesize*' (Marcus (LaRouche), 1973, p. 48).

A final expression of the conflation of idiosyncratic Marxism, authoritarian control and personality change has been a handful of psychotherapeutic sects organised by former activists in the communist movement. One was founded in New York City by Saul B. Cohen (aka Saul Newton), a charismatic former communist social worker and member of the Abraham Lincoln Brigade, who developed his own interpretation of Harry Stack Sullivan's psychiatric theories (FBI, 1967). According to one former member, Newton's 'Sullivanians' believed that 'In psychology there is Freud, Sullivan, and Newton. In politics there is Marx, Engels, Lenin and Newton. We are the vanguard for the world community' (Lambert, 1991). Although the Sullivanians had some influence in New York Left-artistic circles in the 1970s, the group lost membership in the 1980s and does not seem to have survived its leader's death in 1991.

More influential has been a group calling itself the 'Communities for Re-Evaluation Counseling'. Currently established in a number of American cities and abroad, this organisation was founded in Seattle by Harvey

Jackins, a political activist who became a self-taught therapist in 1950, following an anti-communist purge of the labour movement in the Northwest (US House, 1954). In contrast to leaders of other psychopolitical sects, Jackins neither calls his therapy 'Marxist' nor cites explicitly Marxist principles in his many books and pamphlets. His overall strategy is nonetheless an amalgam of individual psychotherapy and class struggle politics.

As Jackins (1977) tells his followers, civilisation has progressed from slavery to feudalism, and then to capitalism, which is 'in the late stages of collapsing' from within. Calling for the 'replacement' of the currently 'oppressive society', through the collective struggle of all 'oppressed people', Jackins identifies 'industrial wage workers' as the one group without whom liberation cannot succeed. As these workers become a majority of Jackins' group, he predicts, their effectiveness in anti-capitalist agitation will be greatly strengthened (Jackins, 1980). In the meantime, the movement will develop by practicing Jackins' version of therapy: the regular purging of childhood traumas through the mutual emotional catharsis (crying, sobbing, shaking) of counsellor and client (Jackins, 1965). Characteristic of therapy sects and rank-and-file labour organising, the trust of new members must be established through one-on-one contact, with counsellors recruiting their clients, who then begin the process again.

Those who follow Jackins' teaching are given increasing responsibility within an organisation which promises the ultimate FreudoMarxist Utopia: a society perfected politically, scientifically, and psychologically. Combining the optimistic bombast of 1950s Lysenkoism and nineteenth-century Spencerian evolutionism, Jackins (1977) proclaims his group to be 'engaged in probably the most fundamental change' in the history of humanity, putting them on 'the very leading edge of the tendency toward order and meaning in the universe' (pp. 3–4). For disbelievers, however, Jackins' combination of democratic centralism and neo-Freudianism is doubly destructive. Both organisational matters and members' own therapy are supervised by a hierarchy of counsellors with Jackins at its pinnacle. Moreover, political differences that arise within the organisation are analysed as emotional blockages – as was done to members who tried to organise against Jackins' view that homosexuality is irrational and abnormal. Reminiscent of the Cold War fate of Freudians in the CP, those who dissent are excluded from the press and activities of the movement. Persistent dissent results in expulsion, which is portrayed in therapeutic terms. In a chilling use of reductionist logic, Jackins (1977) equates oppositionists with their psychological blockages (called 'patterns') and explains 'We can be patient only up to a point and then such patterns must be separated from us' (p. 51).

CONCLUSION: UNFULFILLED PROMISES?

Reflecting upon almost a century of Marxists' uses of psychology in the United States, one finds a record of frequent tactical success. Such was the case at the Brookwood Labor School, for example, when left-socialists were able to use the authority of the New Psychology to justify their more optimistic, militant politics. On a strategic level, however, this history is marked by unfulfilled promises and expectations. Compared with the Marxist left in Italy, France or Britain, the movement in the United States had less visible impact upon the human sciences and produced less substantive, integrated theory. If one were to draw up a list of classic statements of Marxist psychology, it would contain few works written in the United States, and almost nothing written by non-émigrés.

As I asserted when I introduced the fictional Dr Meyers and *The World Above*, this does not mean that the project of joining Marxism and psychology is less historically important in the United States. Rather, its relative lack of results invites an examination of forces at work within (and upon) the political left in the United States. One external factor has been the sporadic anti-communist purges of universities, hospitals, and social service agencies, beginning after the First World War and continuing into the 1960s. Throughout the social sciences and clinical fields, threats ranging from lack of promotion to job loss, blacklisting and deportation (in the case of émigrés) has suppressed the public acknowledgment of interest in Marxism. Thus, the prominent psychoanalysts Judd Marmor and Bernard Robbins contributed to the Marx-Freud debate in *Science and Society*, but did so under pseudonyms (Behr, 1951–52; Stone, 1945–46). More typical was David Rapaport's (1956) complete, career-long silence about his Marxist beliefs. Rapaport, a key figure in American psychoanalysis and clinical psychology after the Second World War, told only a few, trusted friends of the important role that dialectical materialism played in his work, sacrificing opportunities for collaboration for the more pressing needs of job and personal security.

Such public self-censure not only inhibited joint work by Marxists, but has prevented historians from seeing much of the work that *did* take place. As a result, Marxist psychologists and Marxist-inspired discoveries are underrepresented in the history of American psychology; and even the politically-sophisticated reader is denied the sources necessary to construct an alternate account. Thus, one may sense a Marxist or anti-Fascist moral behind the 'Asch effect': the finding that two individuals can resist conforming to a mistaken social norm, while a single person will bend to the majority opinion. But the political cleansing of existing histories prevents us from knowing how Solomon Asch's experience of solidarity with a small political minority – Communist faculty at Brooklyn College – contributed to his discovery of this important principle in social and experimental psychology (Ceraso *et al.*, 1990; Girden, 1985; Holmes, 1989).

Another factor retarding Marxist work in psychology has been the theoretical impoverishment of American Marxist movements, relative to those in Europe. This was true in the American SP in the first decades of the twentieth Century (Sweezy, 1952). It was also true in the CP in the 1940s, where many academic disciplines were not represented by theorists of any significance; in others, such as philosophy, one or two individuals turned out workmanlike versions of Soviet treatises. One looks in vain in the American communist movement for a Jean-Paul Sartre or for the equivalent of Britain's 'visible college' of world-class scientists and intellectuals (Werskey, 1978).

Contributing to this programmatic superficiality has been Americans' feelings of political exceptionalism, and the often unwarranted optimism of the American left. Although this has given American activists a unique energy and vibrancy, their lack of experience with failed revolutions resulted in a less complex view of political and personal dynamics. While the psychoanalysts Wilhelm Reich and Otto Fenichel experienced the crushing of mass movements in which they personally participated, American communist psychiatrists did not, so the latter viewed political activism as more inherently fulfilling. They also they showed little interest in their Party leaders' psychological failings, since no significant mistakes were attributed to the American leadership from the 1920s until the purge of Earl Browder in 1945.

Added to this lack of experience with revolutionary defeat was the American CP's less critical view of events and leaders in the USSR. For post-Freudians in the Party this translated into a personality theory with an ideal Socialist Man as its norm. Based upon that model, American Marxists were left with a simplistic view of the relationship of social structure to unconscious drives, psychosexual stages and structures such as the super-ego. Another obstacle was the relatively uniform intellectual culture within the CPUSA, compared with some European CPs. Although one can find evidence of creative, revolutionary work by the rank and file on a local level, at times of crisis the CP's positions on intellectual issues were classically 'Stalinist': undemocratically determined, autocratically managed, and unrelentingly subservient to the needs of the Soviet leadership.

On issues of psychology, this lack of democracy interacted with the small number of Party intellectuals to produce discussions that were often isolated from the non-CP left. In Britain, by contrast, the Communist Party (CPGB) included figures such as John Strachey, an internationally-respected author who could write for Marxists and non-Marxists alike, and whose public differences with the leadership on psychoanalysis were tolerated long enough to stimulate discussion within the larger Left movement (Thomas, 1973).

Moving from the 1930s to the early 1950s, an equivalent comparison can be made in the ability of British versus American communists to dissent from the Soviets' anti-Freud campaign. Although the CPUSA brooked no internal dissent, in 1953 the *Daily Worker* in London published a mildly positive review of Ernest Jones' biography of Freud, written by British communist T.A. Jackson. Because of Jackson's high status in the CPGB and his record as a critic of Freudianism in the 1930s, California communists felt safe in reprinting his review in their newspaper (Jackson, 1937, 1953). It evoked such criticism, however, that the editors were forced to recant and publish a historically tendentious rejoinder – written by an obscure educational psychologist who had helped purge all non-Pavlovians from the California Labor School (Roberts, 1953).

Given this atmosphere of intolerance within the communist movement, and the repressive anti-communism surrounding it, the lack of progress toward the grand Marxist psychology promised in the 1940s is not surprising. In its place, a number of influential researchers found Marxism valuable as a guide to the philosophical flaws of competing trends and schools of thought. As in the political sphere today, Marxism was most useful in the history of psychology as a critical perspective, rather than as a blueprint for a Utopian human being.

REFERENCES

Bartlett, F.H. (1938) *Sigmund Freud: A Marxian Essay*, London: Victor Gollancz Ltd.

Bartlett, F.H. (1939, October 17) 'Freud's Contribution', *New Masses* **33**, pp. 25–6.

Behr, Z. (1951–52) 'Principles of Rational Psychotherapy', *Science and Society* **16**, pp. 296–312.

Brown, J.F. (n.d.) 'The Impact of Psychology on the Twentieth Century'. Unpublished manuscript in author's possession.

Brown, J.F. (1936) *Psychology and the Social Order*, New York: McGraw-Hill.

Brown, J.F. (1936–37) 'Degree of Freedom of Social Locomotion: A Psychological Concept for Political Science', *Science and Society* **1**, pp. 404–10.

Ceraso, J., Rock, I., and Gruber, H. (1990) 'On Solomon Asch', in I. Rock (ed.) *The Legacy of Solomon Asch*, Hillsdale, NJ: Lawrence Erlbaum.

Chess, S. (1948) 'The Dynamic Interplay Between Child and Environment', *Journal of Child Psychiatry* **1**, pp. 371–7.

Cohen, S., Johnson, R. and West, R. (1956–57) 'Marxist Psychology in America: A Critique', *Science and Society* **21**, pp. 98–121.

Daniels, M. (1923, November) 'A Judgement of Solomon', *Labor Age*, pp. 18–19.

Daniels, M. (1925, April) 'Anna and Apple Sauce', *Labor Age*, pp. 18–19.

Federal Bureau of Investigation, San Francisco Bureau (1967, August 15) Memorandum to Director of FBI. Expurgated photocopy in author's possession.

Finison, L.J. (1976) 'Unemployment, Politics, and the History of Organized Psychology', *American Psychologist* **31**, pp. 747–55.

Freedberg, S. (1984) 'Bertha Capen Reynolds: A Woman Struggling With Her Past'. D.S.W. Dissertation, Columbia University.

Girden, E. (1985) 'Recollections of Psychology at Brooklyn College of the City University of New York', *American Psychologist* **40**, pp. 141–7.

Goodman, P. (1945, July) 'The Political Meaning of Some Recent Revisions of Freud', *Politics*, pp. 197–203.

Grenden, F. (1928, March 17) 'A Rat's-Eye View of the Universe', *New Leader*, pp. 4–5.

Hansberg, H.G. (1982, December) Interview. Tape recording in author's possession.

Harris, B. (1993a) 'Arise ye footnotes!; Repressed sect-uality', *Contemporary Psychology* **38**, pp. 1134–5.

Harris, B. (1993b) '"Don't be Unconscious, Join Our Ranks": Psychology, Politics and Communist Education', *Rethinking Marxism* **6**, no. 1, pp. 44–76.

Harris, B. (1993c) 'Review of *The Myth of Psychology* by Fred Newman'. *Contemporary Psychology* **38**, p. 216.

Harris, B. (in press) 'The Benjamin Rush Society and Marxist psychiatry in the United States, 1944–1951'. *History of Psychiatry*.

Harris, B. and Brock, A. (1992) 'Freudian Psychopolitics: The Rivalry of Wilhelm Reich and Otto Fenichel, 1930–1935', *Bulletin of the History of Medicine* **66**, pp. 577–611.

Harris, B. and Nicholson, I. (in press) 'Goodwin Watson', in J.A. Garraty (ed.), *American National Biography*, New York: Oxford University Press.

Hartmann, G.W. (1936a) 'The Contradiction Between the Feeling Tone of Political Party Names and Public Response to their Platforms', *Journal of Social Psychology* **7**, pp. 336–57.

Hartmann, G.W. (1936b) 'A Field Experiment on the Comparative Effectiveness of "Emotional" and "Rational" Political Leaflets in Determining Election Results', *Journal of Abnormal and Social Psychology* **31**, pp. 99–114.

Hartmann, G.W. (1939) 'Value as the Unifying Concept of the Social Sciences', *Journal of Social Psychology* **10**, pp. 563–75.

Hartmann, G.W. (1941) 'Frustration Phenomena in the Social and Political Sphere', *Psychological Review* **48**, pp. 362–3.

Hilgard, E.R. (1986) 'From the Social Gospel to the Psychology of Social Issues: A Reminiscence', *Journal of Social Issues* **42**, pp. 107–10.

Holmes, D.R. (1989) *Stalking the Academic Communist: Intellectual Freedom and the Firing of Alex Novikoff*, Hanover, NH: University Press of New England.

Hopkins, P. (1922, May) 'Psychology and the Workers: The Creative and Aesthetic Instincts', *Labor Age*, pp. 21–2.

Hopkins, P. (1923, February) 'Running Away from Life', *Labor Age*, pp. 20–1.

Hopkins, P. (1927) *Fathers or Sons? A Study in Social Psychology*, London: Kegan Paul.

Hopkins, P. (1962) *Both Hands Before the Fire*, Bangkok: Boonpring T. Suwan.

Howard, M. (1950) 'A Question from Chicago and an Answer', *Worker*, February 19, p. 9.

Jackins, C.H. (1965) *The Human Side Of Human Beings*, Seattle, WA: Rational Island Publishers.

Jackins, C.H. (1977) *The Upward Trend*, Seattle, WA: Rational Island Publishers.

Jackins, C.H. (1980) 'The RC Community and the Working Class', *Working for a Living*, no. 5, pp. 12–17.

Jackson, T.A. (1937) 'Review of *Freud and Marx* by Reuben Osborn', *New Masses*, July 20, pp. 22–3.

Jackson, T.A. (1953) 'Freud – the First Volume of a Basic Examination', *Daily People's World*, October 30, p. 6.

Laidler, H.W. (1927) 'Post War Socialist Thought: The Psychological Trend to Socialism', *American Appeal*, May 14, p. 3.

Lambert, B. (1991) 'Saul B. Newton, Commune Leader, Is Dead at 85', *New York Times*, December 23, p. C11.

LaRouche, L.H. (1987) *The Power of Reason: 1988, An Autobiography*, Washington, DC: Executive Intelligence Review.

Levine, A. and Robertson, P. (1956) 'Partisanship and Science', *Political Affairs* **35**, October, pp. 56–65.

'Little Psychologist, What Now?' (1936) *Psychologists League News Bulletin*, May, p. 1.

Marcus, L. [Lyndon H. LaRouche] (1973) *Beyond psychoanalysis*, New York: National Caucus of Labor Committees.

Marmor, J. (1949) 'Psychoanalysis', in R.W. Sellars, V.J. McGill and M. Farber (eds) *Philosophy for the Future: The Quest of Modern Materialism*, New York: Macmillan.

'Memorandum on the Jefferson School' (1956) Alexander Trachtenberg Papers, Wisconsin State Historical Society, October 26.

Newman, F. (1974) *Power and Authority: The Inside View of the Class Struggle*, New York: Centers for Change, Inc.

Newman, F. (1991) *The Myth of Psychology*, New York: Castillo International Inc.

Pittenger, M. (1993) *American Socialists and Evolutionary Thought, 1870–1920*, Madison, WI: University of Wisconsin Press.

Polonsky, A. (1951) *The World Above*, New York: Little Brown.

Rapaport, D. (1956) Letter to 'Dear Milek'. David Rapaport Papers, Library of Congress, June 25.

Robbins Institute, Board of Directors (1955) 'The Program of an Integrated Psychotherapeutic Center', *Psychotherapy* **1**, no. 1, pp. 89–96.

Roberts, H. (1953) 'A Comment on Our Review of a New Book About Freud', *Daily People's World*, November 27.

Santa Barbara Public Library, Biography File, Prynce Hopkins (n.d.) Typed summary of article in *Daily News*, 19 January 1925, p. 6.

Schanck, R.L. (1936–37) 'Review of *Psychology and The Social Order* by J.F. Brown', *Science and Society* **1**, pp. 429–32.

Schneirla, T.C. (1949) 'Levels in the Psychological Capacities of Animals', in R.W. Sellars, V.J. McGill and M. Farber (eds) *Philosophy for the Future: The Quest of Modern Materialism*, New York: Macmillan.

Sharnoff, p. (1937)'A Dissent on Jackson's review of "Freud and Marx"', *New Masses*, August 3, p. 22.

Sheen, F.J. (1982) *On Being Human*, Garden City, NY: Doubleday.

Stone, J.T. (1945–46) 'The Theory and Practice of Psychoanalysis', *Science and Society* **10**, pp. 54–79.

Sweezy, P.M. (1952) 'The Influence of Marxian Economics on American

Thought and Practice', in D.D. Egbert and S. Persons (eds) *Socialism and American Life* vol. 1, Princeton NJ: Princeton University Press.

Thomas, H. (1973) *John Strachey*, New York: Harper and Row.

Untermann, E. (1927) 'The laws of the mind', *American Appeal*, October 8.

US House of Representatives, Committee on Un-American Activities (1954) *Investigation of Communist Activities in the Pacific Northwest Area – Part 4 (Seattle)*, Washington, DC: Government Printing Office.

Weinstone, W. (1950) 'A Solid Working Class Base for the Communist Party', *Daily Worker*, May 10, p. 7.

Werskey, G. (1978) *The Visible College: The Collective Biography of British Scientific Socialists of the 1930s*, New York: Holt, Rinehart.

Wilson, B. and Cooper, J. (1952–53) 'The Limits of Rational Psychotherapy', *Science and Society* 17, pp. 351–5.

PART TWO:

CRITICAL TRADITIONS

Some progressive lines of work have survived and developed in psychology against the experimental individualist orthodoxy. Even within the mainstream, surprising connections with Marxism have been forged, and in Chapter 5 Jerome Ulman persuasively argues for a sympathetic critical reception of behaviourism which would provide us with an adequate account of social action. R.D. Hinshelwood, in Chapter 6, brings the history of failed meetings of Marx and Freud up to date with an account of objectification and individuality which also throws light on the vexed question of the relationship between 'base' and 'superstructure'. In Chapter 7 an entirely different tradition of work is described by Wolfgang Maiers and Charles Tolman. Holzkamp's 'Critical Psychology' was elaborated from the late 1960s in Germany, and takes seriously the task of scientifically understanding subjectivity in capitalist society. The tradition that Liam Greenslade describes in Chapter 8, that of Volosinov, has been kept alive in recent years in literary theory and cultural studies, but also provides critical psychologists with a resource for comprehending the work of language which was first developed in the early years of the Russian revolution. In Chapter 9, Lois Holzman argues that Newman's reading of Vygotsky saves that revolutionary tradition of developmental psychology for the present.

5

RADICAL BEHAVIOURISM, SELECTIONISM, AND SOCIAL ACTION

Jerome D. Ulman

Radical behaviourism and Marxism have rarely crossed paths. When they have met, their encounters have been more confrontational than collaborative, yielding more mutual incomprehension than understanding. With few exceptions, these two scientific world perspectives have continued on their respective courses like two ships passing in the night. Those exceptions, those rare occasions of interpenetration (to use a fitting dialectical term), have been marked much more by naivety and misunderstanding than by fruitful exchange of scientific and technological knowledge.

As a case in point, one of the most misinformed critiques of Skinner I have encountered is contained in a book that purports to be both psychological and Marxist: *Mind in the World: A Marxist Psychology of Self-Actualisation* (Lethbridge, 1992). So extensive are its inaccuracies and misrepresentations of Skinner's views, in fact, that the entire body of this chapter may be taken as my reply. For example, Lethbridge (1992) writes: 'The problem with Skinner's antitheory is that he assumes that there is no alternative to idealism but mechanism' (p. 24). Competing as a source of misinformation about Skinner is the book *The Political Economy of Science: Ideology of/in the Natural Sciences* (Rose and Rose, 1976). Consider, for example, the following verdict: 'because Skinner's ahistoric concept [of society] carries conviction only within the atmosphere engendered by a society ... of repressive intolerance, Skinner's position is irreconcilably conservative' (Rose and Rose, 1976, p. 110). These two examples of poor scholarship should be enough to make the point that in order to understand Skinner one must read Skinner and not rely on secondary sources, although there is a new secondary source, Nye (1992), which provides a reasonably comprehensive and credible introduction to Skinner.

RADICAL BEHAVIOURISM:
THE PHILOSOPHY OF THE SCIENCE OF BEHAVIOUR

Radical behaviourism (*radical* in the sense of being root or basic) is the
philosophy of the science of behaviour relations founded by Skinner. Radical behaviourism rejects explanations of behaviour based on the notion of
the psyche or like terms (cognition, mind, etc.), terms which refer to some
immaterial or supernatural inner process in accounting for behaviour or, as
Skinner (1988a) put it, explanations which appeal:

> 'to events taking place somewhere else, at some other level of observa-
> tion, described in different terms, and measured, if at all, in different
> dimensions' – events, for example, in the real nervous system, the
> conceptual nervous system, or the mind (pp. 101–2).

Unlike Watson's behaviourism, Skinner's radical behaviourism considers
inner or covert events as no different in kind than overt events; all behaviour, covert and overt, verbal and non-verbal, is treated as appropriate
subject matter for scientific investigation. And, unlike contemporary
methodological behaviourism or logical positivism, radical behaviourism
does not restrict the science of behaviour to subject matter which must be
observable by more than one person, that is, to interobserver verification
(see Smith, 1986). The real test of a scientific statement is found in
practice; that is, does the statement enable us (even a Robinson Crusoe) to
increase our effectiveness in dealing with the material world? This is a test
which both Marxists and radical behaviourists apply.

   In Skinner's system, there are four and only four kinds of variables which
determine any behaviour: genetic endowment, physiological condition, past
learning history, and the current environment. By construing events which
occur inside the organism as covert behavioural and environmental events
(the environment doesn't stop at the skin's surface), no conceptual vacuum
remains which can be filled in by supposing immaterial entities such as
mind or psyche. Accordingly, for radical behaviourists, the only difference
between overt and covert events is the extent to which they are accessible to
observation (e.g. I can see you write but I cannot hear what you say to
yourself as you write). Thus, radical behaviourists extend the concept of
behaviour to encompass verbal as well as non-verbal behaviour, and overt as
well as covert behaviour (thinking, imagining, consciousness, etc.). In one of
Skinner's ([1945]1988b) most important papers – 'The Operational Analysis
of Psychological Terms' – he explains how phenomena traditionally deemed
purely psychological or mental (thinking, imagining, self-awareness, etc.) can
be reinterpreted materialistically from the radical behavioural viewpoint as,
in his words, *private events*. It is important to understand that Skinner's
'operationalism' (functional analysis) is not at all similar to the operationalism of the logical positivists. The latter type of operationalism characterises
methodological behaviourism, not radical behaviourism (see Smith, 1986).

WHO ARE RADICAL BEHAVIOURISTS?

Among psychologists, radical behaviourism is accepted by only a tiny minority (a subset of those who call themselves behavioural psychologists; in the American Psychological Association, less than 2 per cent of its total membership). It is a controversial position in the extreme. This philosophy of the science of behaviour has received little understanding and even less acceptance in mainstream psychology. Todd and Morris (1983) show that psychology texts frequently misinform students about radical behaviourism. Further, such leading psychology journals as the *American Psychologist* sometimes publish unscholarly attacks on radical behaviourism (e.g. Mahoney, 1989). The reason for these attacks is obvious: radical behaviourism eschews all mentalistic/cognitive constructs – the very subject matter claimed by mainstream psychology – as nothing more than explanatory fictions.

Radical behaviourists are found among professionals in disciplines other than psychology, in such fields as social work, organisational management, education, and health care. Then there are radical behaviourists with graduate degrees in psychology who subsequently identified themselves as behaviour analysts; some remaining ambivalent about their affiliation with psychology, others disavowing psychology altogether. Even among those who call themselves behaviour analysts, however, radical behaviourism is not a majority orientation. Finally, there are those who have gone beyond merely disengaging themselves from psychology as a discipline, and have taken the position that the study of behaviour is an independent science in its own right, a separate discipline termed *behaviorology* (see Fraley and Vargas 1986; Vargas 1991). This basic science of behaviour has taken organisational form with the founding of *The International Behaviorology Association* in 1988 and subsequent publication of the scientific journal *Behaviorology*. Behaviourologists (I count myself among them) are by definition radical behaviourists; additionally, they define their discipline as the study of the development and changes in behaviour (both covert and overt) over time in relation to the *selective effects* of the environment within which the individual interacts. The defining paradigm or explanatory framework of behaviorology is *selection by consequences*. Behaviourologists consider themselves Skinnerians in the same sense that biologists consider themselves Darwinians, and genuine communists consider themselves Marxists.

SOCIAL ACTION

Now that we have identified the players who call themselves radical behaviourists (noting that not all radical behaviourists identify themselves as behaviourologists), just what do they *do* with respect to progressive social action? If social action is taken as action directed toward improving the human condition, most radical behaviourists are committed to the practice of ameliorating behaviour problems case by case, working with one individual or small group at a time. Even among those radical behaviourists who call for change on a larger scale, however, few venture beyond the limits of the programme of gradual, piecemeal reform (see Ulman, in press).

A few radical behaviourists, though, have become radical politically as well, see world socialist revolution as the only realistic solution to the problems facing humanity, and proclaim themselves to be Marxists – some as political independents, others as members of organisations identified as Marxist. Many Marxist-oriented radical behaviourists in the 1980s were members of a special interest group (SIG) of the Association for Behaviour Analysis, Behaviourists for Social Action (BFSA), a politically heterogeneous organisation committed to the application of the science of behaviour in the struggle against social injustice and the defence of the operant analysis of behaviour against undue attack. While the majority within the BFSA (now inactive) were non-Marxists, few if any were anti-Marxists. Their 'social action' was largely in the form of theoretical work, however, most of which has been published in the SIG's journal *Behaviour and Social Issues* (formerly, *Behaviour and Social Action*, 1986–1990; before that, *Behaviourists for Social Action Journal*, 1978–1985). Outside of BFSA, the social action of individual members has been quite varied, ranging from community-based behavioural interventions in poverty areas to active participation in revolutionary politics. Still, to give perspective to 'a few' in reference to the current sum of Marxist-oriented radical behaviourists, we are talking about few more than might fill a minivan. Many radical behaviourists continue to be interested in the design of culture, but in the Utopian fashion of Skinner (1948), rather than the revolutionary fashion of Marx.

SELECTION OR TRANSFORMATION?

One kind of social action is political action, another is scientific practice. Therefore, let us now consider scientific practice from the position that the study of behaviour is an independent discipline in its own right – *behaviorology*, the natural science informed by radical behaviourism. Why should the study of behaviour become a separate science? Basically, the defining paradigms of psychology and behaviorology are incommensurable (Ulman 1992). The paradigm of psychology is *transformational*: some kinds of behavioural observations are made (ranging from oral responses to Rorschach inkblots to precise reaction-time measures) which are then taken to be indices of hypothetical mechanisms operating within the individual (e.g. id-ego-superego psychodynamics, cognitions, self-concepts, traits, hypothesised processes within the conceptual nervous system). The transformation paradigm supposes that:

> some aspect of the world incites the organism to take action; but before that action occurs, the organism engages in a series of operations, typically called mental or cognitive, that determines the significance of the event and thus determines the nature of the action (Vargas, 1991, p. 141)

The organism itself, through (hypothetical) inner structures and processes, is presumed to be the agency of its own action. The transformation is purely an ontological assumption, however, from material (some environmental event) to immaterial (some supposed mental or cognitive process) to material (some action). Thus, observed environment-action relations are merely transposed nominally into presumed mental phenomena.

Whereas the paradigm of behaviorology is selectionist and consistently materialistic (or more specifically, realistic, as in the critical realism of Roy Bhaskar, 1989) in its assumptions: behaviour is defined as the interaction of the organism with its environment and is considered to be selected by some combination of three selective processes: natural selection (phylogenic behaviour), operant selection (behaviour selected by reinforcing consequences), or cultural selection (selection by the special social environment that constitutes one's cultural context – see Skinner, 1981).

Selection as a type of causation is not easy to understand. Perhaps as difficult to understand is the character of the abstraction constituting the subject matter of behaviorology – not the organism itself but its actions, the consequences of those actions, and the circumstances in which those contingent relations occur. The organism itself is viewed simply as a locus of interacting genetic and environmental controlling variables, a part of the context within which the properties of behaviour must be analysed. In short, psychology, based on the transformation paradigm, is concerned with what the organism *is* (e.g. a person's dominant traits); behaviorology, based upon the selection paradigm, is concerned with what the organism *does* in conjunction with the variables that determine those actions. Behaviorology extends this selectionist analysis even to the behaviour of the scientist (including that of the research psychologist). Thus, behaviourologists understand science in terms of the actions of scientists or the resulting products of those actions, focusing their analysis on the variables that select what scientists do and say about what they do (Skinner, 1957).

SOME IMPLICATIONS OF SELECTIONISM
FOR MARXIST THEORY

Radical behaviourism, then, is the scientific philosophy that informs behaviorology, whereas selectionism is the scientific paradigm upon which behaviorology is based. Let us examine some of the theoretical and practical implications of selectionism for Marxist theory. The implications are profound.

If we approach the thinking of Marx and Skinner as two consistent natural science perspectives, then those perspectives, along with that of Darwin, can be synthesised into a comprehensive and totally consistent materialistic viewpoint capable of comprehending all forms of life processes from the reproduction of a single cell to the evolution of entire human social formations along an unbroken event continuum of emergent organic phenomena (Ulman, 1991). In a nutshell, the analogy is that the process of operant conditioning stands to the ontogeny of behaviour as the process of natural selection stands to the phylogeny of species and as the process of historical selection (see Ulman, in press) stands to the transformation of human social formations. But the relations among these three processes are more than mere analogies, they are *causally* related through selection contingencies (Skinner, 1981), one evolving from the other – from natural, to operant, to cultural selection.

In *Dialectics of Nature*, Frederick Engels ([1880]1934) described three general dialectical laws – the transition of quantitative changes into qualitative changes, the unity and conflict of opposites, and the negation of the negation – which he applied to all matter. *Selection, I suggest, is a special dialectical law of the movement of living matter*, from that of a single cell to a social formation composed of millions of people. Selection incorporates the general dialectical laws, but is applicable only to living things. Carl Sagan (1980) thinks that extraterrestrial lifeforms may consist of many of the same basic molecules (proteins and nucleic acids) as those found on Earth – 'but put together in unfamiliar ways' (p. 128). It is at least as plausible as to suppose that such lifeforms may be 'put together' – biologically, behaviourally, and socially/culturally – through the process of variation and selection.

Further, this dialectical law of selection manifests itself in qualitatively different ways at the three levels of life processes: with biological processes functioning as the substrate for behavioural processes, and behavioural processes functioning as the substrate for sociocultural processes. The scientific principles discovered to operate at one level may not operate at another level, however. Independent empirical verification would be required to justify such a conclusion. To disregard this rule of scientific reasoning makes one susceptible to the error of reductionism; or its converse, expansionism (i.e., without justification, applying principles established at a higher level to lower level phenomena). These two kinds of errors are often committed by, respectively, sociobiologists and structuralists (including structuralist Marxists). Concerning the former, Skinner (1990) explains, 'the role of variation and selection in the behavior of the individual is often simply ignored. Sociobiology, for example, leaps from socio- to bio-, passing over the linking individual' (p. 1208). We could add that structuralism leaps in the opposite direction but likewise ignores the linking individual.

Selectionism, like a scalpel in the hand of a skilled surgeon, excises all of the teleological malignancy that has afflicted scientific thinking from the time of the ancient Greek philosophers to the present. Darwin did away with teleological notions of design and purpose in biological science, with the enthusiastic endorsement of Marx and Engels. Skinner has done the same with respect to human actions, those actions we ordinarily consider to be purposive or intentional are analysed as operant behaviour (e.g. in Skinner, 1974), the subject matter of behaviorology. Unfortunately, his anti-teleological theory has been received with considerably less enthusiasm by latter-day Marxists.

Not being a Marxist, Skinner did not prescribe exactly how or under what circumstances new cultural practices are to be designed, but he most definitely did not say that capitalist society is the pinnacle of cultural evolution. In sum, the emergent life processes – biological, behaviourological, sociocultural – appear to be purposive only because a past history of selective consequences has set the process in question on a predictable course. However, when the environment changes drastically, when a future no longer resembles the selecting past, what may now appear to be an adaptive adjustment may become a critical fault. This point is well developed in Skinner (1990) in regard to all three levels of variation and selection: natural selection, operant conditioning, and the evolution of social environments (formations).

Finally, radical behaviourism does away with all traces of Cartesian dualism and does so without partitioning from concern any important *real* phenomena about which dualists talk. Radical behaviourism thus obliterates the last refuge of idealism and fideism, the notion of mind or psyche. By construing all so-called subjective phenomena as covert material events (i.e., the interactions of covert behavioural events within an immediate milieu of either inner or outer events or both), no conceptual space remains for presuming the mind or soul to exist, not even in the pineal gland, as Decartes had hypothesised. Thus, what had been accepted through the ages as separate realms of existence, the physical and the mental, now becomes a seamless and monistic *material* whole. Consequently, philosophical dichotomies such as subjective versus objective collapse into nothing more than relative points on a material event continuum, ranging from inaccessible (covert) to accessible (observable by others) in relation to whatever the speaker may be thinking or talking about (Vargas 1993). Everything real we know about, including ourselves, comes from – to borrow Carl Sagan's expression – *starstuff*. ('We have begun to contemplate our origins: starstuff pondering the stars', Sagan, 1980, p. 345.)

Skinner's explanation of selection by consequences as the causal mode common to all life processes – or, I suggest, as the special dialectical law of living matter – is just as applicable to the history of human behaviour (cultural evolution) as it is to the other emergent life processes. As Skinner (1990) observes, 'The evolution of social environments [through the process of variation and selection] has produced not a single culture but many often conflicting ones' (p. 1207). The essay *Marxism and Darwinism* by the Dutch Marxist and natural scientist Anton Pannekoek (1909), a cogent refutation of Social Darwinism, is thoroughly selectionistic in relating 'human nature' to history. Pannekoek (1909) explains:

Darwinism and Marxism are two distinct theories, one of which applies to the animal world, while the other applies to society. They supplement each other in the sense that, according to the Darwinian theory of evolution, the animal world develops up to the stage of man, and from then on ... the Marxian theory of evolution applies. When, however, one wishes to carry the theory of one domain into that of the other, where different laws are applicable, he must draw wrong inferences (p. 33).

In Pannekoek's view, it would be shortsighted to conclude that Marxism applies only to society and that Darwinism applies only to the organic world. Rather, 'man has developed from an animal, and the laws that apply to the animal world cannot suddenly lose their applicability to man' (p. 36).

Pannekoek continues, 'Sociability ... is a peculiarity which distinguishes man from some, but not all, animals. There are some peculiarities that belong to man only, and which separate him from the entire animal world. These ... are language, then reason. Man is also the only animal that makes use of self-made tools' (p. 42). Here Pannekoek's discussion parallels Engels' ([1896]1972) remarkable (but unfinished) 1876 essay, *The Part Played by Labour in the Transition from Ape to Man*, both requiring only minor qualifications today.

This fundamentally important question about the relationship between nature and history can be elucidated by applying the selectionist paradigm. Vargas (1988) offers a particularly lucid behaviourological (hence, selectionist) account of the characteristic social behaviour which humans share with other animals in comparison with those that are uniquely human. In brief, certain nonhuman animals can exhibit some primary verbal behaviour, but the verbal behaviour of humans is infinitely more complex.

The crux of the matter is that we can comprehend the emergent processes of biological evolution, behavioural evolution, and cultural evolution, as material processes by means of the same *kind* of causal explanation, selection. Skinner (1981) comments, 'as a causal mode, selection by consequences was discovered very late in the history of science – indeed, less than a century and a half ago – and it is still not fully recognised or understood' (p. 502). In the last several years, however, there have been some significant theoretical advances in our understanding of selection as a type of causation.

BEHAVIOUROLOGY OR PSYCHOLOGY?

We are just beginning to appreciate the magnitude of the task involved in the reconstruction of Marx's theory of history on a solid materialist *and* selectionist foundation (i.e., a materially selectionist Marxism); an historically consequential task that will unify biology, behaviorology, and historical materialism while respecting the differential laws of organic development and change that operate at their respective levels of integrated complexity. One aim of this paper is to bring to the attention of Marxists concerned with understanding the actions of individuals the fact that there exists a natural science of behaviour relations – behaviorology – that is *continuous* with 'historical contingency', and that this basic science is the proper microfoundation for scientific socialism.

The time is ripe for Marxists to recognise the science of behaviorology as the basic science for understanding human actions. But to do so requires that we put the science of psychology in proper historical perspective (one helpful source is Hergenhahn, 1992). The origin of psychology as a discipline was in philosophy, specifically, that branch called the philosophy of mind – having its roots in theology – and did not become a separate discipline until well into this century. But what is a mental event and of what stuff is it composed? Is it some as yet unknowable Kantian thing-in-itself or supernatural phenomenon that psychologists will eventually be able to explain when they succeed in unlocking the secrets of the mind? To assert that it is the outcome of the functioning of the brain is no more defensible than to claim the same thing about the existence of the soul. A behaviourologist would answer the question of 'mind' by investigating the variables controlling the verbal behaviour of the psychologist making such an assertion. This is not to imply that behaviorology is absolutely right, and psychology is absolutely wrong. The real issue at hand is the fit of the respective contradictory assumptions of the two disciplines with that of a scientific Marxist analysis.

In addition to demonstrating measurably superior technological outcomes, behaviourology provides alternative explanations for socially important behaviours which once were only construed within a psychological framework. Essentially, behaviourology and psychology are based upon incommensurable paradigms, selectionist versus transformational as discussed earlier; that is, epistemologically and ontologically, they are radically different modes of discourse and simply have little or nothing to say to one another (about *incommensurability*, see Bhaskar, 1989).

Concomitantly, Marxists should become informed of the fact that a real ideological struggle has developed as a legacy of Skinner's scientific contributions – largely, perhaps, as a result of the historical accident of Skinner's decision to attempt to reform psychology rather than to develop the science of behaviour as a natural extension from biology (Skinner 1984; Smith, 1986). Put bluntly, developing a natural science of behaviour as a separate discipline cannot advance within the organisational confines of psychology, given psychology's mandate of unquestioning respect for the divinity of the psyche (or any of its cognate hypostases – mind, cognition, experience, etc.). Behaviorology offers unqualified atheistic interpretations of such teleological and 'soulful' psychological concepts as intention and purpose (e.g. in Skinner, 1974).

At the same time, we should be quick to point out that the alternative paradigm of behaviourology does not imply that behaviourologists can immediately and plausibly explain everything which psychologists have ever talked about. But it does imply that Marxists, as materialistic scientists, should both appraise critically just what it is (and is not) that psychologists claim to talk about in reference to the presumed existence of mental/cognitive phenomena, and learn about behaviourology from the works of behaviourologists. Skinner's works are the best starting point for acquiring a dependable and comprehensive understanding of the assumptions underlying behaviorology, a discipline that is just beginning to explore what its selectionist paradigm implies in the analysis of behaviour and in its relation to other modes of discourse such as Marxism. In comparing psychology and behaviourology, the crucial test for materialists should be based on the question of which discipline enables us to take more effective practical action in the concrete world, the world of both natural science and class struggle.

TOWARD A NATURAL SCIENCE EPISTEMOLOGY

We have seen that behaviourology is opposed to reductionism, teleology, and dualism (i.e., it is a real monistic materialism). Additionally, it offers a natural science epistemology expressed in its own operant terms, a bootstrap epistemology. Behaviourologists, in accounting for a person's verbal behaviour, point to the social environment or verbal community which maintains the reinforcement contingencies responsible for that person's verbal behaviour (including the verbal community of psychologists who maintain the verbal behaviour which we call cognitivism/mentalism). Quite possibly, Skinner's most profound contribution to science will be a natural science epistemology derived from the operant analysis of verbal behaviour. In what he considered his most important and complex work, *Verbal Behavior* (Skinner, 1957), the chapter 'Logical and Scientific Behavior' defines a *scientific community* as one which 'encourages the precise stimulus control under which an object or property of an object is identified in such a way that practical action will be most effective' (p. 419). The ramifications of this epistimological viewpoint for scientifically oriented Marxists are far-reaching (but beyond the scope of this chapter to pursue). Clearly, behaviourologists and scientific Marxists can collaborate fruitfully in investigating the macrocontingency relations maintained by particular verbal communities, scientific and otherwise. For example, social class relations might be studied as relations among different verbal communities (Burton and Kagan, in press; Vargas, 1975). With this natural science approach, we may be able to improve our understanding of such social phenomena as, for instance, ideological control – a topic important to Marxists but which has remained largely one of philosophical discourse rather than of scientific analysis.

I believe that the time has arrived for us to amend Engels' ([1883]1968) analogy in his 'Speech at the graveside of Karl Marx' where he said 'just as Darwin discovered the law of development of organic nature, so Marx discovered the law of development of human history' (p. 429). We should now add, 'and so Skinner discovered the law of development of behaviour, both human and nonhuman'. Beyond that, we should see clearly now that all three of these laws of development of living matter are variations of a superordinate law – or, to use Skinner's (1981) term, causal mode – *selection by consequences*. It is in terms of this special dialectical law that we will discover the fundamental unity in theory and practice underlying the work of these three giants of life science: Darwin, Marx, and Skinner.

Acknowledgement. I wish to thank Ernest A. Vargas for his helpful comments.

REFERENCES

Bhaskar, R. (1989) *Reclaiming Reality: A Critical Introduction to Contemporary Philosophy*, London: Verso.

Burton, M. and Kagan, C. (in press) 'The verbal community and the societal construction of consciousness', *Behavior and Social Issues*.

Engels, F. ([1880]1934) *Dialectics of Nature*, New York: Progress Publishers.

Engels, F. ([1883]1968) 'Speech at the graveside of K. Marx', in K. Marx and F. Engels (eds) *Selected Works*, London: Lawrence and Wishart.

Engels, F. ([1896]1972) *The Origin of the Family, Private Property, and the State*, New York: Pathfinder.

Fraley, L.E., and Vargas, E.A. (1986) 'Separate disciplines: The study of behavior and the study of the psyche', *The Behavior Analyst* 9, pp. 47–59.

Hergenhahn, B.R. (1992) *An Introduction to the History of Psychology*, Belmont, CA: Wadsworth.

Lethbridge, D. (1992) *Mind in the World: A Marxist Psychology of Self-Actualization*, Minneapolis, MN: MEP Publications.

Mahoney, M.J. (1989) 'Scientific psychology and radical behaviorism: Important distinctions based in scientism and objectivism', *American Psychologist* 44, pp. 1372–7.

Nye, R. (1992) *The Legacy of B.F. Skinner: Concepts and Perspectives, Controversies and Misunderstandings*, Belmont, CA: Brooks/Cole.

Pannekoek, A. (1909) *Marxism and Darwinism*, Chicago: Kerr.

Rose, H., and Rose, S. (1976) *The Political Economy of Science: Ideology of/in the Natural Sciences*, London: Macmillan.

Sagan, C. (1980) *Cosmos*, New York: Random House.

Skinner, B.F. (1948) *Walden II*, New York: A. Knopf.

Skinner, B.F. (1957) *Verbal Behavior*, New York: Appleton-Century-Crofts.

Skinner, B.F. (1974) *About Behaviorism*, New York: Knopf.

Skinner, B.F. (1981) 'Selection by consequences', *Science* 213, pp. 501–4.

Skinner, B.F. (1984) *The Shaping of a Behaviorist*, New York: New York University Press.

Skinner, B.F. (1988a) 'Methods and theories in the experimental analysis of behavior', in A.C. Catania and S. Harnad (eds) *The Selection of Behavior: The Operant Behaviorism of B.F. Skinner: Comments and Consequences*, New York: Cambridge University Press.

Skinner, B.F. ([1945] 1988b) 'The operational analysis of psychological terms', in A.C. Catania and S. Harnad (eds) *The Selection of Behavior: The Operant Behaviorism of B.F. Skinner: Comments and Consequences*, New York: Cambridge University Press.

Skinner, B.F. (1990) 'Can there be a science of mind?', *American Psychologist* 45, pp. 1206–10.

Smith, L.D. (1986) *Behaviorism and Logical Positivism*, Stanford, CA: Stanford University Press.

Todd, J.T. and Morris, E.K. (1983) 'Misconception and miseducation: Presentations of radical behaviorism in psychology textbooks', *The Behavior Analyst* 6, pp. 153–60.

Ulman, J. (1991) 'Toward a synthesis of Marx and Skinner', *Behavior and Social Issues* 1, 1, pp. 57–70.

Ulman, J. (1992) 'Behaviorology and psychology are incommensurable paradigms: A rejoinder to Staats', *Behaviorological Commentaries* **2**, pp. 23–8.

Ulman, J. (in press) 'Marxist theory and behavior therapy', in W. O'Donohue and L. Krasner (eds), *Theories in Behavior Therapy*, Washington, DC: American Psychological Association.

Vargas, E.A. (1975) 'Rights: A behavioristic analysis', *Behaviorism* **3**, pp. 178–90.

Vargas, E.A. (1988) 'Verbally-governed and event-governed behavior', *The Analysis of Verbal Behavior* **6**, pp. 11–22.

Vargas, E.A. (1991) 'Behaviorology: Its paradigm', in W. Ishaq (ed.) *Human Behavior in Today's World*, New York: Praeger.

Vargas, E.A. (1993) 'The construction of a science community', *Behaviorology* **1**, pp. 9–18.

6

CONVERGENCES WITH PSYCHOANALYSIS

R.D. Hinshelwood

Nor is there the least doubt that these sciences [Marxism and psycho-analysis] are directly opposites. The question is, are they dialectical opposites? (Strachey, 1937, p. 7).

In 1924 only two societies within the International Psycho-Analytical Association were larger than the Russian Psycho-Analytical Society. The Russian Society was sponsored by Trotsky (1930). A number of émigré analysands of Freud and Jung returned after the revolution, and there were separate Branch Societies in Moscow, Kazan and elsewhere. From 1926 psychoanalysis began to be persecuted and slowly disappeared, being finally outlawed in 1936. During its brief period of success the Society in Moscow established a Clinic for the treatment of patients; the State Psycho-Analytical Institute for train-ing psychoanalysts; and an experimental children's nursery, called the Psycho-Analytical Children's Home and Laboratory run by Vera Schmidt. The latter was for pre-school children run on psychoanalytic lines, contem-porary with, for instance the Malting House School in Cambridge (see Bridgeland, 1971). To this Moscow nursery, Stalin sent his eldest son, Yakov. Although there was some persisting influence on the work of the soviet psychologist Lev Vygotsky and his colleague Alexander Luria (Wertsch, 1985), the Soviet interest in psychoanalysis was a blind trail.

Marxism and psychoanalysis are the major dominant influences in thinking about human nature that have informed the Western world dur-ing this century. To find a link between them would be a twentieth-century philosopher's stone. In fact both frameworks have a good deal in common. Both, from their nineteenth-century origins, claimed to be scien-tific – before the present-day definitions of science. They are both anti-metaphysical and materialist; and, like natural science, they are critical of surface appearances; both are in a sense concerned with false conscious-ness. And then psychoanalysis is, like Marxism, and unlike positivist science, a dialectical method of thinking. They have been jointly attacked as moral systems (for instance, Popper, 1957) and thus pushed into an unexpected alliance.

However the really difficult sticking point is that Marxist theory starts from the social environment (the means of production); whereas psycho-analysis looks to the internal events in the individual's psychic apparatus, only later expressed in derivative social formations. Thus psychoanalysts and social theorists stand gazing in opposite directions. In that back-to-back position both have a limited gaze. Marxism has risked becoming a simple economism, as banal as Thatcherism; psychoanalysis risks the danger of a solipsism. The difficulty for psychoanalysis is to understand the processes of collectivisation, whilst Marxism needs a good theory of the individual which goes beyond the needs for material provision.

PSYCHOANALYTIC MARXISMS

Jacoby (1983) concluded that in the 1930s the attempt to embrace a broad psychoanalysis, one that encompassed social theory as well as individual psychology, was widespread in Europe. Increasingly political as the Nazis dominated more and more of Europe, many psychoanalysts were 'socialists and Marxists. They may even have constituted a majority of the analysts' (Jacoby, 1983, p. 12). Fenichel was a central figure holding together this network of socialist psychoanalysts, increasingly diverse, as they emigrated. Subsequently medicalisation and professionalisation of psychoanalysis has eradicated this radical tradition.

The first generation of Marxist Freudians during the 1920s and 1930s worked against the backdrop of the Stalinisation of Marxism and advanc-ing Fascism. In fact both Marxism and psychoanalysis have moved on since then. Marx had pointed towards, though did not develop, a very much more extensive psychology. This is much better understood since Marx's early manuscripts were published in 1932, notably the sixth thesis on Feuerbach states, 'the human essence is no abstraction inherent in each single individual. In its reality it is the ensemble of the social relations' (Marx, [1845] 1975, p. 423). The negative reaction to Stalinisation sur-faced strongly after the defeat of nazism. In the attempts to de-Stalinise Marxism, some thinkers showed interest in importing psychological approaches into Marxist discourses. The new left sought to include a new version of human beings into a pre-diamat Marxism. For Sartre the subject was an agent within a determining matrix. This new dialectic between self-conscious struggling human nature, and a conforming determining history returned to the early Marx. The Frankfurt School has remained a lively inspiration. Marcuse's work attained high prominence temporarily in the 1960s. That strong return to the dialectical method was continued by Habermas ([1968] 1971) and in the exhaustive history of this topic recounted by Wolfenstein (1993).

The development of the new left has more recently been towards single-issue political campaigns – anti-racism, feminism and the environ-ment – which has linked Marxists in with non-Marxist campaigners. Some have turned to psychoanalysis, in particular feminists (Mitchell,

1974) and anti-racists – but each in their own way. The critical stance of psychoanalysis has been recently employed by some political thinkers in a stand against the political complacency of post-modernism (Frosh, 1991; Rustin, 1991).

At the same time it must be recognised that psychoanalysis has greatly expanded. Contemporary psychoanalytic developments have been towards the investigation of the relations between subject and object. Foremost in this has been the work of Melanie Klein and the British School of psychoanalysis. The important premise of object-relations psychoanalysis is that the human being is in relations with objects from birth. Of course, the first objects which the subject relates to in infancy are not necessarily very accurate versions of them. Nevertheless it is a potentiality from birth to apprehend in terms of relations between subject and objects. The context of the internal world, in particular the internal society, links the psychological with the social (Menzies, 1970, p. 61). The internal society, and the internal complex of relationships that form that society, is regarded as an inheritance in each person. The actual links between the internal and external social relations are complex:

> Individuals may put their internal conflicts [and therefore relations] into persons in the external world, unconsciously follow the course of the conflict by means of projective identification, and re-internalise the course of the conflict by means of introjective identification (Jaques, 1955, p. 497).

The way an individual is constructed from the continuous flow of projections and introjections is the process studied in the practice of a modern psychoanalysis (Heimann, 1952). The important point is that there is an inherited endowment of a potential for an ensemble of relations with objects which comprises an active 'internal society'. However it is important to avoid characterising psychoanalysis as the theory of the internal world and Marxism that of the external ensemble of social relations. Psychoanalysis is an attempt to address the interchange. And indeed Marx describes the internal and the external typically in the following way: 'But what distinguishes the worst architect from the best of bees is that the architect builds the cell in his mind before he constructs it in wax' (Marx, [1867] 1976, p. 284). This distinction is comparable to the psychoanalytic process of turning an internal structure (a 'fantasy') into something external – objectification in Marx's terms. So the idea of the internal society that is current in object-relations psychoanalysis is not a novel addition to Marxism. It may, however, significantly amplify that aspect of Marxist psychology. In this way the external interpenetrates the internal world (of object and subject). So, some recent developments in Marxism have coincided with some in psychoanalysis.

THE INDIVIDUAL AND INDIVIDUALISM

More recent interpretations of the link between psychoanalysis and Marxism rest on the instinctual needs of human beings as a materialist, and deterministic, given. The instinctual needs the psychoanalyst addresses are comparable to the economic needs of a rather crude Marxist psychology. More recently attempts to understand the creation of subjective experience and of individual identity have taken up the material base of human needs.

From a psychoanalytic point of view, the dissolution of the self into fragmented parts possessed by the social context is a process of individual psychology. But from a Marxist point of view it is the pressures of society itself which expropriates the particles of the self. Despite this back-to-back position, we might however examine the processes picked out by the psychoanalyst in order to gain a purchase on the effects of society on the individual. Perhaps if the modernist dilemma is how to sustain a sense of self, the struggles by which the individual does this, or fails to do this, tells us about the obstacles modern society puts in the way of individuality. Referring to this 'crisis' of the self in modern society, Richards (1989) observes of his collection of writers: 'Intrinsic to all the accounts of "crisis" given here is the observation that the external social world is not an inert backcloth to individual enactments of crisis-management' (Richards, 1989, p. 2). There is a concerted effort on the part of individuals to struggle with the crisis that modern society inserts into their sense of being. It is as if the whole of culture is predicated on the need of individuals to establish a stability, continuity and permanence to their own sense of self – a feature which has given rise to the popularity of Lasch's term 'the culture of narcissism' (Lasch, 1979).

This line of thought leads to a very specific reordering of the dialectic between the individual and society; now it becomes the forces which dissolve the individual's sense of self, and those which he uses (often generalised into a cultural form) to defend and stabilise their sense of self. This view has the advantage of giving some purchase on the problem that collectivisation poses for psychoanalysis. If all individuals are struggling with much the same sort of attacks on themselves from contemporary social relations then they will tend to orbit around the same sort of responses to defend themselves. This is one specific instance of the notion that character structure is formed by social structure and it therefore supplements Fromm's correlation.

In an extended series of essays Rustin (1991) brought a Kleinian perspective to bear on many features of cultural and institutional life, including psychoanalytic institutions. Fanon (1952) achieved a use of psychoanalysis in his perspective on racism and colonialism. Feminism particularly has begun to be alive to the potential convergence of object-relations psychoanalysis with political campaigns. But how do these approaches coincide with the specifically Marxist project of liberation from economic class determinism?

These particulate emancipatory claims can be grouped loosely into a pluralist venture (Rustin, 1985), but it is one which has a declining focus on class and social relations in general.

Habermas developed a return to aspects of Hegel and reconsidered some of the essentials of psychoanalytic paradigms in dialectical terms. This has been more systematically and comprehensively achieved by Wolfenstein (1993). It does create arresting new views on old psychoanalytic topics: 'Marx worked dialectically while Freud thought dualistically' (Wolfenstein, 1993, p. 218) – that is only partially true, and therefore a slightly unfair 'dualistic' comparison on Wolfenstein's part. In fact Freud's view of the id and super-ego in a system mediated by the ego has dialectical form. A dialectical process can consist of two points of view, two positions, one of which negates the other – by opposing it. However, in so far as they have in common much of the perceptions, apperceptions and conceptualisations they are said to penetrate each other – or 'interpenetrate'. Then, the negation is countered by a negation of the negation; and if the process is truly dialectical the end result will not be a return to the first position, but to a transformed final position, one which somehow synthesises the originating two. We can take the psychoanalytic example: when the id demands satisfaction it does so with an immediacy. For instance, someone wants to eat because of hunger. This meets a super-ego which demands that the hunger is ignored because, say, the person is sitting in their psychology seminar and it is deemed ill-mannered to eat there. The ego has to mediate this; it may judge that the prohibition should be countered by sucking a sweet which the person has in their pocket – or chewing their pen. But the original demand – to eat – is not returned to without modification.

A great deal of psychoanalysis is concerned with the mediating role of the ego but the ego is not unaided. One of Freud's ([1964] 1933) examples is of the sadist who becomes a butcher. In this instance we can see that the mediating factor is not just the ego. The ego is assisted, even prompted by certain social channels into which impulses can be diverted. The existence of a butchery trade allows the ego to 'find' a transformed synthesis of id impulse and super-ego prohibition. This is known as sublimation, and represents a profound interpenetration of the social into the life of the individual whilst he mediates conscience with desires. In this way we can come to recognise psychoanalytically the interpenetration of the social and the individual: individual impulses are deeply involved in butchery; the butchery trade can deeply mould the developing character of the individual. The collective presence of a whole group or culture creates a pressure towards social institutions whose psychological function is the channelling of impulses; the proviso is that individuals can and will modify their impulses. Such a mutual confrontation and interpenetration between individual and society is a dialectical process. These psychoanalytic illustrations take the dialectical process into the realm of personality development in the psychosocial matrix.

We need to take away the following from this discussion: a recognition of the need for a jointly informed practice; an understanding that social structure is replicated in character formation; the importance of the nature of the individual and the historical relativity of identity; and finally the need to proceed with a broadly dialectical method.

CONVERGENCE

I shall now review in brief some further connections: that between Marx's theory of alienation and the psychoanalytic view of depersonalisation; and that between Marx's theory of the exchange of commodities and a psycho-analytic description of the dispersal of personal identity.

Marx described the impoverishment of the worker confronted with the extent and power of their created products:

> the more the worker exerts himself, the more powerful the alien, objec-tive world becomes which he brings into being over and against him-self, the poorer he and his inner world become and the less they belong to him ... The worker places his life in the object; but now it no longer belongs to him, but to the object ... the life which he had bestowed on the object confronts him as hostile and alien (Marx, [1844] 1975, p. 324).

This process in which the object is in some significant sense a lost part of the subject is reflected in very similar descriptions by Melanie Klein; 'products of the body and parts of the self are felt to be split off, projected into another, and to be continuing their existence there' (Klein, [1955] 1975, p. 142), and 'As far as the ego is concerned the excessive splitting off and expelling into the outer world of parts of itself consider-ably weaken it' (Klein, 1946, p. 8). The close resemblance between these and other passages from Marx and from Melanie Klein's descriptions of projective identification suggest that both are intent on conveying a com-mon human experience. A convergence of these two sets of observation has occurred (see also Hinshelwood, 1983).

The commodities exchanged in the market place in a wage-labouring society have a quality that Marx called a fetish. He was struck by the value that commodities seem to acquire beyond their usefulness. Running besides their use-value is some other value that allows it to have compari-son with any other commodity. Marx called that its exchange value:

> This common element cannot be a geometrical, physical, chemical or other natural property of commodities. Such properties come into con-sideration only to the extent that they make the commodities useful, i.e. turn them into use-values. But clearly, the exchange relation of commodities is characterised precisely by its abstraction from their use-values ... As use-values commodities differ above all in quality, while as exchange-values they can only differ in quantity, and therefore

do not contain an atom of values since they are merely different quantities (Marx, [1867] 1976, pp. 127–8).

Exchanging commodities results in the circulation of an abstract entity without the characteristics of the original commodity or of the producer of it:

> With the disappearance of the useful character of the products of labour, the useful character of the kinds of labour embodied in them also disappears; this in turn entails the disappearance of the different concrete forms of labour. They can no longer be distinguished, but are altogether reduced to the same kind of labour, human labour in the abstract (Marx, [1867] 1976, p. 128).

The circulation of commodities implies in a concrete way the circulation of the labourer's activity that has been divested of its personal connection with him. In social groups a very similar process can be described in which certain aspects of the participant's personal identity can also circulate through the social relations disconnected from himself (Hinshelwood, 1982). The 'affective network' is a term coined to mean the network of relationships in which emotions pass from one person to another, losing their personal reference to any particular person. One illustration of this (Hinshelwood, 1989) described a long sequence of movements of something that has psychological 'substance' but is unattached to persons:

> The affective network [of a group] is an exchange system of human emotions and identity, of reified bits of human beings. In this sense affective networks parallel the exchange systems of commodities which are also reified bits of human relations ... The losing of parts of human emotions and identity in the affective network compares with the expropriation of surplus value in the labour of economic production (Hinshelwood, 1989, p. 82).

There is a convergence between the circulation of surplus value and the circulation of what we might call 'surplus identity'. The network of social relations has this specific property: to allow the exchange and circulation of both material commodities and of aspects of personal identity. Such a network is created and sustained by both the economic system of production, and also the basic conditions of human identity.

These two processes – alienation/depersonalisation and commodity/identity – can be viewed both from an external and from an internal perspective. They are potentially a bridge to link the interpersonal and the intrapsychic, and thus to link Marxism to psychoanalysis. The depletion of the individual due to certain kinds of projective identification is not just an individual process. The depleted parts of the person are found in some other part of the field of social relations, some other part of the institution, and this gives rise to the circulation of parts of the personalities of individuals like commodities within the ensemble of social relations.

BASE AND SUPERSTRUCTURE

Together with the convergent oppression/repression we have discovered a bundle of points of contact between the alternative theories. Of course the theoretical frameworks which correspond to either side of these points of contact are quite different – the psychoanalytic theory of projective identification and object relations on one hand, and the Marxist theory of labour and value on the other. We now need to consider the way these observations and their respective theoretical frameworks are structured. Both Marxism and psychoanalysis construct the world in the form of a material base which gives rise to a 'non-material' superstructure.

According to historical materialism, the methods of technological production prompt a system of economic and social relations around those methods. Not only that but other manifestations occur – a legal system that protects ownership of products, rules about labour relations, etc. Families adapt to those methods – for instance, moving from domestic production to urban dwelling around factory production. These social adaptations and relations that are engendered by the methods of production constitute the culture of a society; it is a non-material superstructure. It progresses in a time sequence driven by technical innovations in productive methods and this results in historical progress. This leads to a curious anomaly: human beings make their own history, but at the same time their lives are determined by the methods of production. Their subjectivity – the consciousness of themselves – is distorted to conceal this anomaly, and such false consciousness is ideology; it depends upon the inherent property of the human mind to render awareness unconscious.

Something rather similar happens according to psychoanalysis. The body represents another material 'base', an observation noted by Timpanaro (1975). Material production is aimed at the material needs of human beings. The body is the instigator of those needs and therefore of production. Hunger, pain, sexual feelings and so on are the primary stimuli which are inherent in having a human body. The body prompts not only the need for a productive industry, but there is another and parallel sense in which the body is a material base. It is the base from which the mind and its potential for object relations emerge. Freud understood the mind to be a locus of transition in which bodily states appear in psychological form. This may be fairly direct, such as hunger which is readily apprehended and gives rise frequently to straightforward behavioural responses. Other states, especially sexual ones, may have a very different route through to sublimated derivatives in the mind – in the character and behaviour of the person – in their object relations.

If economic activity and bodily experiences create separate theories, they also generate separate superstructures – the world of social relations and the world of object relations respectively. The upshot of the second part of this chapter is to show that the two superstructures converge. They lean together and coincide at certain points; we have dealt with three of those points – oppression/repression, alienation/depersonalisation and commodity/identity.

We can ask: how is this convergence achieved? How do the two material bases throw up superstructures which converge? What mediates that convergence from disparate origins? It is consistent with Marxist and psychoanalytic theories that it is the individual person themself that mediates the tension between the internal sources of their object relations and the external sources of their social relations, or at least it is the person in a collective manifestation – group, nation, population. There is here a potential to develop a theory of the individual on the basis of mediator of these superstructures. We have then transformed the dialectical problem from the need to understand the mediation between the individual and society to a quite different problem of mediation – the mediation between two superstructures from separate bases.

We might ask: what is such a theory of the individual going to look like? And what can it do? As Raymond Williams argued (1980) the cultural superstructure is not rigidly determined by the economic base: it has a 'relative autonomy'. The present notion of convergence of the superstructures through the person makes that autonomy more comprehensible if we understand there to be two superstructures, cultural and psychological, which are partially (or wholly) mediated by individuality (i.e. personal identity). Then the influences of one and the other will interpenetrate in a process that is not fully determined by either material base. A field of cultural endeavour opens up between the superstructures, to be explored by the collective individuals. The individual, defined as the struggle to sustain a mediation between the cultural and psychological, drives the progress of both culture and of character psychology in the process of that mediation. Very likely that struggle between the cultural and psychological superstructures is the process which contributes to the sense of agency (will), and our unique consciousness and self-consciousness.

The field of cultural endeavour opened up by this struggle acquires an architecture which is influenced by both the economic relations of production that is extant at the time, the complex of potentialities within the world of object relations and the talents of given individuals of the time. From a psychoanalytic point of view, that field grows within it certain channels down which are drawn the various tractable, moulded impulses of human individuals – the butcher held within the mould of his butcher's shop. It would be one implication of this view that no cultural phenomenon can be fully understood without its potentiality as a channel for human outlet, both for the pioneering spirits, and those routinisers that come after.

The complementarity of the two superstructures relies on the capacity of human beings to find social channelling for the diversion of the instincts in modified forms, but within the constraints of unconscious phantasies and within those of the social relations of economic production. The individual with their constructed identity and the social channels will tend to gravitate towards the place where the superstructures converge.

The convergences are mediated by the individual and simultaneously construct them.

It is no longer possible to sustain a view of the separated personal identity. The psychoanalytic understanding of the dispersal of the person has dissolved the individual into the network of relations (social relations and object relations) in which parts of their identity gather. That depletion and insecurity, in contemporary society, may lead to a profound search for a stable untampered identity – a narcissistic search, as Frosh concluded. However, that construction of the individual is itself socially enhanced and channelled, like the butcher's solution to sadistic impulses mentioned earlier, and such social possession of the individual has to be concealed from him in order to be successful.

Clearly, as economic production develops and creates historical pressures on social forms to change, so the mediation between superstructures will require continual adjustment and modification. The nature of the individual is therefore historically ground anew between the upper and nether grindstones – one of object relations (bodily base) and one of economics (material production). What then is the scope for a negative practice? It is not enough that psychoanalytic practice liberates the individual; and often, incidentally, it does not. Psychoanalysis can only be revolutionary if it has a much wider effect on self-consciousness; in other words on the false consciousnesses of whole classes – or on whole particulate liberatory movements – feminism or racism, as well as political liberation. For this move we have to turn to a psychoanalytic version of group dynamics to consider the points where the social imprint brands the developing individual. The dissolving and constructing processes which occur in the networks of groups have been touched on above (Hinshelwood, 1989); they suggest that there is no finally formed individual which social processes cannot radically reconstruct through the fluid quality of personal identity.

CONCLUSION

These have been the reflections of a psychoanalyst, and therefore in a discourse that is individualistic. However, as a discourse *between* people it is interpenetrated by the social. Psychoanalysis can be dismissed simply as bourgeois ideology; or as irrelevant because it is merely an analysis of a historical period of bourgeois ideology (late nineteenth century). But psychoanalysis is in fact historically relative, and phases in the development of its theory and practice are instantly recognisable – and also in its cultural location. It therefore warrants examination as a socially related and potentially engaged form of thought – both of its time and examining its time. What psychoanalysis is good at is the content of what is collectivised. It has difficulty with understanding the collective itself, and it is difficult to apply the knowledge which Marxism has of the collective to solve that problem for psychoanalysis. Just as it is difficult to supplement the gap in Marxism with the psychoanalytic understanding of the subjective identity of the individual. Complementarity could exist between the two frameworks, but not without a persisting tension – however that tension is reflected, not just between the conceptual frameworks but within the actually occurring problematics at the superstructural level.

Acknowledgements. I am grateful for discussions with David Bell, who commented on a draft of this chapter, with Bob Young and many other colleagues and friends.

REFERENCES

Bridgeland, M. (1971) *Pioneer Work with Maladjusted Children*, London: Staples Press.

Fanon, F. ([1952] 1986) *Black Skin, White Masks*, London: Pluto Press.

Freud, S. ([1933] 1964) *New Introductory Lectures on Psycho-Analysis. SE XXII*, London: Hogarth.

Frosh, S. (1991) *Identity Crisis: Modernity, Psycho-analysis and the Self*, London: Macmillan.

Habermas, J. ([1968] 1971) *Knowledge and Human Interests*, London: Heinemann.

Heimann, P. (1952) 'Certain functions of projection and introjection in early infancy', in M. Klein, P. Heimann, S. Isaacs and J. Riviere (eds) *Developments in Psycho-Analysis*, London: Tavistock.

Hinshelwood, R.D. (1982) 'The individual and the social network', in M. Pines and L. Raphaelson (eds) *The Individual and the Group*, New York: Plenum.

Hinshelwood, R.D. (1983) 'Projective identification and Marx's concept of man', *International Review of Psycho-Analysis* **10**, pp. 221–6.

Hinshelwood, R.D. (1989) 'Social Possession of identity', in B. Richards (ed.) *Crises of the Self: Further Essays on Psycho-Analysis and Politics*, London: Free Association Books.

Jacoby, R. (1983) *The Repression of Psycho-Analysis*, New York: Basic Books.

Jaques, E. (1955) 'The social system as a defence against persecutory and depressive anxiety', in M. Klein, P. Heimann and R. Money-Kyrle (eds) *New Directions in Psycho-Analysis*, London: Tavistock.

Klein, M. ([1946]1975) 'Notes on some schizoid mechanisms', in *The Writings of Melanie Klein, III*, London: Hogarth.

Klein, M. ([1955]1975) 'On identification', in *The Writings of Melanie Klein, III*, London: Hogarth.

Lasch, C. (1979) *The Culture of Narcissism*, London: Abacus.

Marx, K. ([1844]1975) 'Economic and philosophical manuscripts', in *Early Writings*, Harmondsworth: Penguin.

Marx, K. ([1845]1975) 'Concerning Feuerbach', in *Early Writings*, Harmondsworth: Penguin.

Marx, K. ([1867]1976) *Capital: Volume 1*, London: Penguin.

Menzies, I. (1970) 'Psychosocial aspects of eating', in I. Menzies Lyth (1989) *The Dynamics of the Social*, London: Free Association Books.

Mitchell, J. (1974) *Psychoanalysis and Feminism*, London: Allen Lane.

Popper, K. (1957) *The Poverty of Historicism*, London: Routledge and Kegan Paul.

Richards, B. (ed.) (1989) *Crises of the Self: Further Essays on Psycho-Analysis and Politics*, London: Free Association Books.

Rustin, M. (1985) *For a Pluralist Socialism*, London: Verso.

Rustin, M. (1991) *The Good Society and the Inner World: Psycho-Analysis, Politics and Culture*, London: Verso.

Strachey, J. (1937) 'Introduction' to R. Osborn, *Freud and Marx: A Dialectical Study*, London: Gollanz.

Timpanaro, S. (1975) *On Materialism*, London: New Left Books.

Trotsky, L. (1930) *My Life: An Attempt at Autobiography*, New York: Scribners.

Wertsch, J. (1985) *Vygotsky and the Social Formation of Mind*, Cambridge, MA; Harvard University Press.

Williams, R. (1980) 'Base and superstrucure in Marxist cultural theory', in R. Williams (ed.) *Problems in Materialism and Culture*, London: Verso.

Wolfenstein, E.V. (1993) *Psychoanalytic Marxism: Groundwork*, London: Free Association Books.

7

CRITICAL PSYCHOLOGY AS SUBJECT-SCIENCE

Wolfgang Maiers and Charles W. Tolman

We see how the history of *industry* and the established *objective* existence of industry are the *open book* of *man's essential powers*, the exposure to the senses of human *psychology* ... A *psychology* for which this, the part of history most contemporary and accessible to sense, remains a closed book, cannot become a genuine, comprehensive and *real* science. (Marx, [1844]1964, p. 142)

The chief defect of all hitherto existing materialism ... is that the thing, reality, sensuousness, is conceived only in the form of the *object* or of *contemplation*, but not as *human sensuous activity, practice*, not subjectivity. (Marx, [1845]1977, p. 13)

According to Marx, a really scientific psychology would be one that grasped the essential powers of human individuals as reflected in their productive activity, that is, in the practice of which the individual is the subject. Subjectivity here is understood not as mere contemplation or self-reflection but as effective agency, which is achieved only in cooperation with others, that is, in societal, historical relations. Our intention here is to describe, however briefly, how Critical Psychology represents such a science of the subject.

The project known in Germany and other European countries as Critical Psychology has been developing for a quarter of a century. (It is commonplace in Germany, among both supporters and detractors, to refer to this distinct and systematic approach as 'Critical Psychology' (*Kritische Psychologie*), in contradistinction to 'critical psychologies' (*kritische Psychologien*). For further details on the position and its history, see Tolman and Maiers (1991) and Tolman (1994).) It had its origins in the critiques of society and science undertaken by the student movement of 1968 in West Germany and West Berlin. The intention was to replace the dominant, subject-negating psychology with a 'critical-emancipatory' alternative.

In the context of the debate around positivism, Critical Psychology's initial critique was aimed at the nature of science and its relation to societal practice. Discussion focused on the 'crisis of relevance', science's alignment with 'dominance', the nature of scientific truth claims, the interests governing knowledge and the social function of empirical research. The social-theoretical level of the debates was, in retrospect, not always profound. The scandalous uses made of psychological research findings and professional practice in the dominant economic and political interests were evident to anyone who cared to look. The examination of psychology was assisted by works like Baritz's *Servants of Power* (1960). The kind of analysis which was emerging from the debates at that time included analysis of the institutions and functions of mainstream psychology, and served primarily to expose the ideological nature of its concepts and methods. For example, Holzkamp (1972, pp. 35ff) showed how experimental psychology had eliminated the historical aspect of its subject-matter as a consequence of an 'organismic anthropology, which treated the human subject as a natural essence.

A turn to the study of Marx's critique of capitalist political economy (especially the *Grundrisse* and *Capital*) as a complex of contradictory forms of societal practice and consciousness determined by antagonistic social and economic interests marked a new stage in the critique of psychology. The immediate result was concrete, critical insight into the objective partiality of positivist science as it was perpetuated in the pre-established subjective partisanship of individual scientists. What became apparent was the 'necessarily false consciousness' of psychology's misunderstanding of life activity and subjectivity of concrete human beings. Ignoring their historically determined societal conditions, individuals were necessarily understood as abstract. Moreover, these abstracted individuals were set off against a quasi-natural environment which was presumed to be the ultimate determinant of their actions. This objectivistic view was merely the inversion of the subjective idealist counterpart which hypostatised individual experience as the ultimate substance.

Both points of view were now recognised as spontaneous results and reifications of capitalist production. They represented the actually existing inverted relationships which, on the surface, characterised bourgeois society. Each presupposed the privacy of isolated individuals whose societal relations were reduced to natural relations between things. This was not confined to 'individual' psychology. It could readily be seen in that large part of social psychology that remains even today under the sway of Floyd Allport's (1924) definition of the subdiscipline as 'the science which studies the behaviour of the individual in so far as his [sic] behaviour stimulates other individuals, or is itself a reaction to their behaviour' (p. 12).

To the extent that it does not see through the inversion of society and individual in the definition of its subject matter, psychology remains tied to the bourgeois ideology of essentially asocietal human individuals existing in natural and immutable life circumstances. In short, it remains a science that is aptly labelled 'bourgeois'.

One prospect for determining an emancipatory alternative was an historical-materialist analysis of the ways in which problems and discourses related to 'subjectivity' had accompanied the development of bourgeois society, and how these had been distorted as contexts for emerging disciplines such as psychology. Parallel to this, the critical psychological programme undertook a comprehensive, concrete reconstruction of the objects of traditional psychological research (perceptions, feelings etc.) in a manner that would reflect their historicity and the ways in which they had been shaped by bourgeois society.

The transition to Critical Psychology as a programme for unifying critique with continued development of the science started in 1971 (Maiers, 1991). Soviet psychological works such as Rubinstein's *Sein und Bewusstsein* [Being and Consciousness] ([1957]1972) were influential, especially Leontyev's elaboration of the 'historical method of investigating the psyche' (Leontyev, [1959]1973) which had originated with Vygotsky and the cultural-historical school. The philosophical side of Critical Psychology was drawn from pertinent contemporary contributions to the Marxist theory of knowledge, logic of science and methodology. Particularly important, however, was Engels's *Dialectics of Nature* ([1873–86]1972), which led to renewed considerations of the connection between the historical and the natural aspects of human existence, reflecting Marx's maxim that 'history itself is a *real* part of natural history – of nature developing into man' (Marx, [1844]1964, p. 143). The project was further aided by a closer understanding of Marx's *Capital* as a model for the dialectical-historical investigation of historical-empirical subject-matters.

The method of Critical Psychology developed as the result of generalising from Marx's instrumentarium of logical-historical method. It was clear from the start that such generalisation would not be achieved simply by lifting these methods out of *Capital* and applying them unaltered to the psychological subject-matter. Such a procedure, as Holzkamp saw (1991, p. 51), would persist in leaving the 'individual as such' out of reach. Marx's methodological canon had to be used more as a set of guidelines for directing the development of new methods appropriate to psychology's peculiar subject-matter. The most important guideline was that the essential constitution of the historical, concrete object could only be understood from the developmental logic of how it came into being.

According to Marx, a dialectical theory had to be based on a developmental method of thinking which 'ascends from the abstract to the concrete'. 'Abstract' knowledge is such as one would get from a dictionary: we can know that a human being is an animal that walks upright, wears clothing and has soft earlobes. This kind of knowledge is 'true' and it is practical in so far as it allows us to make reliable (and true) distinctions between humans and other creatures. It does not, however, reveal what it means to be human. Marx urged us to rise from this kind of abstract knowledge to grasp the concreteness of our object of concern, that is, to reproduce its concrete nature in our concept of it. The concrete was defined as a 'convergence of many determinations ... and thus a unity of diversities' (Marx, [1857]1974, p. 21; [1857]1971, pp. 631–9). What converges in the concrete individual are of course historical and social relations. The kind of explanation that follows from this method is 'deductive' in a 'genetic-reconstructive' sense, not from arbitrarily universal premises but from the intelligible structure of the object's determinants (cf. Bakhurst, 1991, pp. 138–44).

This particular adoption of Marxist methodology has distinguished Critical Psychology from most other psychology-critical or critical-psychological positions. On the whole, these positions have either rejected the possibility of developing a positive science from the radicalisation of the critique of science, or they have reduced historical materialism to a social theory with nothing to say about individual subjectivity, thus creating the appearance of a need for an independent, supplementary psychology of the subject – usually psychoanalytic (e.g. Lorenzer, 1974). Often, on the basis of the very same premises, the opposite conclusion has been asserted: that individuality might be understood on the basis of a sufficient concretisation of political-economic analysis. Critical Psychology rejects these conclusions because they imply that, on its own, Marxist epistemology cannot provide the basis for the refounding of a psychological science.

Holzkamp's *Sinnliche Erkenntnis* ('Sensual Knowledge') appeared in 1973 and a number of important works were soon to follow (e.g. Osterkamp, 1975, 1976; Ulmann, 1975; Schurig, 1976; Seidel, 1976). This work was aimed primarily at elaborating an epistemology for psychological concept formation, methods and understandings of professional practice which would escape the traditional assumptions of a private existence subjected to a natural environment. It focused on the subject's experience of the world and self, and attempted to develop formulations that would preserve its authenticity and yet allow scientific explanation and concrete generalisation. Among other things, this meant identifying the real possibilities which existed for individuals actively and meaningfully to alter the circumstances of their lives, as distinct from and in addition to the possibilities for merely getting along through willing subjection to societally imposed restrictions.

The analysis began with traditional psychology's theoretical naturalisation of the human being. Common understandings and confusions around the 'natural' and 'social' had to be exposed as purely ideological. At the same time, it was necessary to find a way of overcoming the scientific short-sightedness of these notions. A Critical Psychology which aimed at being a psychology from the standpoint of the subject depended upon the establishment of a substantively differentiated concept of individual subjectivity, the natural and social-historical developments of which form a unity. To overcome naturalism, Marx had suggested in his first thesis on Feuerbach that human reality had to be understood subjectively, that is, from the point of view of practice. If subjectivity was not to be understood as 'free-floating', then practice had to be considered as object-oriented, sensuous-practical activity (Marx, [1845]1977, p. 13).

'Practice' forms the central category in the materialist dialectic for defining the relation between humans and their world. It must be embedded in a comprehensive theory of nature and society. Such a theory of universal interconnection must conceptualise the human being as a special kind of natural being which, within the natural totality, both appropriates nature and productively alters it. There are two theoretical implications here. First, people shape the conditions of their lives by opposing nature, but on the supposition (by no means assured) that they will not end up thereby depriving themselves of this basis for their own existences. In the interests, then, of the human species it is important to understand that nature is not merely a passive object for societal exploitation. It must be understood in its own context of reproduction, which includes considera-tion of the side- and after-effects of human intervention.

The second implication is that psychological conceptions of the subject that 'rest on an unquestioning categorial reproduction of the "obviously" compelling, exclusive opposition of nature and human society' are 'one-sided'. To overcome this, it is necessary to show how societality has developed from natural human existence and how humans as natural beings have developed both the capacity and the need to participate in the creation and alteration of societal conditions. Failure to do this results in two possible forms of objectivism. The 'sociologistic' form degrades indi-viduals to mere points of convergence of societal factors. As such, it pre-vents understanding the sensuous side of individuals' material existence and the subjective necessities grounded in it. The 'biologistic' form con-ceives the sensuous, material individual in terms of an inner nature to which the societal remains external.

If the phenomenal quality of consciousness is to be understood as a reflexive relationship of the person to both world and self; if we want to understand the subjectively grounded action of empirical subjects in condi-tions of concrete societal life; if we want to avoid the 'solipsistic psyche' that renders subjectivity unamenable to scientific investigation; then, at a minimum, an adequately differentiated conception of human nature is required. Marx's dictum that 'history itself is an actual part of natural history, of the development of nature into human nature' (1968, p. 544) remains valid. Critical Psychology rejects the theoretical anti-humanism implied in the structuralist interpretation of Marx which was discussed in the 1960s.

In our view, Marx's 'theoretical humanism' (cf. Maiers, 1985, pp. 117ff; Brockmeier, 1988, pp. 387ff) – which resulted from his rejecting Hegel's idealistic elevation of history over its actual participants – is also valid for understanding the development by which humankind moves toward genuine humanity. On its revolutionary Utopian side, it retains the early and classical bourgeois notion of history as the unity of social progress and realisation of human reason. Contrary to many postmodern readings, Critical Psychology remains committed at the level of a specific science to this aspect of modernity.

Critical Psychology defines its basic categories by a procedure called 'func-tional-historical' analysis. This is an attempt to reconstruct the origin and development of the substantive characteristics of psychical dimensions and functions which can be abstracted from traditional psychological concepts, that is, it attempts to grasp the intelligible structure of, say, motivation or learning. In doing this it appeals to pertinent evidence from biology, paleontology, anthropology etc. The result is a system of more or less hierarchically arranged concepts portraying the developmental logic of psychophylogenesis. The most elementary forms yield the most general concepts; phylogenetic differentiation leads to further conceptual distinctions and these finally develop as concepts reflecting the 'qualitative leaps' in phylogenesis (cf. Tolman, 1994). By means of a kind of historical-empirical decoding of the developmental relationships which are preserved in the dimensions and functional aspects of human consciousness, we are able to estimate the extent to which the traditional basic concepts obscure or illuminate differences between species levels, and what modifications allow them to be retained.

Substantively, such a functional-historical reconstruction leads first to a categorial definition of the qualitative transition from the pre-psychical life process to the genesis of psychical reflection. This reconstruction begins with Leontyev's (1973, pp. 5ff) paradigmatic hypothesis about the emergence of sensitivity (cf. Holzkamp and Schurig, 1973), passes along various intermediate genetic forms, in order finally to reveal the course of anthropogenesis. Most important is the emergence of the societal-economic form of human life, which was first superimposed upon a natural existence and then became the dominant form of human existence characterised by labour. This development is traced from its origins as an evolutionarily determined process governed by biological priorities of species preservation at the prehuman level to its manifestation in societal human nature. This species-specific nature bears the potential for individual societalisation ('vergesellschaftung': see Maiers, 1991, pp. 37–8). This occurs through the utilisation and appropriation in ontogenesis of societally and historically produced possibilities for the development of cognitive activity, emotional-motivational processes and social modes of communication.

Placing human action and experience into its historically concrete societal context, however, requires conceptions of human sociality which go well beyond its natural potential. At this point the method of the categorial reconstruction can no longer be 'functional-historical'. This essentially biological-historical method is restricted to results of a continuous-progressive evolutionary process, including that of anthropogenesis, and hence is no longer appropriate because the fundamental process of development itself changes with a societal mode of existence (Holzkamp, 1983, pp. 48ff and 185ff). Rather, a method is needed which can grasp the unique differentiations and qualifications of psychical ontogenesis that emerge with the universal societal mediation of our relations with the world and one another.

The main achievement of the historical investigation we have sketched has been to reveal – and differentiate categorically – the mediating levels between societal reproduction and the individual life process. The traditional naturalistic reduction of human life activity and subjectivity to a state of unqualified determination by external circumstances conceptually strips sensuous-concrete individuals of their subjective agency. In contrast, it is the 'double-sided' nature of human action that must be emphasised, that is, the relationship between its objective determination by circumstances and determination of the latter by the subject's action. This 'double-sidedness' is also lacking in the idealistic adulation of individual autonomy which, like naturalism, leads to dramatically reduced relevance of so-called scientific psychological theory for everyday and professional practice. The task is to see that the psychological categories reflect the individuals' in-principle possibilities for practical change.

Irrespective of the concrete form of society, the relationship between individuals and their world is universally characterised by 'possibility relations' and 'subjective grounds for action'. Objective social meanings refer to historically produced forms of practice which need to be translated into the action of individual members of society. From the standpoint of individuals, however, they represent only generalised possibilities for action to which individuals can, in principle, relate consciously and from which, within objectively determined limits, they can adopt alternatives for action. Individuals experience needs and interests, which in the last instance reflect the vital necessity to exercise active influence on the societal or natural conditions and resources which are relevant to their need satisfaction and for the maintenance or improvement of the quality of their lives. Depending on the needs or interests which are effective, the objective conditions and meanings – as they are experienced by individuals – function as 'premises' for action-intentions. From this point of view a conception of determinism that is adequate to human 'freedom of action' is one which recognises that behaviour is grounded, via its premises, in its relations. An individual's action becomes, in principle, intelligible for others on the basis that no one acts consciously contrary to his or her actual vital interests as he or she understands them. This is the 'material a priori' of human self-consciousness, of interpersonal understanding and thus also of subject-scientific knowledge.

Definitions of this sort, however, need to be concretised with respect to specified conditions of life, which in our case are the conditions of bourgeois society. This society is characterised by a contradiction between societally produced possibilities for individual development and satisfaction of needs on the one hand and, owing to prevailing property relations, the massive exclusion of individuals from these possibilities for self-determination of societal conditions on the other. This contradiction pervades every aspect of everyday practice in the life world without being necessarily apparent to the individual concerned. Based mainly on studies by Osterkamp (1976), Holzkamp (1983, pp. 249ff) has conceptualised the contradiction between the 'immediacy' and 'mediacy' of meaning-ground relations in everyday practice as a double possibility within every existentially relevant situation. This double possibility offers individuals the alternatives of 'restrictive' and 'generalised' modes of making their actions effective, that is, of achieving *action potence*. The restrictive mode finds action potence within the framework of available or conceded conditions; the generalised mode, taking the risk of failure and negative sanctions, is directed at developing and extending the framework of action.

This distinction between restrictive and generalised action potence is reflected in other important psychological categories. For instance, in cognition, the restrictive mode is represented as a tendency to 'interpretive' thinking which takes things more or less at face value. The generalised mode, by contrast, is characterised by 'comprehensive' thinking which is directed at underlying causes and connections. In emotion, the restrictive mode is linked to 'emotional inwardness' in which emotions tend to be taken as personal problems; in the generalised mode, 'generalised emotional engagement' takes emotion as a response to the world requiring corrective action. In the generalised mode, the more characteristic motivation is self-motivation based on one's actual needs and interests; in the restrictive mode, what appears as motivation is in fact internal compulsion resulting from the introjection of determination by others. These alternatives are not 'types' but tendencies or possibilities for any cognition, emotion and motivation within the framework of bourgeois society. Under the premise that no one is knowingly his or her own enemy, this distinction helps to explain why it can be subjectively grounded for individuals to yield to restriction, even though in the long run it contributes to the reduction of their own bases for life and prospects for alleviating subjective suffering through the help of others. The risks and impediments accompanying the generalised alternative are often simply too overwhelming to contemplate.

Explanation of the lawful characteristics of the subjective situation and action potence is achieved by tracing the subjective grounds for action to the material forms of practice and consciousness (Marx's 'objective thought forms') and thus to the action spaces which are available in the concrete, historical relations between individual and society. This avoids the theoretical limitations which arise – as for example in symbolic interactionism – when we attempt to account for the meaningfulness and groundedness of human action on its own. Such accounts miss the specific nature of the human-world connection, which is also overlooked in the usual opposite move of absolutising the objective conditionality of action.

The subject-scientific analysis of the connections between meanings and grounds for action includes an investigation – 'analysis of meanings' – of social-historical forms of economic, political, juridical and ideological structures in terms of the relative possibilities for action that the various class-and position-specific life worlds contain. Against this background we determine the forms that action potence and subjective situation take in actually dealing with these possibilities. Such an analysis of groundedness is necessary, inasmuch as it is not evident at all times to the subjects concerned – especially after experiencing repeated failures – which possible intentions 'reasonably' correspond with their own interests in a particular situation.

The problem of 'psychological' knowledge in the strictest sense is to discover, in view of the aforementioned 'material a priori', how exactly it can be subjectively grounded for people to make accommodations with oppressive authorities, miserable conditions etc., thus contributing to the consolidation of the restrictive framework. Why, in short, do people opt for the short-term benefits over the longer-term benefits of generalised action potence? For one, the benefits of restrictive action potence are real benefits. They offer relief from conflict, immediate if limited need-fulfilment, and the securing of at least some degree of action potence. Critical Psychology can help to understand this, but it can also indicate steps by which possibilities for action may be extended so as to overcome the contradictions, the reciprocal- and self-impediments, which obstruct life practices.

Subject-scientific empirical research sets in where subjects are systematically unclear about such matters, and thus need clarification of the complex connections they experience between life interests, existential conditions and the actions that can be grounded in them. The starting point of empirical investigation is always a set of problems: inconsistencies among groundings of action (with characteristic defence mechanisms unwittingly maintaining them). Through this individuals obstruct their own life practice, surrender to particular dependencies, and hinder themselves from developing their own ability to gain control of the circumstances which govern the quality of their lives.

Serious problems arise from attempts to extend one's own possibilities at the expense of others, usually owing to ignorance of the premises and grounds of others' actions. This has the paradoxical effect of strengthening the very obstacles and resistances which restricted the subject in the first place. Such self-injurious grounding patterns can be made comprehensible to subjects only to the extent that more effective and practicable alternatives can be made apparent.

Meaning-grounds analyses aim at making comprehensible for the individuals concerned the partial functionality of their restrictive coping strategies. Such hypotheses have their criterion of confirmation in a correspondingly altered, more satisfying life practice for the subject. By the same token, such a 'controlled-exemplary practice', which is fed back to and supervised by the research group, provides an approach to a generalised characterisation of action possibilities which hold for others in comparable life situations. The conception and method of generalisation here take up Lewin's (largely forgotten) proposal (1931) for a kind of generalisation from concrete particular cases to 'such a' case. Holzkamp (1983) calls it 'structural generalisation' or 'generalisation of possibilities'. It is not directed at dimensions of sampled human characteristics, but at the use and extension of subjective 'possibility spaces' for action. The Critical Psychological principle referred to here as that of 'unity of knowing and changing' is rooted in the Marxist conception of practice, both as an epistemological principle and as a definition of the societal function of scientific knowledge.

The research programme which derives from the foregoing is fundamentally at odds with third-person psychology, in which 'subjects' are investigated from the perspective of an observer at a distance. Psychological subject-science is concerned with the subjective experience of objective societal possibilities and restrictions on action. Subjects, as origins of such experience, cannot be made into objects, but must stand on a level with the researchers. By implication the latter are affected by their own cognitive procedures, and hence their interests must be reflected methodologically as an aspect of intersubjective understanding in scientific research. Since specifically human life activity is conducted in the context of groundings of action that are 'first person' – and can thus be dealt with only from the person's own standpoint – it follows that the subject's standpoint must be recognised as a valid vantage point for gaining scientific knowledge. Moreover, psychology must consistently maintain the corresponding 'grounds discourse' in the language of its theories and as an 'intersubjective frame of agreement' in its research practice. It is in this sense of psychological research 'from the standpoint of the subject' that Critical Psychology is a distinct 'subject-science'.

REFERENCES

Allport, F. (1924) *Social Psychology*, Boston: Houghton Mifflin.

Bakhurst, D. (1991) *Consciousness and Revolution in Soviet Philosophy*, New York: Cambridge University Press.

Baritz, L. (1960) *The servants of power*, Middleton, CT: Wesleyan University Press.

Brockmeier (1988) 'Der dialektische Ansatz und seine Bedeutung für die Psychologie', in G. Juttemann (ed.), *Wegbereiter der historischen Psychologie*, München/Weinheim: Beltz Verlag.

Engels, F. ([1873–86]1972) *Dialectics of nature*, Moscow: Progress Publishers.

Holzkamp, K. (1972) *Kritische Psychologie: Vorbereitende Arbeiten*, Frankfurt: Fischer Taschenbuch Verlag.

Holzkamp, K. (1983) *Grundlegung der Psychologie*, Frankfurt: Campus Verlag.

Holzkamp, K. (1991) 'Societal and individual life processes', in C.W. Tolman and W. Maiers (eds), *Critical Psychology*, New York: Cambridge University Press.

Holzkamp, K. (1973) *Sinnliche Erkenntnis. Historicher Ursprung und gesellschaftliche Funktion der Wahrnehmung*, Frankfurt: Athenäum.

Holzkamp, K., and Schurig, V. (1973) 'Zur Einführung', in A.N. Leontyev, *Probleme der Entwicklung des Psychischen*, Frankfurt: Fischer Taschenbuch Verlag.

Leontyev, A.N. ([1959]1973) *Probleme der Entwicklung des Psychischen*, Frankfurt: Fischer Taschenbuch Verlag. English edn 1981, *Problems of the development of the mind*, Moscow: Progress Publishers.

Lewin, K. (1931) 'Der Übergang von der aristotelischen zur galileischen Denkweise in Biologie und Psychologie', *Erkenntnis* 1, pp. 421–66. (English trans. 1931, *Journal of General Psychology* 5, pp. 141–77.)

Lorenzer, A. (1974) *Die Wahrheit der psychoanalytischen Erkenntnis: Ein historisch-materialistischer Entwurf*, Frankfurt: Suhrkamp.

Maiers, W. (1985) 'Menschliche Subjektivität und Natur', in *Forum Kritische Psychologie* 15, pp. 114–28.

Maiers, W. (1991) 'Critical Psychology: Historical background and task', in C.W. Tolman and W. Maiers (eds), *Critical Psychology*, New York: Cambridge University Press.

Marx, K. ([1844]1964) *The economic and philosophic manuscripts of 1844*, New York: International Publishers.

Marx, K. (1968) 'Ueber P.J. Proudhon. Brief an J.B. v. Schweitzer', in *Marx-Engels Werke*, vol. 16, Berlin: Dietz.

Marx, K. ([1857]1971) 'Einleitung zur Kritik der politischen Oekonomie', in *Marx-Engels Werke* 13, Berlin GDR: Dietz Verlag.

Marx, K. ([1857]1974) *Grundrisse der Kritik der Politischen Oekonomie*, Berlin GDR: Dietz Verlag.

Marx, K. ([1845]1977) 'Theses on Feuerbach', in *Karl Marx and Frederick Engels: Selected works in three volumes*, Moscow: Progress Publishers.

Osterkamp, U. (1975) *Grundlagen der psychologischen Motivationsforschung I*, Frankfurt/Main: Campus Verlag.

Osterkamp, U. (1976) *Grundlagen der psychologischen Motivationsforschung II: Die Besonderheit menschlicher Bedürfnisse: Problematik und Erkenntnisgehalt der Psychoanalyse*, Frankfurt/Main: Campus Verlag.

Rubinstein, S.L. ([1957]1972) *Sein und Bewusstsein*, Berlin, GDR: Akademie-Verlag.

Schurig, V. (1976) *Die Entstehung des Bewusstseins*, Frankfurt/Main: Campus Verlag.

Seidel, R. (1976) *Denken: Psychologische Analyse der Entstehung und Lösung von Problemen*, Frankfurt/Main: Campus Verlag.

Ulmann, G. (1975) *Sprache und Wahrnehmung*, Frankfurt/Main: Campus Verlag.

Tolman, C.W. (1994) *Psychology, society, and subjectivity*, London: Routledge.

Tolman, C.W. and Maiers, W. (eds) (1991) *Critical Psychology: Contributions to an historical science of the subject*, New York: Cambridge University Press.

8

V.N. VOLOSINOV
AND SOCIAL PSYCHOLOGY:
TOWARDS A SEMIOTICS
OF SOCIAL PRACTICE

Liam Greenslade

Social psychology in fact is not located anywhere within (in the 'souls' of communicating subjects) but entirely and completely without – in the word, the gesture, the act. (V.N. Volosinov, 1986, p. 19)

The purpose of this chapter is to introduce the reader to the work of the Soviet theorist V.N. Volosinov (c.1894–1934) and to consider some of the implications of his work for social psychology. Although Volosinov produced only two books and a handful of papers in his lifetime, his work is marked by a deep complexity of thought. In a period of a decade he contributed to the development of a number of concepts of considerable contemporary relevance. His writings encompass theories of semiotics, the subject, discourse, linguistics, ideology and communication. Despite long neglect, his work has not significantly diminished in its importance to contemporary critical thought.

The burgeoning interest in his mentor, Mikhail Bakhtin, indicates the significance of ideas developed in the period immediately before and after the Russian revolution to a contemporary context burdened by the nihilistic approach of post-modern theoreticism (Hirschkop and Shepherd, 1989; Callinicos, 1989). My aim is to provide a gloss upon his attempt to develop a Marxist social psychology. I shall concentrate upon three broad areas of his work, which relate to the theories of ideology and dialogism and the critique of the individual in Western discourse. Due to the restriction on space I shall not attempt to place Volosinov in the context of work within Marxism and critical theory which succeeded him, although I regard this as an important task.

VOLOSINOV: A BRIEF LIFE

Almost nothing is known about Volosinov himself. In fact, his entitlement to authorship of the two texts which form the centre of discussion in the present chapter: *Freudianism: A Marxist Critique* and *Marxism and the Philosophy of Language* published respectively in 1927 and 1929 remains a subject of controversy which is still continuing (Clark and Holquist, 1984; Hirschkop, 1986; Metejka and Titunik, 1986).

As far as is known, he was born in 1894 or 1895 in St Petersburg and in 1934 was resident there working at the Herzen State Pedagogical Institute and the State Institute for Speech Culture (Bruss and Titunik, 1976; Shukman, 1988). He was known to be a member of the group gathered around one of the leading St Petersburg intellectuals, Mikhail Bakhtin, to whom authorship of the two books mentioned above has been attributed. At the time of his initial membership of the Bakhtin group, from around 1918 or 1919, he was described as a 'poet and musicologist' (Shukman, 1988) and apart from the two books, he published a series of other papers during the 1920s on linguistics, poetic discourse, sociology, and psychoanalysis (Shukman, 1988). At some point after 1934 he disappeared completely, and his ultimate fate is unknown.

SIGN, IDEOLOGY AND SOCIAL PSYCHOLOGY

The dictum that 'language is practical consciousness' (Marx and Engels, [1875]1974, p. 51) which arises from the necessity of social intercourse in producing the means of subsistence, constitutes at once the point of departure and a problematic which Volosinov's work attempts to address. He does this by focusing upon language as a practical activity: as speech, as writing, as utterances cemented into the fabric of day-to-day existence.

For Volosinov, language is neither the closed system of norms presupposed in structuralist theories of language (e.g. de Saussure, 1974) nor is it the product of the individual psyche acting to attach meanings to stimuli and express them (White, 1984). In contesting the opposition between Saussurean sociologism and Lockean psychologism on the terrain of language, Volosinov opens up the possibility of a social psychology which transcends the binary opposition between individual and social presupposed in western culture. For Volosinov (1986, pp. 19–20) social psychology:

> ... is first and foremost an atmosphere made up of multifarious speech performances ... All these forms of speech interchange operate in extremely close connection with the conditions of the social situation in which they occur and exhibit an extraordinary sensitivity to fluctuations in the social atmosphere.

Volosinov argues that these speech performances are material activities which are shaped, but not mechanically determined, by the relations of production, and contextualised within the socio-political order to which those relations give rise. They are also part of the process by which this order may be changed. Since neither one is reducible to the other these performances therefore have to be studied from two distinct but related viewpoints.

The first of these concerns the materials from which utterances and speech performances can be made up, that is, the range of signs and meanings available for individual speakers to utilise psycholinguistically in formulating social utterances. The second concerns the sociolinguistic process of verbal interaction which is framed by the organisation of social relationships between groups composing society as a whole.

For Volosinov, these dimensions are inseparable. He regards as failed the attempt to split off speech from language or the speaker from the social context of speech (e.g. de Saussure, 1974; Chomsky, 1965; Brown, 1958; Giles and St Clair, 1979). In neither approach is it possible to account for the human ability to engage in symbolic activity in the ways that they do (Silverman and Torode, 1980; Weedon et al., 1980), nor to explain adequately the relationship between language and consciousness.

In order to surmount these problems, Volosinov calls upon two concepts, ideology and sign, to pave the way to the development of a social psychology which links human consciousness to social life. The ability to use signs is, for Volosinov, predicated upon the fact of human social organisation. He notes that (1986, p. 12)

> Signs arise only on *interindividual territory*. It is territory that cannot be called 'natural' in the direct sense of the word: signs do not arise between any two members of the species homo sapiens. It is essential that the two individuals be *organised socially*, that they compose a group (a social unit); only then can the medium of signs take shape between them.

This assertion should not be read as denying that human beings from different cultures or language communities cannot communicate with each other (e.g. by mimetic activity), rather that it is only within socially organised groups, or between groups organised in relation to each other, that fully-fledged signs may emerge. Within this context, signs must be understood not as things in themselves but as functions of complex relationships between signifier and signified in the multilevelled context in which they emerge.

Signs and words are not interchangeable. While all words may be signs, not all signs are words. A sign he defines as something which bears meaning, which depicts or stands for something other than itself. Any object may become a sign. A piece of bread may be transformed into the body of Christ, but only in a particular frame of social practice. Furthermore, signs are not signals. Their relationship to their referent is not direct and unmediated (cf. Skinner, 1957), neither is the relationship between signifier and signified wholly arbitrary, as de Saussure asserts. According to Volosinov (1986, p. 10):

A sign does not simply exist as a part of reality – it reflects and refracts another reality. Therefore it may distort that reality or be true to it, or perceive it from a special point of view.

Words are a special category of sign. They are the most social ubiquitous signs and are implicated in every socio-ideological activity from 'inner' thought to 'outer' conversation. He argues that the countless 'ideological threads' of social life are registered in words and this makes them the most sensitive index of social change. He observes (1986, p. 19):

> The word is the medium in which occur the slow quantitative accretions of those changes which have not yet achieved the status of a new ideological quality ...

Volosinov links the capacity of words and signs to 'reflect and refract' ideology. But his view of ideology is not one in which it can simply be read off from the organisation of the political economy, nor is ideology merely a realm of false perception. For Volosinov, ideology is materially linked to the context (i.e. the economic and political order), and operates as a form of coded constraint upon sign meaning within that context, which varies according to context.

METHODOLOGICAL PRINCIPLES

Volosinov (1986) outlines three basic methodological premises for understanding the relationships between signs, ideologies and social existence, namely:

1 Ideology may not be divorced from the materiality of the sign by locating it simply in 'consciousness'.

2 The sign may not be divorced from the concrete forms of social intercourse.

3 Communication and the forms of communication cannot be divorced from the material basis.

This pithy statement of his methodological premises belies the complexity of their implications. Volosinov's position opposes reductionism by proceeding from the complex (basic acts of human communication) to the structures of complexity (ideological processes borne in the medium of sign-use).

For Volosinov, the constraining boundary of sign use and thus ideological creativity is the organisation of relationships within and between groups composing a society at any time. These relationships are themselves constrained by the prevalent mode of economic organisation and the system of social reproduction and division of labour to which it gives rise.

What this entails is that both the nature of communication and the forms of communication which occur will differ between face-to-face, pre-capitalist societies, where the relationship between social labour and its products is self-consciously recognisable, and commodity societies such as our own where it is not (Newman, 1991). In these contrasting societies, not only do people orient themselves differently to acts of communication (pragmatics) but also what they communicate (semantics) and how they communicate (syntax) will differ.

Furthermore, in a society like our own where the division of labour is highly complex, communication and the forms of communication differ between the groups which comprise it. Bernstein's (1971) observations on the differences between middle- and working-class speech and Spender's (1985) on gendered language illustrate this. The existence of highly specific technical languages in science, religion, and the legal system do so similarly.

Volosinov's second dictum appears self-evident. However, its implications may be less obvious. First, if we wish to understand how a particular sign signifies, we need to understand it in the context of its use. If we take the purest form of ideological sign, the word, then two clear aspects emerge. First, outside of social intercourse words cannot exist: they are acoustic emissions (i.e. noise) or physical entities (marks on paper) and nothing more. The existence of a word presupposes some form of social organisation between word-users. Second, the same sign may signify many different things, exhibiting 'polysemanticity'. The only way of identifying what is meant or understood, which are not necessarily the same, is to locate its use in the context of the particular interaction in which it occurs. Additionally, signs are polysemantic, both synchronically and diachronically.

Furthermore, the concrete forms of social intercourse act as a constraint upon what can be meant or understood in the use of a given sign. Different forms of social intercourse operate to inhibit the degrees of ideological flexibility inherent in ideological signs. In scientific exchanges, for example, a great effort is made to 'operationalise' terms in order that they mean the same thing to every user of them. The same is not true of the words which make up a conversation in a pub.

Finally, his dictum regarding the materiality of ideology is a crucial one. There is no 'realm of ideology', he contends, if ideology is simply to mean ideas which exist independently of the thinkers of them. Ideology is materially expressed in and through the medium of signs. Similarly there is no 'realm of consciousness' upon which ideology as an external phenomenon can be said to operate. Both are functions of the human capacity to use signs, and may not be understood independently of that.

In short, ideology is neither 'out there' waiting to interpellate subjects as sociologism might suggest (Therborn, 1980), nor is consciousness the inner, privately bounded domain as presupposed in orthodox psychology. For Volosinov there is no essential division between ideology and consciousness. All ideological content is capable of being understood and taken into the psyche. Conversely, any outer ideological sign at some point in its development must pass through the psyche. He notes (1986, p. 39)

Between psyche and ideology there exists, then, a continuous dialectical interplay: the psyche effaces itself, or is obliterated in the process of becoming ideology, and ideology effaces itself in the process of becoming the psyche.

The medium of signs is crucial to this interplay. Without signs, neither ideology nor consciousness can exist. That is not to say that some internal sensibility of pain or hunger or physical pleasure could not exist, but it is of the order of that possessed by animals, not by sign-using humans.

Within such a context the so-called 'private' domain of the subjective conscious is, Volosinov argues, thoroughly social. Outside of the material of signs 'there is no psyche' (1986, p. 26): there are merely physiological processes. Consciousness itself is not a distinct ontological or epistemological entity; rather it is a boundary, a punctuation between the organism and the outside world. Psychological experience is the semiotic expression of this boundary, and its primary material is the word or inner speech (cf. Vygotsky, 1962).

DIALOGISM, EXPERIENCE AND THE THEORY OF THE SUBJECT

From the foregoing principles Volosinov develops an approach to social psychological phenomena which departs radically from the dominant tradition in social psychology, which has been characterised by a tension between a biologically based psychologism (e.g. Allport, 1924) and a radical sociologism (e.g. Durkheim, 1938), both of which are nonetheless rooted in an individualistic purview (Greenslade, 1989). In crude terms, social psychology has largely been a domain concerned with 'I/thou', 'self-other' type relationships (e.g. Mead, 1934) and there have been almost no successful attempts to move beyond this.

In the Soviet tradition, however, it has long been recognised that this opposition between individual and social is inherently limiting. Within that tradition, the aim has been to overcome it by recasting the fundamental relationship between individual and social into terms which reflect the historical and collective nature of human social relationships. As Porshnev (1970, p. 71) succinctly puts it:

Social psychology does not become a science until 'we and they' (or 'they and we') are taken as the initial psychic phenomenon ...

Volosinov may be seen as an originator of this line of approach. For him the inner life of the human being is entirely conducted through semiotic material, through signs, through inner speech. But the speaker in this case is not the Cartesian solipsist. It is a human being, a member of groups which are socio-historically constituted both internally and in their relationships to each other.

Although the individual psyche is a boundary, the boundary is not between it and ideology (i.e. between the individual and the social). Volosinov argues that this view is simply false. The correlate of the social is not the individual but nature. He observes (1986, p. 34):

> ... a rigorous distinction must always be made between the concept of the individual as a natural specimen ... and the concept of individuality which has the status of an ideological-semiotic superstructure over the natural individual ...

For Volosinov, the error of Western psychology emerges in its ideological confusion between what he terms the 'I-experience' and the 'We-experience'. Following Bakhtin, Volosinov contends that language, and hence consciousness, is primarily dialogical or polyglossic in nature. Both inner and outer speech consist of 'conversations', as opposed to 'monologues', cross-cut by a multiplicity of social voices, accents and intonations reflecting the purview of the groups to which a person belongs and which s/he encounters in the course of daily life. He notes (1986, p. 85):

> Utterance, as we know, is constructed between two socially organised persons, and in the absence of a real addressee, an addressee is presupposed in the person, so to speak, of a normal representative of the social group to which *the speaker belongs*. The word is oriented toward an addressee, toward who that addressee might be ...

The presupposition of an addressee is what gives experience its ideological form and content. The degree to which an experience is formulable in language is proportionate to the degree of its social orientation. The 'I-experience' and the 'We-experience' represent the two poles of this relationship. A We-experience is characterised by the stable integration of the experiential utterance with its social milieu. It corresponds with the official ideology of the society or the behavioural ideology of a sub-group. It is complex and differentiated and reflects the ability of the consciousness to locate its social roots. Conversely, I-experiences emerge where a social framing, an ideological context, and hence a presupposable addressee, do not exist to give the experience semiotic context, or allow it social intelligibility. Here consciousness struggles to give meaning and expression to experience. Volosinov also notes that such experiences, as far as language is concerned, can tend towards extinction by reverting to the level of physiology. Furthermore, whole groups of experiences can follow this path, a theme he takes up in *Freudianism* (1976, p. 89):

> Motives under these conditions begin to fail, lose their verbal countenance, and little by little really do turn into a 'foreign body' in the psyche. Whole sets of organic manifestations come, in this way, to be excluded from the zone of verbalized behavior and may become asocial.

The neuroses which Freud identified as sexual, Volosinov saw as rooted in the ideological and the socio-political, in the failure of 'official' ideological frameworks to encompass the experiences engendered by its historical conditions. For Volosinov, the crisis of bourgeois subjectivity in the late nineteenth century led to the emergence of Freudianism itself, which constituted an attempt to draw back subjective experience into the compass of an 'official' ideology.

Within this framework, the error of 'psychological' social psychologies becomes clear. Simply, they seek to explain We-experiences in a framework which implies that they are I-experiences. They do so because of their ideological rootedness in the individualistic We-experience of the bourgeois class from which they derives. Such theories assume that the rights, esteem, and social orientation which they presuppose are impelled from within the psyche or the organism, rather than without in the collective complex of a sustained socio-economic situation. They are a specific kind of interpretation of a historically and socially framed We-experience.

BEHAVIOURAL IDEOLOGY AND CHANGE: TOWARDS A REVOLUTIONARY SOCIAL PSYCHOLOGY

Volosinov distinguishes between two categories of ideology, those which he terms 'official' and those termed 'unofficial' or behavioural. The former are the systems of sign organisation where meaning tends to be at its most crystallised or inflexible. They are the accretion of periods of struggle over meaning between the competing social groups within a society. In very crude terms, official ideologies embody what Marx has termed the ruling ideas of the ruling class, or Nietzsche the 'word of the masters'. In their seeming 'neutrality' in relation to context, official ideologies give a specific refraction to signs or, as Volosinov (1988, p. 147) has it:

> The ruling class strives to lend the ideological sign a supraclass, external character, to extinguish or exhaust the struggle of class relations that obtains within it, to make it the expression of only one, solid and immutable view.

This struggle continues throughout language, and it is in the realm of behavioural ideology where it is at its most marked. Although the same language may be used by various classes and groups within a given society, the degree of correspondence between signs and experience differs for each group. It is in the realm of behavioural ideology that signs may be adapted, distorted or invented to draw experience and the means of articulating it into a workable correspondence, to make sense of the world and to function within it.

The objective life experience of the worker is not the same as that of the factory owner, that of the woman in a patriarchy is not the same as that of the man, that of the colonised not that of the coloniser. Their modes of social organisation, their daily practices and, as a result, their languages stand at variance with each other marked by the contradictions and conflicts which characterise relationships between differently empowered groups. These differences are marked most strongly and sensitively in behavioural ideologies which shape the course of all informal interactions and exchanges.

Each of these groups struggles to make experience felt in words and give different accents, evaluations, and intonations to their meanings. In the interstices of official ideologies, of ruling-class hegemony over meaning, behavioural ideologies spring up to resist and challenge the hold which the dominant groups seek to place around meaning. As Volosinov remarks (1976, p. 88):

> In the depths of behavioral ideology accumulate those contradictions which, once having reached a certain threshold, ultimately burst asunder the system of the official ideology.

But before this can occur the semiotic contents of a behavioural ideology must be constituted in the organisation of some form of collective sensibility. It must emerge in the verbal interactions of human beings recognising and reacting to their shared and socially organised life experiences. If this cannot be accomplished, then such ideologies take on, for want of a better term, a 'declassé' status. They will die out as verbalised systems and retreat into the asocial realms of language as 'I'-experience, noise (e.g. schizophrenic 'word-salad') or the body (e.g. 'hysterical' symptoms, eating disorders, self-harm, depression, anxiety, catatonia, etc.) to emerge only as a symptom of the divorce between experience and the means of giving it full social expression (cf. Newman, 1991; Bateson, 1973; Laing and Esterson, 1970) .

The cause of such 'pathologies' lies in the dominant ideological motif of capitalist culture and its attempt to totalise the perspective of its own 'ideal speaker-hearer' upon society as a whole. All the official ideologies of this group, and the hegemonic structures and institutions which accompany them, assume the presence of a white, male, usually heterosexual, private property-owning subject, universal and abstracted from historical process as the core 'addressee' of all semiotic material. This is true of art (i.e. in the dominance of perspective), religion (in the Protestant assumption of an unmediated relationship with the deity) as it is in science (the observer distinct from the observed) and the legal system (e.g. British common law). The disruption of human social experience which this ideological purview generates is immense. The mystification of subjectivity and social relations which it entails necessarily leads to alienation at every level, from the economic to the existential. The point is that the total individual which it constructs is an ideological refraction, and nothing more.

Following Volosinov, it becomes clear that the speaking subject is not a total, self-enclosed entity. In a society such as our own in which there are many different groups constituting the language community as a whole, the assumption of homogeneity becomes not merely disabling but also pathological. Volosinov's 'heteroglossic' subject speaks with not one voice but many, each one cross-cut by its own meanings and ideological accents, which may concur or conflict. The monologue of bourgeois subjectivity makes no allowance for this polyvocal aspect of experience.

I do not speak as a subject in and of myself: I speak as a member of several groups and real communities whose relationships constitute me (*inter alia* white, Irish, male, working class, heterosexual) historically, socio-emotionally, economically, and ideologically. All my experience is historically conditioned by these relations and constrained by the degrees of free-play amongst them.

Within this context, the task of a revolutionary social psychology is not to produce official ideological accounts of my 'inner-life' from the perspective of an imaginary monologue, neither is it to explain, account for, and adapt me to my degrees of behavioural or emotional deviance from the norms of bourgeois hegemony: it is to reconnect me with the experience of my language communities in order that I may make sense of a shared world and give voice to it, and to locate me in history, the only 'natural' state for all human beings (Newman, 1991).

This is a long-term project and not easily accomplished. But in the so-called 'new times' in which we live it is a pressing one. For in our present context, as Baudrillard (1983) asserts, the commodity signs of the real have become a substitute for the real itself. It becomes increasingly hard to look beyond the surface of events to unmask the structuring relationships beneath them. Increasingly the leading edge of critical thought and practice concerns itself with concepts more amenable to an economy based on the needs of individuated consumers, of clients and customers dominated by advertising and the media. Our task as social psychologists must entail the long-range strategy of re-connecting us as communities to our historical experience, to give us back not merely our voice but our memory of who we are and what we might become. For as Volosinov (1976, p. 91) himself has put it:

Where the creative paths of history are closed, there remain only the blind alleys of the individual 'livings out' of a life bereft of meaning.

Acknowledgements. My grateful thanks for their help in the development of this chapter go to Meredith Ralston, Alan Fair, Paul Brown, Eric Woods, Alan Blair, John Maclean and other members of the Graduate School, University of Sussex, 1982–1986. Thanks also to Valerie Walkerdine, John Broughton and the editors of the present volume. Responsibility for errors is my own.

REFERENCES

Allport, F.H. (1924) *Social psychology*, Cambridge, MA: Houghton-Mifflin.
Baudrillard, J. (1983) *Simulations*, New York: Semiotext(e).
Bateson, G. (1973) *Steps to an Ecology of Mind*, London: Paladin.

Bernstein, B. (1971) *Class Codes and Social Control (Vol. I)*, London: Routledge & Kegan Paul.

Brown, R. (1958) *Words and things*, New York: Free Press.

Bruss, N.H. and Titunik, I.R. (1976) 'Preface', in: V.N. Volosinov, *Freudianism: A Marxist Critique* (trans I.R. Titunik), New York: Academic Press.

Callinicos, A. (1989) *Against Postmodernism*, London: Polity Press.

Chomsky, N. (1965) *Aspects of the Theory of Syntax*, Cambridge, MA: MIT.

Clark, K. and Holquist, M. (1984) *Mikhail Bakhtin*, Cambridge, MA: Harvard University Press.

Durkheim, E. (1938) *The Rules of the Sociological Method*, Glencoe: Free Press.

Giles, H. and St Clair, R. (eds) (1979) *Language and social psychology*, Oxford: Blackwell.

Greenslade, L. (1989) 'Worlds Apart: Towards a Materialist Critique of the Cognitive-Social Dualism', in A. Gellatly, D. Rogers, and J.A. Sloboda (eds), *Cognition and social worlds*, Oxford: Clarendon Press.

Hirschkop, K. (1986) 'A Response to the Forum on Mikhail Bakhtin', in G.S. Morson (ed.) *Bakhtin: Essays and Dialogues on his Work*, Chicago: University of Chicago Press.

Hirschkop, K. and Shepherd, D. (eds) (1989) *Bahktin and Cultural Theory*, Manchester: Manchester University Press.

Laing, R.D. and Esterson, A. (1970) *Sanity, Madness and the family*, Harmondsworth: Penguin.

Marx, K. and Engels, F. (1974) *The German Ideology*, London: Lawrence & Wishart.

Mead, G.H. (1934) *Mind, Self and Society*, Chicago: University of Chicago Press.

Metejka, L. and Titunik, I.R. (1986) 'Preface' in V.N. Volosinov (1986) *Marxism and the Philosophy of Language* (trans L. Metejka), Cambridge, MA: Harvard University Press.

Newman, F. (1991) *The Myth of Psychology*, New York: Castillo International.

Porshnev, B. (1970) *Social Psychology and History*, Moscow: Progress Publishers.

Saussure, F. de (1974) *Course in General Linguistics*, London: Fontana.

Shukman, A. (ed.) (1988) *Bakhtin School Papers*, Somerton: RPT Publications.

Silverman, D. and Torode, B. (1980) *The Material Word*, London: Routledge & Kegan Paul.

Skinner, B.F. (1957) *Verbal Behavior*, New York: Appleton Century Crofts.

Spender, D. (1985) *Man Made Language*, London: Routledge & Kegan Paul.

Therborn, G. (1980) *The Power of Ideology and the Ideology of Power*, London: Verso.

Volosinov, V.N. (1973) *Marxism and the Philosophy of Language*, New York: Seminar Press.

Volosinov, V.N. (1976) *Freudianism: A Marxist Critique*, (trans I.R. Titunik), New York: Academic Press.

Volosinov, V.N. (1986) *Marxism and the Philosophy of Language* (trans L. Metejka and I.R. Titunik), Cambridge, MA: Harvard University Press.

Volosinov, V.N. (1988) *The Word and its Social Function* (trans J. Andrew), in A. Shukman (ed.) *Bakhtin School Papers*, Somerton: RPT Publications.

Vygotsky, L.S. (1962) *Thought and Language*, Cambridge, MA: MIT.

Weedon, C., Tolson, A. and Mort, F. (1980) 'Theories of Language and Subjectivity', in S. Hall, D. Hobson, A. Lowe and P. Willis (eds), *Culture, Media, Language*, London: Hutchinson.

White, A. (1984) 'Bahktin, Sociolinguistics and Deconstruction', in F. Glover-Smith (ed.) *The Theory of Reading*, Brighton: Harvester.

9

NEWMAN'S PRACTICE OF METHOD COMPLETES VYGOTSKY

Lois Holzman

Lev Vygotsky, who many consider the most significant and relevant Marxist psychologist of the early years of the former Soviet Union, was 21 years old when the Bolsheviks seized power in 1917. For the next 17 years until his untimely death from tuberculosis in 1934, and against the background of Stalinism, he wrestled with political and methodological issues raised by the creation of the first socialist state. Vygotsky recognised that socialism could not succeed unless 'a new human being' was developed. People, Marx had made plain, are not merely determined by the existing conditions: we collectively transform the very conditions that determine us (which include, of course, 'us'). More a dialectician than a vulgar materialist, Vygotsky disagreed with those of his colleagues who believed that simply transforming the economic mode of production would 'naturally' transform human subjectivity.

Vygotsky's life-as-lived was a search for a new psychology in the service of a new human being, in the service of a new society, culture and civilisation. It was a search for a science of/for human development. It was Marx's methodology – his dialectical-historical monism – rather than the rationalistic empirics in his analysis of capitalism, which Vygotsky took most seriously. In turn, Vygotsky's revolutionariness and brilliance was as a methodologist, not as a laboratory psychologist. For him, a new psychology required a new unit of study, and a new unit of study required – indeed, was inseparable from – a new method for studying it. The search for method was central to understanding uniquely human activity; it was 'simultaneously prerequisite and product, the tool and the result of study' (Vygotsky, 1978, p. 65).

Vygotsky described his activity as finding out 'how science has to be built'. He likened the task to 'creating one's own Capital' (Vygotsky, 1978, p. 8). It has been 128 years since Marx created his *Capital*, 78 years since the Bolshevik Revolution, 61 years since Vygotsky's death and with it the end of any serious Soviet search for method, and five years since the collapse of the Soviet Union and the demise of the first socialist state. Is a new society possible? A new human being? Can we create 'our own Capital'? Can we create 'our own psychology'?

Fred Newman, the controversial American Marxist psychotherapist and political strategist, has taken up where Vygotsky left off; he 'completes' Vygotsky. Vygotsky became important to me in the late 1970s when his writings proved invaluable to me and my academic co-workers in our critique of cognitive psychology as 'ecologically invalid' (Cole et al., 1976; Hood et al., 1980). During my years of collaboration with Newman, I came to appreciate that questions of method were central to the continued development of human beings. Vygotsky came to play an increasingly important role in our work. It is aided by his voice that I, with the perspective of a revolutionary Marxist and developmental psychologist, will discuss the practice and significance of Newman's method.

Through the mid-1970s, Newman developed a successful radical therapy collective, studied left politics, and got involved in community organising in New York. These years saw the development of a radical politics-radical psychology synthesis best characterized as having a 'serve the people' politic. In an increasingly conservative environment, Newman and his co-workers sharpened their tactics – moving toward the creation of independent institutions, particularly in electoral politics and psychology – which were necessary, they believed, to bring into existence a new, politically defined working class in the United States (Newman, 1983). The new psychology – social therapy – is the focus of this discussion (see Fulani, 1992 and Goldberg, 1992 for a history of independent politics in the United States and their electoral tactics).

Newman's background in methodology and philosophy of science shapes his practice and understanding of both psychology and Marxism. In relation to psychology, for example, philosophical training made him well aware that the reification of 'inner life', mental acts and cognition within psychology and psychotherapy are philosophically and methodologically problematic. Wittgenstein's later writings (1953; 1965; 1980), which he had studied, were especially valuable in this regard. However, a fascinating thing occurred when Newman himself entered semi-traditional psychotherapy in 1968 – he found it remarkably helpful. Not only could one talk about one's inner life', but doing so was valuable – despite the fact that there is no inner life! It was, he posited, the activity of talking to another person about how one feels which is therapeutic. Psychology's 'presenting problem' for him became: how could the therapeutic activity be so helpful when the science upon which it was based is so flawed? The development of social therapy is Newman's response to this question.

In 1979, when the New York Institute for Social Therapy and Research opened its doors in New York's (then) liberal Upper West Side community, the collective of community activists, social workers and academics had two goals: to create a therapeutic approach that did not harm anyone, and to eliminate poverty (Hood and Newman, 1979). From the beginning we believed that a revolutionary politics demanded a revolutionary psychology. Within the sophisticated network of institutions of social control which characterises the contemporary Western world, psychology is perhaps the most powerful for being everpresent. We live in a highly psychologised culture which socialises women and men to an anti-developmental world view – where life is a viewed as a series of problems to be solved, where what is possible is only what already exists, where 'you can't change the world' but only 'yourself'. Many Marxists and non-Marxists have discussed this characteristic of postmodern capitalism. With social therapy, Newman and his colleagues created a practical-critical environment for a developmental world view as human activity – an anti-psychology, a developmentology.

Like Vygotsky, Newman saw Marx's brilliance in his (never complete) denunciation of both idealism and vulgar materialism. Marx's statements about method – e.g. that history is not devoid of premises, but that the premises are people 'in their actual, empirically perceptible process of development under definite conditions' (Marx and Engels, 1973, pp. 47–8) – seemed sufficiently non-dualistic and non-instrumental to be considered seriously in the formation of a new psychology. In addition, Marx had identified the fundamentality of human productive activity (labour and labouring) for a non-perceptualist theory of knowledge. Human beings are not primarily perceivers or cognisers, but producers; more specifically and most significantly, producers of 'revolutionary, practical-critical activity' (Marx and Engels, [1845]1973, p. 121), producers of their own continuous development. For Marx, then, both the object of study and the method of study are practical, that is, practical-critical: they are revolutionary activity.

In transforming the object of study – from abstractions to real people in their everyday practice – Marx indeed challenged the philosophical tradition which held to a dualistic, ahistorical and idealist conception of premises as separate from what follows from them. For Marx, human practice becomes the starting point for an interpretation free science. But, following Derrida, isn't a starting point (a premise) itself an abstraction (Morss, 1992)? One can always find a starting point to impose on a seamless life-as-lived. The question Newman poses (following the later Wittgenstein's critique of explanation) is: what if we don't need any, in the sense that none is required to understand and, therefore, there is none that makes any difference? In our most recent work, we discuss these methodological limitations of Marx's method of practice. Marx's method leaves unanswered how it is that the discovery that premises are people was made – surely, it cannot be that what is discovered is identical with the act (or activity) of discovering it. Marx's method does not self-reflexively engage what the discovery of discovery (including his own discovery) is. Marx does not replace Descartes' method of doubt with a method of affirmation or discovery, with a dialectical theory of learning. To answer these questions we must go beyond Marx's method of practice to its seeming inverse – the Vygotskian social-therapeutic practice of method (Newman and Holzman, 1993b, p. 62).

The question 'what is discovery?' embodies the question 'what is method?' These questions turn out to be essential in a practical-critical way for revolutionaries and therapists. In spite of its commitment to dialectics and materialism, Marx's method of practice (and to some extent, Vygotsky's) fails, in the hands of the revisionists, to break completely with the dualism and idealism of the Western scientific 'observer-observed' paradigm. The 'method of practice' methodologist (or more precisely, practitioner) views history – the object of analysis – still from the vantage point of an observer, not from the vantage point of a participant in history. Dialectics, for Marx a characteristic of seamless history, transforms into a tool used in the ortho-dox Marxists' observations. The result of applying this tool (for result) is a dialectical materialist interpretation of history (in spite of Marx's admonition that the point is not to interpret the world but to change it). The practice of method, in sharp contrast, is not interpretive. There is no object of knowl-edge and no knowledge separate from the activity of practicing method (Vy-gotsky's tool-and-result). It is not about history (it is not about anything at all). Social therapy, as the practice of method, is the making of history.

Perhaps you are now thinking that this is either a trivial point (after all, as Marx told us, it is people in their everyday life conditions who make history, and social therapy is but one of those life conditions) – or a vast overstatement. I think it is neither. I think it is a fairly precise formulation of the central characteristic of Newman's social therapy. According to Marx, history is most clearly recognised and experienced in the midst of Revolution because the institutionally overdetermined organisation of any given event breaks down in the context of Revolutionary Activity. One can most directly relate to history during Revolution, but Revolutions occur sporadically and relatively rarely. If one makes history during Revolutions, then how can ordinary people in non-revolutionary times make history? And how can they do that in psychotherapy? There is a critical distinction to be made here between Revolution (the making of the revolution, seizing state power) and revolution (transforming ordinary, everyday human actions into revolution-ary activity). For Newman, Marx's statement that 'communism is only possi-ble as the act of dominant peoples "all at once"' (Marx and Engels, [1845]1973, p. 56) suggests this distinction. For Marx, communism is not a state of affairs, but an activity; more specifically, an activity with a 'world-historical existence', engaged in by 'individuals whose existence is directly linked up with world history' (p. 56). Thus, in order for communism – the activity, the social process – to occur 'all at once', it must take place in history.

Revolutionary process, then, occurs not through the application of a fixed method but through practicing methodology. 'The *real* movement that abol-ishes the present state of things' is the continuous transformation of mun-dane, specific life activities into qualitatively new ways of life. Social therapy is simultaneously the creating of an environment for the transformation of mundane life activities and the transformation of these activities into a qualitatively new ways of life. The tragic consequences of the failure continu-ously to create a new psychology consistent with Marx's discovery of revolu-tionary activity are evident in the failed Soviet experiment. With the benefit of hindsight, we can see that the Soviet communists tried to bring into existence a qualitatively new human being with an outmoded psychology and methodology, which included nineteenth-century rationalist and mechanistic methods of teaching and modes of communication. To Newman, embracing 'a new human being' does not come 'after the Revolution' but is itself the revolutionary process.

WHAT IS VYGOTSKIAN COMPLETION?

Vygotsky's goal of creating a science which could both shed light on the historical development of human beings/human culture and address the myriad challenges faced by the new socialist state led to a life-long concern with the relationship between development and learning/instruction. He made several important discoveries about how children develop and learn, about speaking and thinking, and about the developmental role of play. Of greatest relevance to an evolving practice of method (creating one's own psychology) is how his methodology and empirical findings reveal the tool-and-result character of human life. In his work are the seeds of a dialectical theory of learning, the method of affirmation and discovery which Marx never formulated.

The dominant view of the relationship between learning and development is that how a person learns is dependent on her/his level of development. Vygotsky criticised this perspective on both methodological and pedagogical grounds. To Vygotsky, learning and development are neither independent of each other nor a single process; they are in a relationship of dialectical unity (learning-and-development). Further, the very notion of 'pure development' is an idealisation – abstract, ahistorical and acultural. Vygotsky made the provocative claim that in the unity (learning-and-development), learning leads development. The revolutionariness of learning-leading-development is completed by Vygotsky's discovery of the 'zone of proximal development' (zpd). The person, the mind, psychological processes such as thinking, speaking, remembering, problem solving, etc., are produced through participation in and internalisation of social-cultural-historical forms of activity. Simply put, the zpd is the difference between what one can do 'with others' and what one can do 'by oneself'. Vygotsky was neither the first nor the last to notice that children and adults can 'do more' in collaboration with others, but he specified the social-cultural-historical process by which this occurs. Learning-leading-development both creates and occurs in the zpd.

The zpd strongly suggests that individual and species development depend on the continuous practice of tool-and-result methodology, on the creative process of tool-making. We could never develop if we only employed tool for result methodology, if we were only tool-users. At least since Piaget, human development has been described as an active process: children 'come to know the world' through 'acting upon it' or 'constructing' it. But such a view (held by social constructionists, neo-Vygotskians, and orthodox Marxists as well as Piagetians) embodies a separation of human being and the world, resulting in the necessity of employing an abstract explanatory mode in order to understand how an individual ever develops 'in the world'. Children and adults, to be sure, use tools, but the 'active process' which human beings engage in which is developmental (qualitiatively transformative) is that of tool-making.

In our recent explorations of Vygotsky's methodology and its influence on social therapy (Newman and Holzman, 1993a; 1993b), we describe the zpd as the life space in which we live inseparable from the we who produce it. The zpd 'is where and how human beings totally transform our circumstances (making something new); it is the location of human (revolutionary) activity. The zpd, then, is simultaneously the production of revolutionary activity and the environment which makes revolutionary activity possible' (Newman and Holzman, 1993b, p. 29).

Vygotsky identified the language-learning environment of the infant and very young child as a natural and, perhaps, paradigmatic, zpd. Playing with language – using the predetermined tools to create something other than what is predetermined – is the 'joint activity' (a meaning-making activity) which occurs in the zpd of early childhood. What is the role of the adult in this zpd? Mothers, fathers, grandparents, and older siblings who jointly create the developmental environment (zpd) for the young child becoming a speaker are obviously more developed as language users. How do they use their expertise to create an environment in which learning leads development? What they don't do is relate to the child's developmental level. No, they relate to babies as speakers. By relating to children in this way as 'ahead of themselves', by admitting them into the human community of language makers and language users, adults are supporting children to perform ahead of themselves (to do what they don't know how to do), thereby creating the revolutionary (joint) activity of learning-leading-development.

Vygotsky further identified the specific activities that are dominant in this linguistic zpd. It is imitation which makes it possible for the child to do what s/he is not yet capable of; not the rote imitation or mimicry of the parrot, but an imitation that produces something new. For Vygotsky, imitation is 'the source of instruction's influence on development' (1987, p. 211). In imitating in the zpd, the child is being related to as relating to her/himself as a speaker and a writer and a social being. The 'product' is something other than (beyond) imitation – it is a new total environment of speakers. The capacity to speak and make meaning is inextricably connected to transforming the total environment of speakers. Put another way, you can't be 'ahead of yourself' by yourself. In the joint activity of creating the linguistic zpd, the child imitates the more developed speaker and the more developed speaker completes the child. In making this claim, we are advancing on Vygotsky's notion of completion, which evolved as he struggled to articulate a dialectical materialist theory of the relationship between speaking and thinking. According to Vygotsky, speaking and thinking are a dialectical unity, in which speaking completes – rather than expresses – thinking. 'The structure of speech is not simply the mirror image of the structure of thought ... Thought is restructured as it is transformed into speech. It is not expressed but completed in the word' (Vygotsky, 1987, p. 251).

The implications of language completing thought are profound. The dominant Western paradigm which serves as the foundation for most studies in communication, linguistics, education, and psychotherapy rests on the assumption that language expresses thought. Vygotsky does not merely reverse the order; he rejects the bifurcated and static view of language and thought, and thereby does away with any need to 'reconnect' them. Gone is the overdetermining conception that language denotes, represents, expresses – in other words, the overidentification of language with use and reference. Language completing thought (the unity thinking-speaking) identifies language as fundamentally activity.

The mother who responds to her infant's 'ma-ma' by smiling and saying 'Are you hungry? Yes, Mama will get your bottle' is completing for the child. She is not saying anything about what the child said, not probing for its underlying meaning or referent. She is engaging in a discourse style that is completive and cooperative. She is using her expertise as a speaker – not as an authority on correct language use, but as a co-creator of language activity – to create continuously a developmental environment by relating to her non-speaking child as a speaker. The total discourse environment of early childhood is completive, not competitive.

Vygotsky's focus on activity and notion of completion fits well with the later Wittgenstein's views on language. Language games, for example, 'bring into prominence the fact that the speaking of language is part of an activity, or a form of life' (Wittgenstein, 1953, p. 11). Much of Wittgenstein's philosophical enterprise was an attempt to see and show language as activity (a form of life), rather than simplistically to identify meaning and use. He claimed that this could not be done without stripping away the abstraction and reification of denotation (language expressing thought). He showed the extent to which our thinking is overdetermined by presuppositions about language and ways of thinking which derive from its reification and identification as passively mentalistic (as opposed to socially activistic). For Wittgenstein, the institution (not the activity) of language is a carrier of pathology. He tried to cure philosophers of their obsession with interpretation and explanation, and their need for order, causality and consistency. In short, he tried to cure philosophers of doing philosophy! (Newman and Holzman, 1993b.)

Wittgenstein was well aware that the views and values of science and philosophy greatly inform 'common sense'. In fact, his philosophical enterprise was arguably as much directed toward ordinary people as toward philosophers. Ordinary people (non-philosophers) are just as socialised to a metaphysical world view as are philosophers. The difference is that ordinary people have the disadvantage of being unselfconscious that the way we speak affects how we think and feel and experience our lives. How we speak and think is profoundly metaphysical, anti-activistic and anti-developmental (filled with causal connections, all manner of dualisms, including inner life and outer reality, and an obsession with explanation). Everyday conversation is replete with what Wittgenstein calls 'pictures that hold us captive': 'the thought just popped into my head'; 'I couldn't get out of bed because I was so depressed': 'I just can't learn math; I don't have the head for it': 'No wonder he beats her; he was abused as a child'.

The dominant discourse style of contemporary culture is equally metaphysical, anti-activistic; common conversation in everyday life is interpretive and essentially competitive. The total adult communicative environment is not conducive to creating jointly new meanings. People take turns 'expressing' their thoughts, identifying with what someone else says, and trying to figure out its deeper meaning and significance. The completive, activistic discourse modality that is jointly created in the linguistic zpd of early childhood is nearly universally practiced, but it is rare after childhood and even, for many, difficult to imagine. For Newman, the continuous creation of 'new human beings' which Vygotsky described as occurring in/by creating the zpd, and that includes a completive mode of discourse, can be reinitiated by a revolutionary methodology – a practice of method. To see and show language as activity requires us to create a philosophical environment, a Wittgensteinian zpd (wzpd) (Newman and Holzman, 1993b).

In retrospect, it is more than a coincidence that the arena for Newman's 'completing' of Vygotsky is psychotherapy. Two factors are at play: the fact that so many people are emotionally underdeveloped, and the nature of the psychotherapeutic environment itself. By emotionally underdeveloped, Newman does not mean that a person is stuck at a particular stage or that one's emotional responses are causally determined by culturally-biased societal conditions. Neither does underdevelopment imply a cultural or moral hierarchy. To Newman, emotional development is the unlimited capacity of human beings continuously to create new emotions. In Wittgensteinian fashion, an approach to reinitiating emotional development must be sensitive to the fact that limitations on emotional growth (creating something new) are intimately related to the limitations of our emotive language. As one example, in our culture we are socialised to speak of emotions as individual possessions which have a cause, are located within us, and 'get expressed' (like our thoughts supposedly do). Further, when it comes to speaking about our emotional lives we have a remarkably restricted vocabulary. Social-therapeutic practice helps adults see that the emotional language they have learned is part of their 'pathology' through their participation in building an environment in which they can become free of the constraints of emotive language, allowing them to develop emotionally. Just like mothers and other adults help create a zpd for language learning-and-development, Newman is concerned to create a zpd for emotional learning-and-development – an ezpd.

CREATING AN EZPD IN PSYCHOTHERAPY

One of the few places in which emotive discourse takes centre stage is in psychotherapy. The psychotherapeutic environment is an especially rich one for evolving a practice of method, precisely because of the nature of therapeutic discourse. That the talk occurring in 'the talking cure' is different from other forms of communication is acknowledged by experts and experienced by therapists and clients, but it is very little understood. Two recent sociolinguistic analyses begin to delineate the uniqueness of psycho-therapeutic discourse. Lakoff (1990) points out that, of all forms of com-munication, it is psychotherapy which takes language most seriously. She sees language primarily as instrumental; it is, among other things, 'the major means for transmitting information from client to therapist and from therapist to client', and 'an instrument of healing; interpretations – the right understanding in the right form – create change' (p. 59). A more constructionist view is presented in Ferrara's (1994) discourse analysis of several individual psychotherapy sessions, in which she attempts to expli-cate the nature of psychotherapy as an emerging speech event, to under-stand how the norms of interaction come to be established through dis-course, and to show how discourse can be therapeutic. She states, 'lan-guage is paradoxically both the method of diagnosis and the medium of treatment in this cultural practice' (p. 4). Both Lakoff and Ferrara note the lack of attention which therapeutic discourse receives, given how important it is to the psychotherapeutic process. Even before the emergence of dis-course analysis, the tendency among philosophers, linguists, and psycholo-gists interested in language has been to ignore emotive language, focusing instead on cognitive language (a practice, no doubt, which is a product and perpetuation of an overly masculine view of what language is and what is of scientific value).

In Newman's view, the nature of psychotherapy is such that the self-reflexive concern with language makes it possible for the discourse itself to have a transformative influence on the environment. In most institutional arrangements where people engage in discourse, the nature of the environ-ment determines how and when we talk, how what we say will be under-stood, etc. The organisation of the discourse presupposes maintaining the institutional, societal and ideological roles and rules which make that environment what it is: in other words, the environment overdetermines the discourse. Therapeutic environments are more like philosophical envi-ronments than they are like pragmatic, consumerist environments. New-man has extended therapeutic discourse in a self-consciously philosophical therapy. Creating an environment in which people can develop emotionally involves 'doing philosophy' because of the degree to which our everyday thinking, feeling and experiencing is permeated with metaphysical presup-positions, despite how disinterested ordinary people, even those who come to therapy, are (Newman and Holzman, 1993b). Creating a philosophical environment involves, in Vygotskian terms, relating to people as ahead of themselves; it involves supporting them to do what they don't know how to do – philosophy. It entails deconstructing the existing environment (competitive and interpretive), and reconstructing a new environment (completive and activistic) – through the activity of discourse.

Social therapy is an unusual environment in which discourse, far from being completely determined by the institutional arrangements of the loca-tion of the discourse, gives transformative shape to the environment. Building the philosophical/therapeutic environment – the Wittgensteinian, emotional zpd (wezpd) – is the revolutionary process of continuously transforming one of life's most pervasive mundane, specific activities. When Newman speaks of the patient as revolutionary (1991b), he does not mean that social therapy politicises people or 'makes them' Revolutionaries. He is not referring to the beliefs, values or intentions of particular individuals. People in social therapy become revolutionaries by virtue of functioning within a revolutionary historical environment – inseparable from their participation in creating that environment. They are participating in an historically specific revolutionary activity – the reshaping of the existing elements of the environment (rule-governed emotionality and discourse about emotionality) into something qualititatively new (new emotional activity, a new activity of speaking, etc.). They are creating their own psychology and, thereby, reinitiating their development. The experience closely replicates the conditions of Revolution where institutionalised arrangements and ideological constraints are collectively and self-consciously broken down, providing an opportunity to understand, study and participate in history. A new historical subjectivity develops. By practicing methodology, social therapy patients/clients are doing the very ordinary and human, but very rare in the postmodern world, activity of creating their lives.

REFERENCES

Cole, M., Hood, L. and McDermott, R.P. (1976) *Ecological Niche-picking: Ecological Invalidity as an Axiom of Experimental Cognitive Psychology*. Working paper of the Laboratory of Comparative Human Cognition. New York: Rockefeller University.

Ferrara, K.W. (1994) *Therapeutic Ways with Words*, New York: Oxford University Press.

Fulani, L. (1992) 'Who killed the economy?' in *When democracy is on the job, America works*. New York: Lenora B. Fulani for President National Campaign Headquarters, pp. 18–29.

Goldberg, P. (1992) 'The Independent Tradition gives Birth to America's premier Black Independent, Lenora B. Fulani', in *When democracy is on the job, America works*. New York: Lenora B. Fulani for President National Campaign Headquarters, pp. 1–17.

Hood, L., McDermott, R.P. and Cole, M. (1980) 'Let's try to make it a nice day – Some not so simple ways', *Discourse Processes* 3, pp. 155–68.

Hood, L. and Newman, F. (1979) *The Practice of Method: An Introduction to the Foundations of Social Therapy*, New York: New York Institute for Social Therapy and Research.

Lakoff, R. (1990) *Talking Power: The Politics of Language*, New York: Basic Books.

Marx, K. and Engels, F. ([1845]1973) *The German Ideology*, New York: International Publishers.

Morss, J.B. (1992) 'Making waves: Deconstruction and developmental psychology', *Theory and psychology*, 2 **4**, pp. 445–65.

Newman, F. (1968) *Explanation by Description*, The Hague: Mouton.

Newman, F. (1983) 'A Tendency towards Vanguardism', *Practice*, 1 (2, 3), pp. 7–17.

Newman, F. (1991a) *The Myth of Psychology*, New York: Castillo International.

Newman, F. (1991b) 'The Patient as Revolutionary', in F. Newman (ed.), *The Myth of Psychology*, New York: Castillo International.

Newman, F. and Holzman, L. (1993a) *Lev Vygotsky: Revolutionary Scientist*, London: Routledge.

Newman, F. and Holzman, L. (1993b) *Don't explain: A Study of Social Therapy as a Vygotskian–Wittgensteinian synthesis*. Manuscript submitted for publication.

Vygotsky, L.S. (1978) *Mind in Society*, Cambridge, MA: Harvard University Press.

Vygotsky, L.S. (1987) *The Collected Works of L.S. Vygotsky. Vol. 1*, New York: Plenum.

Wittgenstein, L. (1953) *Philosophical Investigations*, Oxford: Blackwell.

Wittgenstein, L. (1965) *The Blue and Brown Books*, London: Routledge.

Wittgenstein, L. (1980) *Remarks on the Philosophy of Psychology*, Oxford: Blackwell.

PART THREE:

EVERYDAY LIFE

This part focuses on an arena of action and experience which the discipline of psychology claims to have made its own, and which Marxism is often accused of neglecting. These chapters illustrate different ways in which Marxists critical of the ideological functions of contemporary common sense need not neglect the everyday life which sustains it. Mike Michael, in Chapter 10, deals with this issue by taking seriously Utopian hopes in social psychology, and setting these against post-structuralist and postmodern critiques of such hopes for social improvement. In Chapter 11, Grahame Hayes addresses some of the attempts of 'post-Marxist' writers influenced by post-structuralism, and argues that one of the principal ways in which ideology and resistance is expressed is through the activity of individuals in relation to others in social categories. Paul Hoggett points out, in Chapter 12, that such attempts to link structure with experience have been attempted by those on the Left who have addressed emotion in politics. He looks back at the libertarian critiques of bureaucratic 'Marxism', and, with the help of group-analytic ideas, brings some of those arguments to bear on present-day practice. Kum-Kum Bhavnani and Angela Davis argue, in Chapter 13, that a Marxist understanding of oppression – which in their case example is the oppression suffered by Black women in American prisons – has to be able to connect theory with the experience of control. Ian Parker, in Chapter 14, argues that the personal and the political can be linked in a reading of the lives of those who resist, and that these individual case examples operate as forms of 'revolutionary psychology'.

10

PICK A UTOPIA, ANY UTOPIA: HOW TO BE CRITICAL IN CRITICAL SOCIAL PSYCHOLOGY

Mike Michael

In this chapter, I want to consider one dimension of Marxist critique and its relation to Critical Social Psychology (CSP). The aim is to draw out this dimension, to show how it operates in CSP and to suggest how it might be better integrated into the overarching project of formulating an emancipatory social psychology. The dimension to which I am referring is that of utopian critique – the articulation or projection of some state of affairs in which the equality, liberty, community, self-development and so on are fully realised. This then is used to identify the relations of power, texts, ideologies, discourses, economic and political circumstances that variously occlude, hinder or facilitate the route to such a state of affairs. As Bauman (1976) notes, Utopias (specifically socialist Utopias) serve several functions: they relativise the present by 'exposing the partiality of current reality, by scanning the field of the possible in which the real occupies merely a tiny plot, utopias pave the way for a critical attitude and a critical activity ...' (p. 13); they allow for the extrapolation of the present; they 'split the shared reality into a series of competing project assessments' (p. 15); and they exert an actual influence on the course of history. I will concentrate on the first of these functions.

However, before going on to look at the relation between the two 'traditions' of Marxism and CSP, I will explain some terms. By Critical Social Psychology, I have in mind the recent trends in social psychology which have attempted to address those structures, including those that inhere in orthodox, experimental psychology that serve in the domination of various groupings – women, 'racial' minorities, the disabled, the non-heterosexual, the working class, the 'mentally-ill'. Much of this critique stemmed from the crisis in social psychology and the related attempts to 'socialise' it, that is, to bring into being an approach that appropriately encompassed meaning, society and politics (cf. Parker 1989). Some of these trends traced a direct lineage to Marxism – dialectical social psychology (e.g. Larsen 1986; Georgoudi 1983) and critical social psychology

(Wexler 1983). More recently, in keeping with the disaffection with Marxism (cf. Anderson 1983) there has been a turn to post-structuralism and anti-foundationalism in their various forms, e.g. deconstructionism (Parker and Shotter 1991), Foucault (Henriques *et al.* 1984); social constructionism (Shotter and Gergen 1989; Potter and Wetherell 1987; Edwards and Potter 1992; Kitzinger 1987; Shotter 1993). However, there has also been a resurgence of a critical foundationalism drawing on the works of Bhaskar (e.g. Parker 1992). Of the melange that I have called CSP, I will focus on the post-structuralist, anti-foundationalist perspectives, primarily because these seem to me presently to comprise the dominant trend in CSP.

My argument is that these often entail a visionary aspect – say, a model of the 'happy person' or of the 'free society' – that provides a positive 'other' from which to launch critique – or what Geuss (1981) calls a positive ideology – a desideratum for a particular society, a constellation of beliefs (or texts) that allows a group or class to realise its real interests. These remain, with few exceptions, latent in these CSP texts and thus immune from scrutiny. In so far as they are invisible, and indeed, ahistorical, they will tend to suffer from the same foundationalist, modernist problem whose absolutism is potentially as destructive as it is constructive.

But what of Marxism? Well, Marxism likewise has an Utopian kernel. Though rarely articulated, it is spread across the writings of Marx and Engels and serves as the necessary counterpoint to the critiques of the conditions of the working classes. It reaches its greatest articulation perhaps in the work of Marcuse (1955, 1970; Held 1980; Geuss 1981). More importantly, it has certain substantive commonalities with the implicit Utopias of CSP, specifically around the enlightenment ideal of self- (or selves) actualisation. But also, there is a similarity in the form of deployment of Utopian critique (i.e. it is latent for both Marx and CSP); to the extent that these Utopian others can be excavated and scrutinised, then it becomes possible to begin to more fully explore the possibilities of what used to be known as post-revolutionary society or the higher stage of communism. The importance of this is that we do not fetishise such Utopias – they are not simply prefigurative models, but standpoints for critique and as explicit standpoints they are, I will suggest, necessarily modest and circumspect.

MARXIST UTOPIAS

It is commonly assumed that Marx was not keen on Utopias, Utopian thought and Utopian thinkers. In Marx's words, he had no inclination to engage in the Utopian pursuit of writing 'recipes for the cookshops of tomorrow' (cited in Kumar 1991, p. 98). After all, Marx's historical materialism was much more concerned to root political activity in contemporary political and economic conditions, rather than in the aspiration toward some golden future world. As Geoghegan (1987) notes, for Marx and Engels, communism was not an ideal state of affairs but a movement that abolishes the present state of things. But precisely what constituted this movement was historically contingent. If the revolutionary strategy of the proletariat that would bring about the death of capitalism was wholly contingent, it was also the case that the Utopias were themselves of their time. As Marx and Engels note in their comments on Utopian socialism and communism in The Communist Manifesto, while these writings are revolutionary in that they 'attack every principle of existing society' (Feuer 1959, p. 80), the writings of Utopians St Simon, Fourier and Owen accordingly arose in the undeveloped phase of capitalist relations of production in which the full nature and potential of the proletariat was yet to emerge. Marx and Engels' point is that for all their critical and propaganda value, Utopias had by their time become irrelevant to, or detractions from the real work of class struggle.

And yet, as numerous writers have argued, an Utopian vision nevertheless informed the writings of Marx and Engels. This is not surprising for, as Manuel and Manuel (1979) document, Marx and Engels were steeped in the works of the Utopians (Engels being the more sympathetic). So, what is this vision? Marx and Engels in The German Ideology ([1845]1964) write: '... in the communist society, where nobody has one exclusive sphere of activity but each can become accomplished in any branch he [sic] wishes, society regulates the general production and thus makes it possible for me to do one thing today and another tomorrow, to hunt in the morning, fish in the afternoon, rear cattle in the evening, criticize after dinner, just as I have a mind, without ever becoming hunter, fisherman, shepherd or critic' (pp. 44–5). Later, they remark that in 'a communist society there are no painters but at most people who engage in painting among other activities' (p. 432). What appears to us here is a remarkably contemporary decentred self, but one based in labour and practical activity. In contrast, as we shall see, the decentring that is articulated and promoted by some writers in CSP is 'discursive'.

It is worth reflecting that this form of critique is not the only one available. The forms of critique were perhaps best articulated in the works of Frankfurt School theorists such Marcuse, Adorno and Horkheimer, and Habermas. As Geuss (1981) and Held (1980) note, there were two forms of critique – internal or immanent, and transcendental or Utopian, and critical theory is committed to the principle of 'immanent criticism'. 'Just as critical theory is supposed to contribute to agents' self-knowledge, so the proponents of the critical theory recognise as "valid criticism" only what could in principle be part of the self-criticism of the agents to whom it is addressed' (Geuss 1981, pp. 64–5). This is because there are no·a priori grounds for criticism – the only ones we have available are those derived from the eventuality that the audience will recognise its value, will acknowledge false consciousness, will, in sum, validate the critique. And as Held notes in relation to Horkheimer, such criticism is not relativist (despite the lack of some transcendent bedrock), rather it is historically objective in that 'it implies the recognition that justified positions for critique will not be justified "for all time". Such standards and values are relative to certain contexts but, nevertheless, can, within these, be objective'

tive' (p. 187). In contrast, the latter refers to the postulation of an ideal state of affairs which has been denied us by the prevailing conditions of capitalism. In the case of the Marcuse of *Eros and Civilization* (1955), an ideal human pycho-historical condition (non-repressive de-sublimation) is posited through which happiness and freedom are to be realised; for Habermas it has been the 'ideal speech situation' which models both the transcendent conditions for the possibility of communication and the promise of a truly unfettered communication in which all speakers have equal rights and resources.

However, I would argue, counter to the notion of immanent critique, that if the critic is to provide a critique that resonates with her audience, then this can still be Utopian or visionary. For such models of a better world have long been with us – much longer than Marxism or socialism. Moreover, our very perception of the contradictions and ideologies which obscure 'what is really happening' rests on a tacit vision of some better state of affairs. This might not entail full-blown Utopias, but they are nevertheless Utopian in the sense of projecting preferable states of affairs (cf. below, Giddens 1990).

CRITICAL SOCIAL PSYCHOLOGY (CSP)

In this section I will examine the way in which Utopias are presupposed as means to realising the 'critical' in Critical Social Psychology. The first two examples I give will be shown to have some marked similarities with the Utopian dimension of Marxism mentioned above. The third makes an explicit appeal to an Utopian ideal but it is of a rather different type from that to be found in classical Marxism. However, the function of this reflection is that it allows us to properly expose such assumptions, to open them up to scrutiny and possible problematisation in a way that the preceding two examples do not.

Deconstructionism and Dialogism

With the introduction of deconstruction into psychology, especially via the volume edited by Parker and Shotter (1990), a new avenue of critique was opened up. Perhaps the most influential exponent of this perspective has been Sampson (1989, 1983). In Sampson's deconstructive treatment of the subject of psychology, namely the self, he mentions two other means of undermining the apparent 'naturalness' of the western conception of the individual – cross-cultural and historical comparison. However, in his deconstruction of social psychology and the Western self, he attempts to show how these presuppose certain suppressed but necessary 'others'.

Sampson argues that the meaning and practice of the subject and subjectivity are constituted through language. In order to get at what the subject is, therefore, it is necessary to deconstruct the signifying system in which it is embedded. For the deconstructionist, it is assumed that Western metaphysics is characterised by phonocentrism and logocentrism, in which our proximity to voice and words serves to generate and reproduce the impression that the meanings that they carry are present within them, privileging speech and presence. Against this, following Derrida, Sampson argues that it is writing and absence that constitute meaning where writing is conceptually refashioned to mark the absence of the speaker and the spatiality of signifiers which gain their meaning only by their difference from one another. Thus, for Sampson the absent is always already active in the present – the absent is both different from, and adds to, the present. This constitutes the supplement. This is best encapsulated in Derrida's use of Freud's metaphor of the mystic writing pad. When the writer inscribes upon the upper sheet marks appear, but when this is lifted, the upper sheet loses any marks while the lower retains the traces. For Sampson, then, the upper level always rests on a series of traces that remain obscured. Consciousness always reflects these absences.

Sampson goes on to apply this series of metaphors to psychology's subject. Accordingly, there can be no pure centre of awareness: self-consciousness is always already mediated by the trace and people are always decentred by their relation to the symbolic system. The self as an integrated whole is likewise a fiction: people are systems in flux rather than fixed centres. For Sampson, then, the other is the suppressed signifer – the absent upon which the present(ed) rests. Where the dominant network of signifiers consists of the pure centre of awareness, the self as an integrated whole and identity as unpolluted by others, we discover underlying it – and this embodies Sampson's Utopian vision – a dispersed awareness, a fragmented self and a dissipated and multiply-populated identity.

More recently Sampson (1993) has embarked on an attempt to outline how we might go about recovering the suppressed other. His reworked project is a 'celebration of the other' which entails a transcendence of the confines of self-celebratory monologism in which there is a 'construction of a serviceable other, one constructed on behalf of the particular needs, interests and desires of the dominating group' (p. 4). The upshot is the (re)production of a model of the self as self-contained, individual, the owner of one's own capacities. In contrast to this monologism, Sampson recommends a genuine dialogism. This requires that we recognise that 'we gain a self only in and through a process of social interaction, dialogue with others in our social world; that the only knowledge we can have of ourselves appears in and through social forms – namely, others' responses' (p. 106). From this model, Sampson derives a dialogical ethics: dialogism 'recasts the meaning of freedom: we are free jointly to construct our lives together, and are therefore of necessity responsible beings by virtue of this feature. "I" cannot be free, only "We" can be free' (p. 171). However, actually to realise this dialogism, one needs 'a democratic and egalitarian context' for 'not only does democracy issue from dialogism, but without a genuinely democratic and egalitarian society, dialogue themselves are not possible' (p. 187).

Sampson's text provides us with a narrative of the predominance of an untruth – that of, self-celebratory monologism – which has usurped the (ontologically) rightful place of dialogism. The work of feminist authors is used to illustrate how dialogism has been suppressed and how the 'other that is woman' is excluded from representations in which what passes for the universal human gaze is actually the male gaze. Representations of identity as monologic have arisen historically, at numerous sites (Sampson also points to the African-American as other) and it is implicitly possible to recover, in part, this history by close scrutiny of monologic texts (psychology furnishing some of these). While an old-fashioned origin story is avoided, there is an implicit appeal to one: once there was a dialogic arcadia (or one day there will be, or might be, a dialogic Utopia).

The Social Psychology of Postmodernity

The multiplicity entailed in the ideal of dialogue with numerous critical 'others' also finds expression in some social psychologists' representation of the postmodern condition, and the corollary self that is dispersed, decentred and multiplicitous (Gergen 1991; Michael 1991, 1994; Kvale 1992). This is particularly the case in Gergen's (1991) *The Saturated Self*. Here, the actual break-up of the sorts of longstanding features of Western, patriarchal, modernist selves are grounded in a reading of contemporary history. Thus, Gergen contrasts the postmodern or saturated self to the romantic and modern selves. The romantic self hinged on a vocabulary of 'passion, purpose, depth and personal significance' (p. 27) and the 'romantic individual was forever a mystery – the vital essence quixotic and out of reach' (p. 47). By comparison, the modernist self is infused with reason – it is 'reliable, self-contained and machine-produced' (pp. 44–5) and as such it is fundamentally knowable and measurable. However, in the wake of what Gergen calls the 'Technologies of Social Saturation' (p. 49) – that is, the variety of high technologies such as air travel, video and television and new information technologies such as electronic mail, faxes, satellites, computers – there is a population of the self which opens 'relationships to new ranges of possibility' and renders 'subjective life ... more fully laminated' (p. 71). 'We find a profound sea change taking place in the character of social life during the twentieth century ... A multiphrenic condition emerges in which one swims in ever-shifting, concatenating and contentious currents of being' (pp. 79–80).

Gergen contrasts this fluidity to the strictures and constraints of pre-postmodern everyday conventionality. Where the postmodern entails serious play in which the rules are changeable, rules circumscribe modernist everyday life. Of course, Gergen is fully aware of the possible drawbacks of this postmodern scenario, especially for the way that such a transition threatens our perception of personal authenticity. Nevertheless, Gergen's postmodernity points to the potential 'flowering forms of relatedness, a growing consciousness of interdependence, an organic relationship to our planet, and the withering of lethal conflict' (p. 259).

Ironically, Gergen's account extends from a modernist historical reading of contemporary change, in which the latent or emergent characteristics of the present epoch can be read off more or less unproblematically (cf. Michael 1992). Now, Gergen clearly recognises that such a reading is itself a representation and a construction: as an instance of academic work, it is clearly also prone to the 'bursting of postmodern consciousness into the academic sphere' in which 'attention (has been) removed from the "world as it is" and centres instead on our representations of the world' (p. 16). Nevertheless, within his own narrative of the rise of postmodernity, and its realisation in, and impact upon, such 'postmodern' academic trends, we find an, albeit dispersed, framework of causes that have led up to the condition Gergen calls postmodernity and its human corollary, the saturated self. As such Gergen does not differ from many other treatments of the 'postmodern' – treatments which do not overly problematise the histories, or rather historiographies, out of which the postmodern emerges (e.g. Harvey 1989; Lash and Urry 1987; Giddens 1990, 1991). The common feature of these approaches is their deployment of a more or less traditional, that is to say modernist, analytic armoury to narrate the supposed rise of postmodernity (and its variants, late or high modernity). The point is that we can now ask, where does such a vision of the promised self of postmodernity come from? How is it constructed from the evidence and anecdotes Gergen furnishes us with? I would suggest that there is again an Utopian vision in operation here, one in which multiplicity, difference, shifting perspectives is valorised. There is an echo of Nietszche's Dionysianism (Nietzsche, 1956/1971; Benedict, 1935). The point is that Gergen presents us with this as if it were an emergent property of contemporary Western life, one to which we can have unproblematic access without construction. In constructing such an emergence we deploy our own language game and this is partly, at least, Utopian.

Rhetoric and Ideological Dilemmas

Michael Billig's pioneering work on rhetoric, argumentation and ideological dilemmas ranks as one of the major contributions to recent social psychology (e.g. Billig 1987, 1991; Billig et al. 1988). In developing a rhetorical social psychology, Billig (1991) proposes a dual movement: on the one hand, social psychology must come to analytic terms with rhetoric; on the other, it must 'recognise that the processes of everyday thinking can be processes of "ideology"... this means that common sense not only has a wider history, but that it also possesses present functions, which relate to patterns of domination and power' (p. 1). For Billig, ideology is necessarily paradoxical, at once structuring human thought and providing the terrain upon which individuals invent or create discourse. This is a paradox that needs to be encompassed by social psychology, not resolved. The importance of rhetoric derives, in part, from its capacity to render accessible the argumentativeness, sociality and contradictoriness of human thought and common sense. Thus in order to understand the meanings and functions of people's utterances and writings, it is necessary to reflect upon what it is they arguing against (Billig 1991, p. 17).

However, such a perspective is subject to the charge of relativism, misplaced though this might be (cf. Eccleston and Stenner 1994; Ashmore 1989). In the simplest terms, if all is rhetorical and argumentational, how do we justify any critical stance we might take? Where in all this mapping of argumentational manoeuvres is there a politically-informed recourse to judgments about what are good or tactical or emancipatory discourses? In deflecting such an accusation of relativism, Billig points to the existence of a Utopian vision at the heart of rhetorical social psychology when he writes: 'The rhetorical turn ... is neither a flight from argument, nor an abandonment of ideological critique ... a moral vision can be placed at the centre of the rhetorical perspective to enable such critique. The turn to rhetoric can be formulated as a celebration of argument. At its core can be placed the utopian vision of everyday philosophers arguing in conditions of enjoyment and freedom, with their arguments soured neither by stupidity nor by the social conditions of distortion' (Billig 1991, p. 26). Unlike Sampson and Gergen, Billig explicitly reflects upon the Utopian 'other' – a sort of ideal speech situation – at the heart of his social psychology; and with this he exposes the political and visionary dimensions of his social psychology to critique.

CONCLUSION

In the foregoing I have identified the tacit Utopias of Marx and Engels, Sampson and Gergen. These bear a surprising similarity to one another. While these writers reflect the divergent concerns of the mid-nineteenth and late twentieth centuries – labour and language respectively – they nevertheless share an Utopian vision that hinges on difference, movement and multiplicity. In the case of Marx, the (higher stage) communist individual is multiplicitous in the sense of being able to nomadically engage in an array of different labours. In contrast, for Gergen and Sampson, this difference entails taking up the perspective of multiple others. Unlike Billig who at least excavates, albeit defensively, his Utopian commitments, these other writers end up ontologising in one way or another their implicit utopias. Thus, Marx and Engels' reluctance to articulate fully their vision of the post-revolutionary mode of being serves to dehistoricise it (for example, no vegetarian would be happy with the picture they draw). While this functions as the hidden 'other' from which aspects of their critique flow, by virtue of its hiddenness, it can also limit critique. In the case of Sampson, dialogism is elevated to a metaphysical level – it is always present and always an ideal: it is both the conditions of possibility for communication and the victim of history (patriarchy, capitalism, imperialism). As an Utopian vision however, it too is outside history and outside critique – where does such a vision come from? what are the possible alternatives? in what ways does it further or detract from particular political struggles? All these questions need to be addressed –

but in order for this to be possible, a much more articulated and reflexive account of dialogism needs to be presented – one that acknowledges its Utopian character and historical roots. Finally, the promising postmodern self that Gergen identifies is more clearly historicised, yet the history from which it emerges is presented as an empirical observation: from what historical contexts and Utopian lineages have the discourses, representations and metaphors that have facilitated this construction of the 'saturated self' sprung?

My central point is, then, that it is necessary to draw out the constructed character of these 'good' or desirable others. One way in which this may be achieved, is through the representation of these as Utopian. That is to say, one way of articulating the critical stance of social psychology is to consider it as a creative medium for the production of representations of Utopia. As Kumar (1991) puts it: 'Utopia builds upon existing reality but is not imprisoned by it. It is formally forbidden to be some neutral, "scientific" reflection of reality ... Utopia confronts reality not with a measured assessment of the possibilities of change but with a demand for change' (p. 107). Obviously this is no easy task, but it is possible to draw upon models of this sort of critique from other disciplines. One instance of Utopian meditation takes place in Giddens' (1990) volume *Consequences of Modernity* in which he adopts the position of 'utopian realism': 'we can envisage alternative futures whose very propagation might help them be realised. What is needed is the creation of models of utopian realism' (p. 154). But, in contrast to Kumar's formulation, Giddens wishes to 'keep to the Marxian principle that avenues for desired social change will have little practical impact if they are not connected to institutionally immanent possibilities' (p. 155). As such he seeks these potential Utopian realities in what he calls 'life politics' – or the politics of self-actualisation (p. 156). That is, those 'radical engagements which seek to further the possibilities of a fulfilling and satisfying life for all, and in respect of which there are no "others"' (p. 156). In seeking out resources for such a trajectory, he turns to the role of social movements, such as the ecology movement.

Now, for all the reservations we might have about the content of Giddens' Utopian tactics, critical social psychology can nevertheless engage with the form of his argument, namely the active and reflexive deployment of the Utopian. How, then, do we set about this task? Clearly, in relation to content, one option is to survey Utopian or quasi-Utopian representations of society and social psychological functioning. To this end, anthropological and historical accounts are an important, not to say, traditional, resource. However, there are also political science and literary texts. As regards the former, there is the young Marx's work ([1843–44]1975) to consider further. But also, the recent works of such theoreticians as Bookchin (1982), Marcuse (1955; 1970), and Gorz (1985). As regards the latter, the Utopias of the later Huxley (1976), Le Guin (1975) and Piercy (1979) provide models of social relations which can be used in the critique of prevailing modes of conduct. However, overarching this would be an engagement with the field of Utopian Studies which examines the context and function, as well as the form and content of Utopian writings (e.g. Mannheim 1960; Levitas 1990; Kumar 1987, 1991; Manuel and Manuel 1979). By elevating this to an integral aspect of Utopian critique, it is possible to reflexively subject the Utopian 'other' itself to interrogation.

This brings us to the question of the political efficacy of such a critical strategy. Obviously this is an issue that arises for any social psychology with emancipatory pretentions. If we agree with Gergen (1989; also see Giddens 1991, for a similar account of the social sciences in general) that psychology is a repository of terms for self-elaboration, then a visionary psychology adds emancipatory options to this storehouse. Over and above this, however, the practitioners of a modest, visionary Critical Social Psychology would also render such concepts exploratory, provisional or contingent by virtue of stressing their Utopian pedigree and their historical context. They would not only point to a vision of society where communication, reflection and openness proceed unimpeded, but begin to exemplify such a vision.

REFERENCES

Anderson, P. (1983) *In the Tracks of Historical Materialism*, London: Verso.

Ashmore, M. (1989) *The Reflexive Thesis: Wrighting Sociology of Scientific Knowledge*, Chicago: Chicago University Press.

Bauman, Z. (1976) *Socialism: The Active Utopia*, London: George Allen and Unwin.

Benedict, R. (1935) *Patterns of Culture*, London: Routledge.

Billig, M. (1987) *Arguing and Thinking: A Rhetorical Approach to Social Psychology*, Cambridge: Cambridge University Press.

Billig, M. (1991) *Ideology and Opinions*, London: Sage.

Billig, M., Condor, S., Edwards, D., Gane, M., Middleton, D. and Radley, A. (1988) *Ideological Dilemmas*, London: Sage.

Bookchin, M. (1982) *The Ecology of Freedom*, Palo Alto, Cal.: Cheshire.

Eccleston, C. and Stenner, P. (1994) 'On the Textuality of Being', *Theory and Psychology* 4, 1.

Edwards, D. and Potter, J. (1992) *Discursive Psychology*, London: Sage.

Feuer (1959) *Marx and Engels: Basic Writings on Politics and Philosophy*, New York: Anchor Books.

Geoghegan, V. (1987) *Utopianism and Marxism*, London: Methuen.

Georgoudi, M. (1983) 'Modern Dialectics in Social Psychology: A Reappraisal', *European Journal of Social Psychology* 13, 1.

Gergen, K.J. (1989) 'Warranting, voice and elaboration'. In J. Shotter and K.J. Gergen (eds) *Texts of Identity*, London: Sage.

Gergen, K.J. (1991) *The Saturated Self*, New York: Basic Books.

Geuss, R. (1981) *The Idea of a Critical Theory*, Cambridge: Cambridge University Press.

Giddens, A. (1990) *Consequences of Modernity*, Cambridge: Polity.

Giddens, A. (1991) *Modernity and Self-Identity*, Cambridge: Polity.

Gorz, A. (1985) *Paths to Paradise*, London: Pluto Press.

Harvey, D. (1989) *The Condition of Postmodernity*, Oxford: Blackwell.

Held, D. (1980) *Introduction to Critical Theory*, London: Hutchinson.

Henriques, J., Hollway, W., Unwin, C., Venn, C. and Walkerdine, V. (1984) *Changing the Subject: Psychology, Social Regulation and Subjectivity*, London: Methuen.

Huxley, A. (1976) *Island*, London: Panther.

Kitzinger, C. (1987) *The Social Construction of Lesbianism*, London: Sage.

Kumar, K. (1987) *Utopia and Anti-Utopia in Modern Times*, Oxford: Blackwell.

Kumar, K. (1991) *Utopianism*, Buckingham: Open University Press.

Kvale, S. (ed.) (1992) *Psychology and Postmodernism*, London: Sage.

Larsen, K.S. (ed.) (1986) *Dialectics and ideology in psychology*, Norwood, N.J.: Ablex.

Lash, S. and Urry, J. (1987) *The End of Organized Capitalism*, Cambridge: Polity.

Law, J. (1994) *Organizing Modernity*, Oxford: Blackwell.

Le Guin, U. (1975) *The Dispossessed*, London: Panther.

Levitas, R. (1990) *The Concept of Utopia*, Syracuse, N.Y.: Syracuse University Press.

Mannheim, K. (1960) *Ideology and Utopia*, London: Routledge and Kegan Paul.

Manuel, F.E. and Manuel, F.P. (1979) *Utopian Thought in the Western World*, Cambridge, Mass.: The Belknap Press of Harvard University Press.

Marcuse, H. (1955) *Eros and Civilization*, New York: Vintage Books.

Marcuse, H. (1970) *Five Lectures: Psychoanalysis, Politics and Utopia*, Boston: Beacon Press.

Marx, K. ([1843–44]1975) *Early Writings*, Harmondsworth: Penguin.

Marx, K. and Engels, F. ([1845]1964) *The German Ideology*, Moscow: Progress Publishers.

Michael, M. (1991) 'Some Postmodern Reflections on Social Psychology', *Theory and Psychology* 1, 2.

Michael, M. (1992) 'Postmodern subjects: Towards a transgressive social psychology'. In S. Kvale (ed.) *Psychology and Postmodernism*, London: Sage.

Michael, M. (1994) 'Discourse and Uncertainty: Postmodern Variations', *Theory and Psychology*, 4, 3.

Nietzsche, F.W. ([1956]1871) *Birth of Tragedy, and the Genealogy of Morals*, New York: Doubleday.

Parker, I. (1989) *The Crisis in Modern Social Psychology – and How to End It*, London: Routledge and Kegan Paul.

Parker, I. (1992) *Discourse Dynamics*, London: Routledge.

Parker, I. and Shotter, J. (eds) (1990) *Deconstructing Social Psychology*, London: Methuen.

Piercy, M. (1979) *Woman on the Edge of Time*, London: The Women's Press.

Potter, J. and Wetherell, M. (1987) *Discourse and Social Psychology: Beyond Attitudes and Behaviour*, London: Sage.

Sampson, E.E. (1983) 'Deconstructing Psychology's Subject', *Journal of Mind and Behaviour* **4**, 1.

Sampson, E.E. (1989) 'The Deconstruction of the Self', in J. Shotter and K.J. Gergen, (eds) *Texts of Identity*, London: Sage.

Sampson, E.E. (1993) *Celebrating the Other*, Hemel Hempstead: Harvester Wheatsheaf.

Shotter, J. and Gergen, K.J. (eds) (1989) *Texts of Identity*, London: Sage.

Shotter, J. (1993) *Conversational Realities*, London: Sage.

Wexler, P. (1983) *Critical Social Psychology*, Boston: Routledge and Kegan Paul.

11

THE PSYCHOLOGY
OF EVERYDAY LIFE:
SOME MARXIST REFLECTIONS

Grahame Hayes

Studies in the history of psychology, with few exceptions, have neglected the social and economic conditions contributing to the formation of psychology as a separate discipline. Instead, the focus of most extant histories of psychology have been on psychology's break from (speculative) philosophy, the development of a 'scientific' methodology, and the contributions of the 'great men' of psychology associated with the various 'schools'. In effect, the histories of psychology are profoundly ahistorical, devoid of any sense of the conjunctural, and hence political, nature of the origins of disciplinary knowledge of the human condition. Psychology has been more concerned with an abstract human essence, than with the potentially more empirical reality of the human condition.

Assessing psychology's contribution to the understanding of the human condition, and the consequent alleviation of the problems associated with it over the last hundred years, would be to invoke a political and moral dimension uncharacteristic of the discipline. However, over the last decade, the hegemony of positivist and neo-positivist conceptions of knowledge in psychology have increasingly been challenged. Questions of values, of the political complicity of psychological knowledge, of the masculinist bias of psychological theorising, and of the problems of racism have been discussed and debated within a range of alternative or counter-hegemonic discourses within psychology. Examples here are the important contributions of certain Althusserian strands in psychology (Henriques *et al.* 1984); feminist psychology (Wilkinson 1986; Burman 1990; the journal *Feminism and Psychology*); discourse theory (Shotter and Gergen 1989; Parker 1992); and even the recent ascendancy of qualitative and interpretive methodology (Denzin 1989; Silverman 1993).

While these texts represent a significant shift from the hegemony of a restrictive scientist and positivist psychology it hardly amounts to a serious incorporation of social theory as an integral part of psychological theorising. In the main, the social still remains theorised as simply additive to an understanding of psychological processes. The constitutive status of the social is not realised in many of the accounts emanating from radical psychology, and there seems to be a presumed ontological primacy of (the) psychological datum in (the constitution of) social life. No wonder that Marxist approaches in psychology have been so scarce. A serious engagement with Marxism in psychology would entail questioning the ontological constitution of the psychological in a manner radically different from current conceptions in psychology, even 'radical psychology' conceptions.

So what then would be the status of a Marxist engagement with or in psychology? Whether a Marxist psychology is possible or makes sense is still an open question, but this chapter will explore the more restricted, and the potentially interesting intersection of Marxism and psychology in the study of everyday life and experience. Marxism as a social theory has contributed to a critique of contemporary capitalism, albeit at a predominantly structural and abstract level. Marxism has, disappointingly, had far too little to say about how ordinary people experience their lives under capitalism. On the other side psychology as the theory of the human individual has also operated at a very general and abstract level, and in its search for universals has avoided the particularity of people's experience. The affinity between Marxism and psychology points to psychology as the study of historical consciousness, and Marxism as the science of history, or more aptly, in the words of Lucien Sève:

> It is ... impossible to found a science of individuals on a different basis from the science of history. But *it is equally impossible to found the science of history without at the same time founding the theory of the historical production of individuals* (Sève 1978, p. 90, my emphasis).

In the current anti-Marxist climate of post-Marxism and the triumphalism of the 'new world order', writing about Marxism and psychology might appear to be an act of intellectual recidivism. How does one justify taking Marxism seriously these days, and then linking it to the most unlikely of disciplines, psychology, that so-called science of the individual? And yet in a strange and unexpected way, the collapse of the Eastern European communist governments, and the break-up of the Soviet Union, have created spaces for a re-emergence of the tradition of critical Marxism. The political dominance of Marxism-Leninism in the countries of actually existing socialism in many ways foreclosed a critical appraisal and reappropriation of Marxist theory. After all, socialism had supposedly been achieved and the society was functioning according to scientific principles. Furthermore, it could be argued that the calamities of social life in Eastern Europe and the Soviet Union have also allowed consideration of psychological questions that bear on people's everyday lives: the rise of fascist and neo-Nazi groups in the face of chronic unemployment, the disappointments of the failed promises of what capitalism was going to do for ordinary people's lives, the persistent civil wars being fuelled by the hatred inscribed in the identities of micro-nationalism, and so on.

Answering these fundamental questions contributes to the possibilities for the revitalisation of Marxism and psychology, and especially the (re)vitalisation of the *relationships* between Marxism and psychology. Let this be stated in its most stark and bold form: the future of Marxism depends on an engagement with the psychology of everyday life, and the future of psychology depends upon its insertion into and comprehension of social life. This assertion is not as bizarre and grandiose, and at best utopian, as might at first sound. Is it not true that one of the crises facing Marxist theory has to do with its rather inadequate account of human agency? This is not to suggest that psychology as a discipline is going to 'save' Marxism from the crises that it faces, but that unless Marxism starts to develop a sophisticated account of the interstices of human action and of the problems facing human agency in everyday life, it will at best be incomplete as a theory, and at worst remain crisis-riven. Is it also not true that one of the crises facing psychology is the criticism that the discipline is especially silent with regard to people's experiences of everyday life? This is not to suggest that Marxism as a social theory is going to 'save' psychology from its practical irrelevance, but unless psychology engages with the reality of people's everyday lives, it will continue to be overtaken by *ex cathedra* developments concerning the theory of everyday experience. Marxism and psychology are not being collapsed here into a new form of left syncretism, but used as a counter to the ideological proposition that Marxism has nothing to do with our personal lives, and also that psychology can continue to claim objective status as a discipline without engaging social theory.

MARXISM AND EVERYDAY LIFE

Addressing some of the issues of social theory takes us right to the heart of the problems, crises, and tensions of Marxist theory. Marxism is a theory of the social totality, and especially of capitalism as an over-arching totality. This might seem an extremely impudent and unrepentant thing to be saying given the postmodernist and post-Marxist critiques of grand narratives, and totalising theories. However, if theories do not try to generalise, they are not very useful. The task of theorising the social totality should however not be confused with creating essentialist social categories which then 'become' the social totality. Ernesto Laclau, discussing the crisis of the concept of social totality, writes that:

we tend nowadays to accept the *infinitude of the social*, that is, the fact that any structural system is limited, that it is always surrounded by an 'excess of meaning' which it is unable to master and that, consequently, 'society' as a unitary and intelligible object which grounds its own partial process is an impossibility (Laclau 1990, p. 90).

In trying to comprehend the social totality, Marxist theory must resist its *totalising* tendency, and grapple rather with the theoretical insight of the 'infinitude of the social'. The theoretical 'impossibility of society' should be all the more appreciated by a theory like Marxism which is constituted as the study of dialectical determinations. While one might be critical of some of the theoretical shifts in Laclau's project, for instance the stress on 'the infinite play of differences', and the focus on 'discursive practices', he is certainly not guilty of lapsing into a relativism in this critique of the notion of social totality. A critical Marxism must remain open to the theoretical impossibility of the social totality, while at the same time preserving a political analysis of capitalism as an over-arching totality.

The will to totality which Laclau and others have laid at the feet of Marxism has had a number of negative effects, both theoretical and practical. The one effect of Marxism as a totalising theory of society has been to remove agency and subjectivity from any serious consideration of its critique of capitalism. The slippages inherent in human identities and subjectivity do not lend themselves to the closure implied in a totalising theory in search of determinate objects of analysis. A totalising, scientistic, and structuralist Marxism only had place for human agency as the (passive) effect of social processes and relations.

The declaration of the importance of the psychological domain should not be confused with an argument concerning the ontological primacy of human nature. Marxist theory is correct to insist on the rather uncontroversial point that we should take seriously the order of (material) determination as being the physical world, the natural world, the socio-economic world, the psychological world. To say that the material conditions of the natural world precede the production of works of art, is not to say that nature 'causes' or determines culture. Acknowledging the material foundations of life, still leaves open the explanation of the complexities of human life and social relations. Asserting the importance of human agency, is for Marxism a political decision, with implications at the level of epistemology and ontology.

Marxism's characterisation of questions concerning human agency and individuality as inherently idealist, bourgeois, and individualist has had the consequence of rendering the theory of everyday life inadequate and incomplete. Psychological dimensions of people's lives are not intrinsically personalistic and solipsistic. The personal and the private are social and historical constructs, and the contradictions of bourgeois ideology need to be challenged in the process of bringing about a social order where people could have (truly) personal and private lives. The triumph of the cult of the self, the defence of personal choice, and the guarantee of privacy in the context of the interventions and intrusions of the state and the market under capitalism are a mockery of human freedom, not its celebration. A Marxism of everyday life cannot be achieved by surrendering questions and issues of human nature, human agency, and individuality to bourgeois thought. That a detailed account of everyday life and human individuality should be an integral part of Marxist theory is one of the explicit propositions of these reflections.

The other negative effect of Marxism in its will to totality is what we can term 'Marxism in power'. While conservative social and political theory has tried to lay the blame for the economic, political, ecological and other disasters of the 'communist regimes' at the feet of Marxism, the Left has been somewhat remiss in adequately explaining the material circumstances which gave rise to the crises of 'Marxist oriented' governments and states. As Therborn (1980) stated in a slightly different context, what is lacking is a Marxism of Marxism. It is unacceptable to suggest that the problems of the societies of Eastern Europe and the former Soviet Union have nothing to do with Marxism really, because these regimes were in 'breach of faith' of a proper understanding of Marxist principles, and hence the practical, societal applications are historical deviations. The previous point about the *theoretical* impossibility of society or the social, is that Marxism, or any other social theory for that matter, cannot (totally) 'run' society. To suggest that a proper application of the scientific principles of Marxism was not undertaken in most of the societies of actually existing socialism, is to miss the point completely. The point is that Marxism should be a critical theory of the social, and not a totalising theory of society.

The collapse of the communist states of Eastern Europe and the Soviet Union was not needed to tell us that there are some serious problems within Marxist theory. This is not to say that Eastern Europe and the former USSR are incidental to a critique of Marxism. They tell us a great deal about the problems of Marxism, which we should heed, otherwise Marxism will become a less than useful theory of social life. The problem of 'Marxism in power' points to a tendency of totalisation and determinism in its theory and practice of social life. It is no good saying that there is not really a problem here, as the problem is about Marxism-Leninism and not really about Marxism *per se*. We have to address the problems of the link between Marxism in power, Marxist governments, and the problems of totalitarianism. There *is* a tension in Marxist theory between its critical and explanatory capacity as a theory, and the bothersome tendency to theoretical totalisation and societal totalitarianism. A necessary vigilance with regard to the tendential problems of Marxist theory would begin to curtail the societal and political excesses committed in the name of a liberatory social theory.

The problems of Marxism in power, range from questions of the nature of the state and the rise of micro-nationalisms, to the catastrophes of central planning, and yet these important issues should not be seen as separate from the 'accounts of everyday life'. After all, one of the main emancipatory features of Marxism is its ability to comprehend the complex interrelatedness of the social totality as a social formation. Furthermore, Marxism as a philosophical anthropology (and there is no reason to abandon this conception) tries to give an account of human life (under capitalist social relations). It might well be that there are idealist strands in Marx's early conceptions contained in the *Economic and Philosophical Manuscripts, The German Ideology,* the *Grundrisse,* and even *Capital* (if one looks properly). To argue for a materialist philosophical anthropology is not to suggest that this was Marx's, or Marxism's, most central project. Clearly Marx's main body of work was to offer a thoroughgoing theoretical and political critique of the capitalist mode of production. However, thankfully, Marx was not a narrow economist, and hence his devastating critique of nineteenth century capitalism in particular, and capitalism as a system and way of life in general, wandered as a matter of course into other kinds of commentaries on social life under capitalist relations of production and reproduction.

Contrary to the post-Marxist ideas which are current, Marx's work still offers brilliant insights and critiques of late twentieth-century capitalism. Given the barbarism of the 'new world order' we should not be too excited about how 'advanced' late twentieth-century capitalism is. Clearly, also, there are some silly ideas, dead-ends, contradictions, and much more in Marx's work, and hence any slavish and eponymous adherence to Marxist principles and writings certainly does not benefit the cause of socialism. Against this, it is the main thrust of Marxism to criticise, and *change* the world. Marxism is an unashamedly political and moral body of thought (and practice).

Marxism is still able to offer an incisive analysis of contemporary capitalist society. This is not to suggest that it is the only social theory adequate to a critique of contemporary societies, and that Marxist ideas should remain unchanged from their classical formulations. Marxism is one of the few social theories that is prepared to judge the outcome of its analyses and critiques, and to suggest alternative ways of living. Furthermore, to do this Marxism is necessarily implicated in a (totalising) theory of society. This also seems unavoidable if we are to suggest different ways of living. With the criticisms levelled at meta-narratives it might seem impertinent to want to disregard the problems associated with grand theoretical discourses. However, surely the issue is rather about *how* theories of society are produced, and their relation to political power. These are very difficult conceptual and practical issues, but are not solved by a dismissal of grand theory in favour of a flowering of theoretical pluralism and particularism. There is a noteworthy difference between the acknowledgment of the problems posed by grand (social) theory, and the conclusion that (all) theories of society are a bad thing. What are all the microsocial theories if not theories of society? We do not escape the problems of grand narratives by simply dismissing them. Or rather the problems facing theories of society are not overcome by a disavowal of grand or totalising theories. The problems of the role of theory or theories of society have to be confronted for us to begin to understand and grasp the nature of contemporary social life.

PSYCHOLOGY AND EVERYDAY LIFE

The psychology, or everyday-ness of social life seems to have been most neglected and absent in Marxism. Not only has the structuralism of much Marxism sidelined human agency, but an opportunity has also been lost to account for the contradictions of social life in contemporary societies (capitalist or socialist). For example, what does it mean to live in Britain in the 1990s as a signalman on the London underground? what does it mean to be a Ghanaian woman trying to eke out a living on the streets of Accra? or a South African shackdweller wanting a decent house? Of course Marxism can tell us a lot about these different social circumstances, but why could we not add to this an account of the meaning and experience of these people's lives, and the possibilities for social action?

The historical antagonism between Marxism and psychology has contributed to the lack of an adequate account of everyday life and experience. The irony and tragedy of Marxism and psychology is that they are both potentially theories of the ordinary, the everyday, and yet both have remained aloof from the promise of their theoretical possibilities. Psychology, as the study of the individual, has surprisingly little to tell us about how individuals live their lives and try to make sense of their lives in ever-stressful circumstances. This is not a call for a return to phenomenological psychology which tends to eschew theory in the hope of understanding human experience through the uncontaminated, extended descriptions of human lives. The recent resurgence of interest in biography is in part an attempt to capture the openness, the contradictions, and lived reality of human lives. The problem with the focus on biography is that the accounts can end up highly descriptive, eulogising (in their individualism), and atheoretical. The argument for a (materialist) psychology of everyday life is not to suggest that this is achieved simply through the detailed account of the uniqueness of particular individuals. The concrete materiality of individuals' lives must be sought in the situatedness of lived experience, as well as in the dialectical development of a theoretical language able to explain the contradictions of everyday life experience.

Too often it seems that Marxist projects in psychology have concentrated on a defensive response to bourgeois psychology, and have tried to outdo the theorisation of the psychological principles of scientific psychology, at the expense of rehabilitating the many-sided individuality of everyday life (e.g. Tolman and Maiers 1991). Psychology, in its zest for scientific status, has produced a commendable theoretical materialism, and scientific psychology has also ensured an empirical grounding to its theoretical insights. It is not these dimensions of psychology with which one would necessarily want to find fault, but rather the processes that have determined what has counted as the object of psychological investigation, and the spurious claim of political neutrality guaranteed by (positivist and neo-positivist) scientific methodology. It is a great waste of intellectual effort that much of psychology over the last century has refused the moral imperative contained within the pursuit of the 'science of the individual'. A critique of the ideological in psychology soon exposes the vested interests served by the production of psychological knowledge. An objective study of the psychology of everyday life has the potential to disturb the complacency of the psychological world and its practitioners, a complacency ensconced within the class privilege and petit bourgeois ideology of psychology's social location. There are very few examples from the history of psychology where the production of knowledge has consistently and unambiguously been in the service of the majority, of ordinary people, of the poor and unemployed, of the working class, or of the mad.

There have, however, been some attempts to develop a psychology less removed from everyday experience: Examples include phenomenological psychology, the work of Harre *et al.* (1985) on the psychology of action, and the unfortunately disappointing work of Billig *et al.* (1988) which had the promise of penetrating the psychology of everyday life with the notion of 'lived ideology' had it not got caught up in a rather facile polemic caricaturing Marxism. All these accounts take people's experiences seriously, as they do people's ability to reflect on their lives. This does not mean that people's accounts or reflections of their lives equals knowledge, but rather that we cannot have knowledge of people's lives *without* their accounts. It is indeed a strange psychology that has a disdain for ordinary people's attempts at making sense of their lives. The raw material of a psychology of everyday life surely resides in the richness of our 'expressions' of our lives. However, a theory of the psychology of everyday life requires the development of a theoretical conceptualisation which takes us further than people's accounts themselves.

One of the theoretical tasks facing Marxism in psychology, is to make sense of people's everyday experience, and develop an explanation of what it means to live in particular social formations in specific historical conjunctures. In a different, but related, psychoanalytic register, Lacan once asked: what should the writing of a psychoanalyst be like? In other words, how do we write about the unconscious? Similarly, we should ask what a psychology of everyday life, that is sensitive to the questions of Marxism, should consist of? What terms, what forms of language, what type of discourse should constitute this project? The difficulty in answering this points both to psychology's, and Marxism's, distance from ordinary working and unemployed peoples' experiences. How do people speak about their lives? Why does human and social knowledge have an inherent distrust of the potential articulateness of the ordinary language of social life? This is not to suggest that what we say as people trying to live and make sense of our lives translates into a coherent theory of ordinary experience. Theory is not only developed through the alienation of common discourse. Thinking theoretically entails saying something beyond the descriptions that people give us about their lives, attempting to explain some of the quandaries which people face about their lives, developing an understanding of the nuances, interstices, and contradictions of lived reality, and penetrating beyond the appearances, beyond the saids, beyond the inconsistencies. Thinking theoretically, as Marxists, entails developing some responses to the conditions, emotional and material, of people's lives which undermine and oppress them.

To the extent that Marxism continues to refuse to talk about the personal, about emotionality, it allows the ideological interpellations of a psychology which is at best trapped within a neo-positivist empiricism, and which is at worst reproducing an idealist individualism, to determine the content and substance of human identity and individuality. There is a significant difference between accepting bourgeois ideology's construction and identification of human nature and human life, and abandoning the issues facing human nature and human life as bourgeois issues. Marxism needs to become involved, embroiled even, in understanding people's personal lives, so that they can become exactly that: personal. One of the most startling contradictions of so-called personal life under capitalism, is that it is not personal at all. The state and capital are all over our lives. We literally are the 'administered society', deceived into believing that we truly exercise our own free will and make meaningful individual choices about our lives. Much of individuality, and personal life today, reflects what Marx called 'abstract individuality'. We will know that substantial social changes have taken place when there is a shift from abstract individuality to concrete individuality. We will know that substantial social change has taken place when concerns of how best to organise the economy are replaced by concerns of how best to organise our emotional lives. The only thing that is really personal and private under capitalism, of course, is private property, and hence the importance of the continued alienation of concrete individuality in the form of abstract individuality. The social relations that maintain the system of private property impel the abstract logic of creating 'subjects of' capitalist social life. Concrete individuality is potentially full of the threat of human agency, of human action, of political will.

ABSTRACTION OR POLITICAL COMMITMENT

In many ways, psychology and the other social and human disciplines have become the proud 'sciences' of the abstract with regard to human individuality and experience. The faceless abstraction that much of psychological theorising is, ensures a theoretical and experiential distance from the subjects of psychological study. Psychology hardly even studies people in the abstraction of their situatedness (the unemployed, black mineworkers, Kings Cross crack addicts), but rather pursues that elusive subject – the universal human, and until relatively recently, the universal man. Psychology has very little to say about the psychology of ordinary human experience. What do we know about sections of the working class, the unemployed, the homeless, middle-class single-parent women, AIDS sufferers, the mad? The list is an interminable indictment of the silence of the psychology of everyday life. This is not to say that the whole of psychology should be devoted to the study of the psychology of everyday life. Clearly not, but the continued silence can only be interpreted as a political choice of intended neglect of this aspect of social life.

Where psychology has avoided the political implications of its researches, Marxism has avoided the psychological implications of its politics. Getting any consensus on the exact definition of Marxism is unlikely, and yet there would be wide agreement that Marxism is a theory of social change, a theory of revolution, a theory contributory to a socialist society. Put more simply, Marxism as praxis, is committed to a society free of exploitation and oppression, where people can live in fulfilment of their potential. A society in which people would not want for basic human and social needs, where people will have the possibilities of fulfilling their potential as human and social beings, and dare we say it, enjoy their lives and be happy. Within certain variants of scientific psychology and scientific Marxism, these notions of needs, potentialities, human happiness must surely sound like a retrogressive retreat into New Age humanism. But what is Marxism if not a theory of a better social order where people will live less adversarial lives, and again, there is no need to surrender the language, and idea, of human happiness, to bourgeois humanism.

The repression of a theoretical language of quotidian experience reflects the politics of exclusion to which the majority are subjected. A Marxist project in psychology at least has the political will to give a voice to ordinary human experience. It remains for psychologists and Marxists, especially those 'settled' within the comfortable confines of academic life, to assert a political commitment in their intellectual pursuits. For too long now, we have reneged on these duties as intellectuals.

REFERENCES

Billig, M., Condor, S., Edwards, D., Middleton, D. and Radley, A. (1988) *Ideological Dilemmas: A Social Psychology of Everyday Thinking*, London: Sage Publications.

Burman, E. (ed.) (1990) *Feminists and Psychological Practice*, London: Sage Publications.

Denzin, N.K. (1989) *Interpretive Interactionism*, Newbury Park, Calif.: Sage Publications.

Harré, R., Clarke, D. and De Carlo, N. (1985) *Motives and Mechanisms: An Introduction to the Psychology of Action*, London: Methuen.

Henriques, J., Hollway, W., Urwin, C., Venn, C. and Walkerdine, V. (1984) *Changing the Subject: Psychology, Social Regulation and Subjectivity*, London: Methuen.

Laclau, E. (1990) *New Reflections on the Revolution of Our Time*, (London: Verso.

Parker, I. (1992) *Discourse Dynamics: Critical Analysis for Social and Individual Psychology*, London: Routledge.

Sève, L. (1978) *Man in Marxist Theory and the Psychology of Personality*, Hassocks: The Harvester Press.

Shotter, J. and Gergen, K.J. (eds) (1989) *Texts of Identity*, London: Sage Publications.

Silverman, D. (1993) *Interpreting Qualitative Data: Methods for Analysing Talk, Text and Interaction*, London: Sage Publications.

Therborn, G. (1980) *Science, Class and Society: on the Formation of Sociology and Historical Materialism*, London: Verso.

Tolman, C.W. and Maiers, W. (eds) (1991) *Critical Psychology: Contributions to an Historical Science of the Subject*, Cambridge: Cambridge University Press.

Wilkinson, S. (ed.) (1986) *Feminist Social Psychology: Developing Theory and Practice*, Milton Keynes: Open University Press.

12

EMOTION AND POLITICS

Paul Hoggett

CHANGING THE WORLD?

Looking back on over 20 years in different kinds of politics what strikes me now is how rarely any of the groups or parties in which I have been involved were actually engaged in praxis. It is vital to remember the distinction between process and praxis; between action in which the subject is missing and action where it is present as a thinking, creative and imaginative being; between the group as object borne along upon processes beyond its comprehension and the group as co-determining subject, determined and self-determining. One must also remember that the group has to negotiate two processes – the flow of external events in which the other (the state, other groups and parties, civil and political society) is encountered and the flow of internal events (the group process, the inter-group process) through which the group encounters itself.

We kid ourselves. We say that we join a group to take action, to do something about the world, and yet we spend much of our time going through the motions. In politics we seem to deceive ourselves more than in any other realm of life. I can remember leaving a revolutionary group in the 1970s and becoming a community worker and suddenly finding myself engaged in more real action in a few months than in the previous three years. And I can remember being an active local Labour Party organiser in the 1980s and realising one day that, outside of routine electioneering, my branch with 180 members had not engaged in a single political intervention in the locality for several years.

So why do we sleep so much and yet kid ourselves that we are awake and alert (unlike the slumbering masses)? It is just possible that this sleep of ours owes something to the times we have been through, that after a decade or more of political reaction the left has gone into a kind of hibernation from which one day it may awake. But it is equally likely that 15 years of reaction were only possible because we were already half asleep. Looking back I realise that the malaise has existed for many years. In 1975 the Solidarity group published Maurice Brinton's pamphlet *The Irrational in Politics*. Three years later a collective I was a part of produced a pamphlet called *Revolutionary Politics as a Hobby* (Masters 1978) and two years later still another political companion and I wrote an article entitled 'Creativity and Pathology in Organisation'. The article concluded with these reflections:

> Any group with a subversive political intent is in business precisely in order to raise awkward questions. We may conclude that a group which cannot tolerate thoughts which threaten to subvert its own functioning cannot then in turn hope to be particularly subversive of external reality. Rather it will confront reality by using the '3 R's' – routine, ritual and repetition. (Davis and Hoggett 1980)

On the other hand there have been times when politics has been very alive and creative. In Bristol and the South West and parts of Scotland the Anti-Poll Tax Campaign was like this. It was creative precisely because political parties largely had nothing to do with it. Reflecting on this I started to ask myself some questions, particularly about party politics. Why is politics so uncreative, indeed why does politics appear to fear creativity? Why is it that the practice of engaging in politics is so rarely seen as an object of study and a resource for learning? Why, therefore, do we insist on being so politically stupid and why, in that sense, does politics shun any form of reflexivity?

POLITICS AS UNREASON

I will begin by stating an assumption. To take politics seriously means to take the world seriously and these days only crazy people take the world seriously.

On those occasions when I have roused myself from slumber it has been because of a burning sense of injustice or outrage at the destructiveness which I have sensed around me. My guess is that in most people's lives there are critical moments like these when you say to yourself 'we've just got to do something about X'. You seek others who feel the same way, you take a kind of pledge to act and then you plunge into what feels like the cold water of public life. Even when you are part of a mass movement, like during the Anti-Poll Tax Campaign, taking responsibility to act – to organise others, to mount demonstrations or pickets, to run street stalls – does not come easily. You feel anxious, at times you sense that a part of you yearns to be back by the fireside, dozing safely inside. But often there is no mass movement, indeed no movement at all, just you and a handful of others.

What I am trying to say is that real politics, as opposed to going through the motions (i.e. the simulation of politics), puts you close to the edge of society. It makes you stand out, makes you visible, subject to the public gaze and constitutes you as peculiar, as out of the ordinary. People who take politics seriously like this have to be mad – 'look at that woman handing out leaflets', the body of the passer-by stiffens and he averts his gaze. The activist is a threat for she ruptures our routines. Like a dog turd on the pavement, for a moment she takes the pleasure away from the visit to the shops.

Most people I know who take politics seriously engage in it with an equal measure of terror and excitement, a terror which comes both from within you and which is projected into you from outside, through the other's gaze. Furthermore when we engage in public politics we take part in *the group without limits*. The crowd has no boundaries, even when enclosed by a room it spills out of itself. We may endeavour to provide some structure but the group without limits always promises to transgress. Reich (1972) used to speak of the emotional plague, a pestilence of unpredictable nature which swirls around like liquid swilling inside a container, thrilling and terrifying. Bion (1961) talked of the cathexis of the individual to the group in terms of *valency*, an automatic and unreflexive fusing of the emotional life of the one with the many. So what have we here? Terror, hatred, love, hope, envy, compassion, faith – a stew of raw emotion seeking an object, a channel or a focus; energy unbound, the horse without a rider.

Besides fear there is this great, burning almost inexpressible hope present too. Surely this is what Gramsci has in mind when he speaks of *will*, the passion which grows out of the sense not just of 'what ought to be' but also from the conviction of its possibility – the 'ought' as an ends for which the means can be found, indeed has to be found. In contrast *faith* is nothing other than 'the clothing worn by real and active will when in a weak position' (Gramsci 1977, p. 337). Imagine hope and faith as if they were electrical currents switching across an open field – what binds faith but religion and is it not politics which binds hope, gives it a home, channels it? But hope can so easily become faith, an active, imaginative longing can so easily become a passive and deluded form of waiting. For Marxism, built upon a theory of immanent contradiction, the slide towards the dogma of imminence has been so easy and has had such tragic consequences. We speak of *the sects*, and indeed this is what they are, quasi-religious organisations masquerading as the political. As Wilson (1975) noted in his observations of the Paliau movement on the Admiralty Islands this is not to say that there is no element of rationality within the sect nor that it is incapable of intervening in the historical sense, it is simply to say that when the intervention comes it is blind and the consequences cannot be foretold.

Fear and hope, the emotional foundation of politics. For wherever there is political action there is emotion. In the past some (e.g. Brinton 1975) have spoken of *the irrational in politics*. As a counter to the blindness of the left to emotional life this has its value. And yet the danger is that it sets up a misleading counterposition – the irrational is bad, rationality is good – from which we draw the conclusion that we need to know of irrationality to overcome it in our politics. But what is the irrational, the unreasonable? Do we not have an obligation to be unreasonable these days when so much which passes for reason is actually a kind of madness? We might on the other hand equate the irrational with the emotional and the rational with intellect and consciousness. But this is equally useless for, as Bion (1962) has made perfectly clear, thinking is as much an emotional as an intellectual process. We are passionate beings and the idea that passion can in some way be mastered or suspended is a quaint notion held to only by the tired remains of ego-psychology. No, the idea of irrationality is obsolete; what we need now is an understanding of *the emotional in politics*, an understanding which reveals both the destructive and creative role of individual and group emotion.

Why is the left still so afraid of emotionality? Why is it unable to identify and speak of that which surrounds it, saturates it and runs through it? Men have clearly played a role – male activists, leftist male academics. The intelligentsia is only comfortable with ideas, after all this is how they ply their trade and maintain their dominance. But dear old Lenin still has a lot to answer for. The idea that consciousness is brought to the masses from outside by the intellectuals is a conceit still adhered to as vigorously by the social democrat as the upright revolutionary. This really is a conspiracy against the laity for, so it is said, left to their own devices all 'the masses' can manage is a fluid and potentially dangerous form of populism.

Goodwyn's (1991) recent analysis of American and Polish populism provides an object lesson in an approach to historical analysis which treats collective sentiments seriously. Goodwyn challenges the notion that ideas are endowed with some special potential to generate action:

> most 'ideas' do not translate into 'action' because people are afraid to act upon them: they simply do not know what is safe to do. The problem is one of power and the social fear that authority can implant in people. Power intimidates in ways that are immobilising. Visible here is what may be described as the barrier of fear. It is a central component both of 'culture' and of 'consciousness' ... People who object to one or more features of the received culture, ie., most people, but do not seem to do anything about it, are considered 'apathetic'. Here 'consciousness' comes abruptly into play: to become real, ie., to become historical actors, apathetic people must have their consciousness 'raised'. (Goodwyn 1991, p. 48)

Using the experience of the Solidarity movement in Poland, Goodwyn proceeds to indicate the impact of collective action upon inherited power relations and the fear which is embedded within them. As he notes, 'it is the psychological impact of this organising achievement on inherited patterns of cultural intimidation that pushes people through the barrier of fear into public life' (p. 49).

POLITICS AND THE IMAGINARY

Despite such dissenting voices, for the majority on the left the diagnosis has been clear – what the masses need is ideas, our ideas, more and more of our ideas, constantly refined and honed until they constitute a foolproof catalyst which will convert the class-in-itself into the class-for-itself. For the revolutionaries, at one time, this found expression in a kind of obsessional tinkering with Trotsky's *Transitional Programme*, for the British social democrats in recent years this has occasionally found expression in the search for the *Big Idea*. Think of it, in Britain after 15 years of the most cynical reaction are people really that stupid that they do not know what's going on? And, for that matter, think of Thatcherism, did it gain its strength and power from the sophistication of its ideas? One only has to ask the question to reveal its ridiculousness.

Now entertain for a moment the possibility that the average person engages in political life with the heart as much as the head, that when they make political choices their behaviour is informed as much by feelings, bad and good, as by ideas. What we might conclude from this is that those who are successful in politics may be those who can most adroitly handle these feelings, harness a million hopes and fears into a set of collective sentiments which give life and vigour to a specific moral and political project. What I am suggesting is that our engagement with politics is fundamentally an imaginary one, not because we are irrational but because we are imaginative beings who live in an imaginary world.

At this very moment I can hear people jumping to a false conclusion. There you are, they say, proof if proof was needed this bloke is a hopeless idealist, clearly he doesn't believe that there's a real world out there at all. The horrors of Bosnia are not imaginary, nor the creeping centralisation of the British state. These things are facts. This I would not dispute but the point I simply seek to establish is that our relationship to such facts is nevertheless an imaginary one. What is Bosnia forced to contain for us that we cannot bear to own in ourselves – our murderousness, our hatred of the family next door? How convenient that this conflict is portrayed as a civil war between three tribes, one of which is given the name *the Muslims* (as Primo Levi noted it was the lost, grey zombies of the concentration camps who were called *Mussulman*, i.e. *the Muslims*).

Our inability to discriminate between the irrational and the emotional–imaginary goes right back to Freud. For Freud the space between illusion and delusion was not that great – while artists and religious activists might not be crazy, they almost certainly were neurotic. In his most infamous statement on the issue, Freud (1927) clearly sees the illusion as something which we labour under because we have been insufficiently educated to reality. At times Freud speaks of reason as if it were a cold shower that only the brave dare stand beneath, the timid among us construct gods, write poetry or believe in fairy stories. It took psychoanalysis a full 30 years to recover from this and my feeling is that a proper understanding of the creative and positive role of illusion was only fully developed in the work of Winnicott (1951, 1971) in the 1950s and after. For Winnicott the realm of illusion is the realm of human culture, through play the creative unconscious and the external world are fused in the interminable unfolding of imaginative production. The space of illusion is the space of transition between inside and outside, between me and not-me, between the future and the past. As such it is the space of human possibility, a third space neither inside nor outside but both inside and outside. Winnicott invites us not just to endure but to celebrate the paradox that is this space in between and repeatedly draws our attention to the crucial distinction between delusion, through which reality is denied, and illusion, through which reality is both accepted and denied.

And is this not the stuff of politics? Is not our task both to accept reality and to deny it? Could the Vietnamese have defeated the might of American Imperialism without harbouring the illusion that as a people they had the strength to overcome whatever this vast foreign power could throw at them? Could the postwar welfare state in Britain have been built without the illusion of a community of common interest through which the middle class was drawn into a political alliance with the labouring masses (Baldwin 1990)? And is it not now commonplace for us to reflect upon the events in May 1968 in France and say that what was so significant was not what was achieved but what was imagined? To say that we engage in politics at the level of the imaginary is not to be a hopeless idealist but to be a realist. Political life just cannot be understood if the emotional–imaginary foundation of humanity is denied. I don't want to have to labour the point but I feel it may be necessary. Look now at our failures rather than our successes. Brinton (1975) begins *The Irrational in Politics* with a catalogue of the political catastrophes which have befallen the left this century, I will recount one particularly telling example:

> In the early 1930s the economic crisis hit Germany. Hundreds of thousands were out of work and many were hungry. Bourgeois society revealed its utter incapacity even to provide the elementary material needs of men [sic]. The time was right for radical change. Yet at this crucial juncture millions of men and women (including very substantial sections of the German working class) prefered to follow the crudely nationalistic, self-contradictory (anti-capitalist and anti-communist) exhortations or a reactionary demagogue, preaching the mixture of racial hatred, puritanism and ethnological nonsense, rather than embark on the unknown road of social revolution. (p. 12)

The idea that the left can construct the more powerful illusions needs laying to rest. Throughout this century the reactionary has proved far more adept at harnessing the emotional–imaginary in order to pervert and corrupt it. Unencumbered by a well meaning intelligentsia the right appears to be quite content to let the left have all the best ideas, they know what makes people tick. While it is true that reaction is the enemy of thought (Thatcher in particular saw thoughtfulness as antithetical to her project (Lousada 1993)) the left has yet to learn that passion cannot be made reason's slave. We need a passionate reason or, as Marcuse (1969) put it, a playful reason if our politics is to emerge from the dull and instrumental calculus in which it is stuck.

POLITICS AS IMPROVISATION

There are three forms of politics. First, there is going through the motions. The mannerisms, the rituals, the rigmarole of executive committees and resolutions provides a superb performance but one which knows absolutely nothing about itself. Indeed this is not just a metaphorical way of speaking for in the kind of politics I have in mind the process of 'passing motions' is actually one of the main forms of ritual. What a marvellously unselfconscious phrase to describe this way of shitting on the real thing.

Alternatively, you can do the real thing but keep it safe, premeditated and deliberative. This is a politics which knows precisely what it wants to achieve, which leaves nothing to chance. Planned, top down, obsessively thought through but a politics nevertheless where the unexpected is dangerous, disturbing, grit in the machine. A politics of distrust which fears spontaneity and therefore fears life. If it moves control it or, alternatively, bore it to death.

Finally, there's that other kind of politics which thrills in the face of the abyss, where you make it up as you go along, a politics which is open to the unexpected. This politics is a performance art and one which knows of itself. You don't plan it, you improvise it. The improviser invites chance into the process of production, accepts it as part of the flow through which action proceeds. It is not arbitrary, there is nearly always some kind of structure but it's not there in the beginning, rather it is something that emerges, a pattern which connects (Mintzberg 1985). In machine politics strategy is something which is imposed, like a formal composition in which everyone knows their place, when to come in, what note to strike. Of course it can work, something like the original intent may be realised once the production is complete, there may be room for a bit of interpretation here and there, but it is eminently predictable and workmanlike.

But if politics is to be based on the imagination then the idea of play must be placed at its heart. Like art, this kind of politics challenges the prevailing principle of reason because of its commitment to the pleasure principle. From this perspective activists are artists and the public sphere is their canvas. Their art is the art of the possible and the skill that they must develop is the skill of intervention. To intervene within a dynamic field of forces in a way which always takes the opponent by suprise requires a capacity to avoid the rut of predictable cliché.

Looked at from this perspective even the most basic political act is exciting. Something has to be done, but what? The world spreads before us, its weft of routines waiting for disruption. Each intervention is a step into the unknown, into the wide open space of the public theatre. As Balint (1959) noted in that much undervalued work *Thrills and Regressions*, to face a terrain without familiar objects to cling to and yet thrill to the possibilities that exist requires a particular psychological disposition which he called philobatism – after the Greek term for acrobat. This is a counterphobic attitude, the exact opposite of the fearful clinging to dogma and routine that much of the left has exhibited for so many years.

Of course this is not to say that there should be no repetition or ritual in politics but where cliché is used it must be an act which knows of itself and therefore is capable of irony and self parody. Politics is a serious business but it should never be taken too seriously, there must always be a capacity for play, for a lightness of touch. Without play there can be no praxis either in terms of the flow of external or internal events.

REFLEXIVE POLITICS

Without play the group becomes heavy and inert, a thing-in-itself, something which just *is* – a lifeless, inorganic piece of machinery. Reflexivity has become a very fashionable word these days. Let us remember its origins in psychoanalysis, in the idea that the individual can view herself and her history as if it were something external to her, a history which can be known and changed, made and, within some limitations, remade. But there is a second way in which psychoanalysis developed the idea of reflexivity, this time as the reflexive practice of the analyst, i.e. her capacity to get a distance from her own experience as it happens in the here and now. Without this capacity the use of the transference and countertransference in analytical work would be impossible. It is this notion of reflexive practice which has the most vital implications for a new form of politics. The group must take itself and its own experience in the here and now as an object for under-standing and intervention, i.e. for reflexive practice, if a genuine form of praxis is to be achieved. What feelings dominate the group at this moment in time and how are they affecting its behaviour? What splitting processes are at work as the group struggles to contain the hope and fear which are so much a part of its life? What is the group unable to contain and how does it project this into the other (the other group, the state, the masses)? What for this group is unthinkable – what sticks in its throat draining its energy, corrupt-ing its purpose, inhibiting its imagination? In terms of the development of a reflexive practice so little has been tried other than the work of Touraine (1981) with the anti-nuclear movement in France. And as a consequence there is virtually no accumulated wisdom through which those engaged in politics might understand their own practice. Compare this state with the sphere of management – here a vast body of work exists on the nature of organisational processes, the dynamics of teams, the process of strategy formation, the play of power and difference, etc.

A POLITICS WITHOUT CORNERS

Bion (1962) tells us that if emotional experience cannot be contained and digested it will lodge in the psyche as a quasi-poisonous material made up of what Bion calls Beta elements which act like accretions of stimuli awaiting discharge. The normal form of discharge is through language but in using this vehicle the Beta elements corrupt language so that it becomes a medium for getting rid of poison rather than a mode of communication. 'Communication' thus becomes agonistics, a process of attack and counter-attack, lunge and parry, through which bad feeling which cannot be thought about is projected out, projected back, re-projected, introjected, and re-introjected. This is the emotional plague that Reich spoke of. Hinshelwood (1989) speaks of it as an *affective network* through which 'bits of experience, affects, emotions, feeling-states, are moved around' (p. 77). In other words, what flows around in the group is reified bits of human experience which are passed between individuals who feel increasingly depersonalised.

Whoever says politics says emotion. As I noted earlier the problem for the political group is the weight of fear and hope it carries, both for its members and for the other. But whoever says politics also says differences, and differences become conflicts and, if the group cannot handle the emotion it necessarily contains, the conflicts soon become splits. How to handle differences without splitting, fragmenting or imploding – this is the key collective–emotional task facing the political group.

How many times do we see it happen? There is a difference of opinion, a mild emotional charge is attached to the engagement and, to reify things for a moment, it is as if this flicker of emotion acts as a signal for the plague to be released. The differences become positions, and the positions become redoubts which in turn become fortresses, and the fortresses gather armies around them and we go to war and spend our time fighting each other rather than the enemy without. OK, so this is a parody, but it has so much truth in it.

We, on the left, are emotional illiterates more often than not borne helplessly along upon powerful sentiments we neither understand nor know how to use. The political is personal, our emotional lives constantly order and structure our political practice. An entirely new approach to political practice is necessary, one in which group and mass psychology is integrated into the heart of politics. Only then might we develop a politics which can transcend the familiar and tragic dramas of self-sabotage and move towards a politics of the imagination, one where there are no corners in which to hide or to place the enemy.

REFERENCES

Baldwin, P. (1990) *The Politics of Social Solidarity*, Cambridge: Cambridge University Press.

Balint, M. (1959) *Thrills and Regressions*, London: Hogarth Press.

Bion, W. (1961) *Experience in Groups*, London: Tavistock Publications.

Bion, W. (1962) *Learning From Experience*, London: Heinemann.

Brinton, M. (1975) *The Irrational in Politics*, London: Solidarity Pamphlet.

Davis, M. and Hoggett, P. (1980) 'Creativity and Pathology in Organisation', *Chartist* **81**, 15–17.

Freud, S. (1927) 'The Future of an Illusion', in James Strachey (ed.) *The Standard Edition of the Complete Psychological Works of Sigmund Freud*, **21**, pp. 3–56.

Goodwyn, L. (1991) 'Rethinking 'Populism': Paradoxes of Historiography and Democracy, *Telos*, **88**, 37–56.

Gramsci, A. (1977) *The Prison Notebooks*, London: Lawrence and Wishart.

Hinshelwood, R. (1989) 'Social Possession of Identity', in Richards, B. (ed.) *Crises of the Self*, London: Free Association Books.

Lousada, J. (1993) 'Self-defence is no offence' *Journal of Social Work Practice*, **7**, 2, 103–13.

Marcuse, H. (1969) *Eros and Civilization*, London: Abacus.

Masters, J. (1978) 'Revolutionary Politics as a Hobby', *Interventions*, **2**.

Mintzberg, H. (1985) 'Of Strategies, Deliberate and Emergent', *Strategic Management Journal*, **6**, 257–72.

Reich, W. (1972) *Reich Speaks of Freud*, London: Souvenir Press.

Touraine, A. (1981) *The Voice and the Eye An Analysis of Social Movements*, Cambridge: Cambridge University Press.

Wilson, C. (1975) *Magic and the Millenium*, London: Panther Books.

Winnicott, D. (1951) 'Transitional Objects and Transitional Phenomena' in Winnicott, *Through Paediatrics to Psycho-Analysis*, London: Hogarth Press.

Winnicott, D. (1971) *Playing and Reality*, London: Tavistock Publications.

13

INCARCERATED WOMEN: TRANSFORMATIVE STRATEGIES

Kum-Kum Bhavnani and Angela Y. Davis

The prison plays a central role in the policing of individuals in capitalist society, and so an attention to the different forms of oppression which are reproduced, through the layering of sex and race upon class exploitation in this institution, should be an important part of the agenda for Marxist psychologists. The development of women's prisons in the United States and Britain over the last 150 years is informed by and in turn informs a history of social attitudes toward women and an attendant history of gendered and racialised punishment practices. Both men's and women's prisons rely upon physical discipline and surveillance, as well as psychological strategies of control and self-surveillance (McDermott and King 1988). Psychological strategies emphasising self-esteem and domestication are especially central in the conceptualisation of rehabilitation programmes for incarcerated women. Discourses of self-help and counselling permeate much of the literature on women's incarceration. Yet, despite this deployment of psychological techniques of control and rehabilitation, that often are mutually contradictory, feminist and Marxist psychologists have not produced a significant body of work on women's imprisonment. Therefore, we hope that this chapter – tentative though it may be – will stimulate further discussion among feminist psychologists. Kum-Kum Bhavnani trained as a social developmental psychologist and now works in feminist and cultural studies. Angela Davis, is trained in philosophy and now works in critical race theory and Black studies. We collaboratively conducted the research which informs this chapter in order to provoke public debate on the future prospects of abolishing jails and prisons as normal punishment for women.

Even as imprisonment is ideologically represented as the surest way to 'keep criminals off the streets' and therefore to assuage the socially constructed fear of crime, the incarceration of greater numbers of people has never had the result of diminishing the number of potential prisoners. On the contrary, the very efforts to invoke the prison as the solution to crime have always resulted in the expansion of carceral institutions and the populations they contain. The number of imprisoned individuals has spiralled steadily in the United States: between 1980 and 1992, the male prison population increased 160 per cent; the female population during the same period increased 275 per cent. While women constitute a relatively small minority of all prisoners – in 1991, there were 87,000 women in state and federal prisons (Bloom and Steinhart, 1993) – the rate of increase among women is proportionately higher than among men. Rather than recognising this alarming tendency toward ever larger incarcerated populations as a serious domestic crisis in the United States, elected officials – both Democrats and Republicans – have manipulated the figures of 'the criminal', 'the welfare mother', and 'the immigrant' to embody profound social fears. The 'criminal', with its underlying racial implications, now serves as one of the major figures against which the nation imagines its identity. In the meantime, incarcerated men and women in the United States – disproportionately people of colour – constitute what many prisoners refer to as a throw-away population, and there are continued calls nationwide for more severe sentencing. In the state of California, for example, 'three-strikes-and-you're-out' legislation has taken a deep-rooted hold with the recent passage of Proposition 184, which precludes legislative interference with the 'three-strikes' law. The 'three-strikes-and-you're-out' law mandates a life sentence for any individual convicted of three felonies.

Although there is a substantial body of literature in criminology and related disciplines on the inefficacy of the prison as a site of rehabilitation, there is a relative paucity of literature examining the policy implications of research on women's imprisonment. There are notable exceptions (Burkhart 1973; Carlen 1985, 1988, 1990; Dobash et al. 1986; Eaton 1993) but it is generally agreed that women have been marginalised in the development of prison policies (Hancock 1986). For example, recent studies on prisons, prisoners, and prisoners' movements (Berkman 1979; Wilbanks, 1987; Braithwaite 1989; Selke 1993) focus exclusively on men. With the exception of Selke (1993), none of these authors even acknowledge the gendered character of their own analyses.

While we are sympathetic to Jeffrey Reiman's (1990) arguments that crime is produced by legislative policy, by policies that govern police and prosecutorial work, and by sentencing policies, his rather simplistic and mechanical class analysis ignores critical moments in the production of crime. Specifically, it lacks insight into the ways gender, race, and sexuality act as cross-cutting influences on the construction of criminal justice policies. While we would both classify ourselves as Marxist, we do also feel that Marxist accounts should not be reductive to class, but, rather, should seek to understand and change the practices that reinforce the many forms of systematic oppression under capitalism.

Where work has been done with or on women prisoners (e.g. Giallambardo 1966), these tend to emphasise the passivity of women prisoners. While women prisoners are systematically infantilised, this does not mean that they are entirely without agency. In this sense, there are parallels between incarceration and the historical system of slavery in the United States. As slaves found ways to resist, while simultaneously camouflaging their acts of resistance, so women prisoners often develop creative ways to challenge the dehumanisation of the prison system (but see Clark and Boudin 1990 for an exception). Yet, for the most part an implicit, but also often explicit, set of discourses organises conceptions of women prisoners as incapable of interpreting, let alone exercising any control over, their situation (e.g. Foster 1975; Cookson 1977; Kruttschnitt 1983; Arnold 1990; Kampfner 1990; Fletcher *et al.* 1993).

Women Prisoners: A Forgotten Population by Fletcher *et al.* is a recent compilation of studies edited by a group of self-described multi-ethnic social scientists who developed a Project for Recidivism Research and Female Inmate Training in Oklahoma. The researchers chose Oklahoma because it has the highest rate of incarceration for women in the United States, 3.8 per 1,000. Their study was comprised of a 142-question survey administered to more than 80 per cent of all women incarcerated in Oklahoma jails in March, 1991 – 557 women in all. In addition, the researchers surveyed 60 per cent of the 163-person co-ed prison staff. The project's central aim was to study recidivism rates among women prisoners. We greatly appreciate the researchers' commitment to women prisoners, their willingness to address issues of 'race' and its intersections with gender and class, and their scholarly efforts to seek liberatory strategies for incarcerated women. However, the articulation of 'recidivism' as a problem emanating primarily from individual life histories diverts their analytical gaze from the institutional and structural forces that serve as a magnet, inevitably attracting former prisoners back into the system. In addition, while the central aim of the Oklahoma researchers was to present a comprehensive, triangulated study considering 'race' as important as gender to theorising the women's prison population in Oklahoma, they manage to construct women prisoners mainly as social victims. A further reservation we have about this particular approach is that the editors rely on 'A National Profile of the Woman Prisoner' produced in 1990 by the American Correctional Association. This profile provides a normative description of incarcerated women as single women of colour in their late twenties who have been physically abused, have dropped out of high school, have had children, and have been arrested at least twice by the age of 15 (Fletcher *et al.* 1993). Without labouring the point, such descriptions create stereotypical notions of incarcerated women, do not problematise discursive representations of criminalised women based on statistical averages, and thereby deny the women any agency.

However, there are exceptions to the type of work that leads to these narrow conclusions. Dobash *et al.* (1986) aim to avoid constructing incarcerated women as passive human beings or mere victims of their social circumstances. Instead, the authors rely upon a Foucauldian perspective, even as they are critical of Foucault's refusal to engage with gender as a category of inequality. Foucault's (1977) work is useful alongside Marxist accounts of crime and punishment under capitalism, but is also necessary to be critical of it. Dobash *et al.* examine official discourses on criminality and imprisonment of women, and interrogate how such official discourses translate into government practices, both past and present. The authors also spent four months conducting intensive observation in a women's jail in Scotland in the mid-1980s; they interviewed a total of 59 women prisoners.

The prison they worked in, Cornton Vale, was built specifically for women and is described officially as a therapeutic community (Dobash *et al.* 1986). The suggestion that women prisoners are more 'difficult' than men prisoners descends from a nineteenth-century view of women in jail, an assumption that remains relatively unchanged in contemporary discourse. Dobash *et al.* also demonstrate that motherhood is a controlling ideological conception invoked in judgments about imprisoned women. The attitude common among senior sentencers is: 'If a woman is a good mother then I don't want to put her in jail, and if she isn't, it doesn't matter' (Dobash *et al.* 1986, p. 195).

As is clear, we found their study to be very helpful in allowing us to develop our own work with incarcerated women. However, the authors do not discuss issues of 'race' and racism for incarcerated women – which means that the racialised dynamics of women's incarceration are hidden from view. As a result, a key process in the incarceration of women is not analysed in their work. At the same time, we do think it important to give serious consideration to the Dobash *et al.* study of women's imprisonment – and, indeed, their work has been extremely influential in settings such as official Scottish policy on jails. However, the authors' arguments are confined to ideas about prison reform, only rarely raising the possibility of the abolition of prisons. In light of our own interest in stimulating discussion about the prospects of strategies and institutions that do not rely foundationally upon imprisonment, this is indeed a significant silence.

One work that departs from this pattern is Pat Carlen's (1990) *Alternatives to Women's Imprisonment*. Carlen highlights the difficulty of conceptualising a penal system in which incarceration does not necessarily serve as the punishment of last resort. She also effectively argues for the recognition of women prisoners as autonomous human beings, i.e. not only as social victims. We are especially impressed by her dramatic proposal of an experimental five-year period in Britain in which only a small number of cells would be made available for women that judges wish to sentence to prison. Thus, rather than assuming that prisons constitute the ultimate site where social rehabilitation can occur, Carlen contextualises her analyses and her calls for reform within an overarching strategy for the reduction and abolition of jails and prisons. Again, we found the arguments in Carlen's work to be of considerable value, but would, again, point to her silence on 'race' and racism as an aspect about which we have reservations.

Our work has been conceptualised in light of the silence of and about women prisoners, and the silence on the ways in which 'race' and racism are implicated in the process of incarceration for women. In addition, our work aims to depart from the current emphasis in existing academic literatures on women prisoners as victims and on prisons as institutions to be reformed rather than abolished. We will briefly describe our work in one prison to illustrate the ways these issues appear in practice, and to draw out some of the threads from a complex set of structures of oppression that are not reducible to either class, nor to any other single category.

THE PRISON

Inmates at San Francisco County Jail #7 in San Bruno are misdemeanants sentenced to less than one year, or they are awaiting trial and/or possible transfer to one of the state prisons. At the time of our work there, the jail dormitories, separated according to gender and status, housed approximately 200 men and 100 women. This jail is a 'program facility', which means that all the sentenced prisoners must participate in mandatory educational programs. In this sense, it is a jail-based alternative to traditional jails. It seeks to recruit racially diverse deputies who are sympathetic to the idea that jail should not only mean control and punishment, but should provide a wide range of multicultural educational opportunities for inmates.

The Program Facility is a 'New Generation Jail', defined in corrections theory as a significant advance over the prevailing organisation of jails. County Jail #7 thus incorporates the latest innovations in jail architecture and in inmate management practices, that are informed by a number of theoretical assumptions about the reasons jails have not worked in the past. While the new generation jail has discarded the model of cells along corridors and the use of multiple sets of bars, its open architecture, complemented by direct supervision practices on the part of the deputies, necessitates a more total form of surveillance.

County Jail #7 has six dormitories – two for women and four for men – each holding up to 60 people. The dorms are laid out in a circular arrangement around an elevated plexiglass control tower from which virtually every square inch of the dormitories can be monitored. Surveillance is also achieved via remote video cameras which are placed inside each dormitory, and recorded images are transmitted to a bank of video monitors in the control tower. Deputies are present in the control tower 24 hours a day, and can turn to any camera for a closer view of any part of any dormitory. This system is a twentieth-century version of Jeremy Bentham's panopticon.

The dorms are shaped as wedges, with the broad part of the wedge having a passage out into a small yard at the back of the building, and the narrow part forming the main point of entry into the dorm. The ceilings are at least 40 feet high. Bunk beds line the back walls, and there are single beds placed close to each other in the middle of the area bounded by the bunk beds. At the front of the dorm is the guard's desk, along with notice boards displaying jail rules, four telephones, and a white board with the names of women who will perform the routine in-dorm tasks such as serving food and cleaning. In addition, at the front of the dorm near the guard's desk are five bench-style metal tables, each with twelve small stools around it. The dorm furniture is bolted to the floor. There is also some exercise equipment in one corner of the dorm, with the communal toilets and shower cubicles (with clear shower curtains) on the opposite side of the room. Many women referred to the dorms as 'warehouses'.

The inmate management practices of this jail call for a 24-hour per day deputy presence inside the dormitory. This is a strategy of control that is very different from that of jails where inmates are locked up in cells containing four to eight women, where the guards look periodically through the bars to ensure that the women are not 'misbehaving'. Thus, the fundamental organising principle of all new generation jails is pervasive surveillance. What is represented as 'progressive' in this new process is the rendering obsolete of old-style inmate–guard relations that rely exclusively on bars and weapons. The new arrangement is meant to foster an educational rather than punitive environment. In fact, both of the women's dorms displayed a quote attributed to Malcolm X, printed in English and Spanish on a large poster reading:

A prisoner has time that she [sic] can put to good use. I'd put prison second to college as the best place for a woman to go if she needs to do some thinking. If she's motivated in prison, she's motivated to change her life.

Most of the women in the two dorms were women of colour, with the majority being African-American women. Despite the dramatic increase in incarceration rates for Latina women in the past decade, there was a relatively small population of Latinas. There was a very small number of women who could be identified as 'Asian-American', although in San Francisco's city jail at 850 Bryant Street, out of the 40 women we saw on the sixth floor in late October 1993, there were at least six Asian women. One woman we interviewed told us that she was of Indigenous American origin. White women were few in number.

Women's uniforms consist of a T-shirt, a pair of sweat pants, and a sweat shirt. All three items were supposed to be monochromatic – blue, yellow or orange. Blue clothing is worn by women who have been sentenced and are eligible for 'outside clearance' – in other words, who are not a 'flight risk'. This group of women is able to work in the jail garden, as well as possibly attend computer classes, held in a small building next door (the old women's jail). Yellow clothing is worn by women who have been sentenced, and orange clothing worn by women who have not yet been sentenced. This last group, it was explained to us, is rarely allowed outside the building, as they are considered much more volatile than the rest of the population. However, because of the shortage of clothing of all colours at any one time, many women wear a combination of yellow and orange. Interestingly, some of the women interpreted the clothing colours as symbolising a racial hierarchy.

There is yet another means by which each woman's classification can be identified. Each prisoner is required to wear a wrist band bearing each woman's jail number. White wristbands are worn by women who have been sentenced, orange by unsentenced women, and blue by sentenced women who have outside clearance. Thus, the wristband is a visible and accurate way of identifying a woman's classification in the jail system. Again, interesting comments were ventured by many of the women regarding identity construction based on institutional classification.

WOMEN'S BODIES – CONTROL, SURVEILLANCE AND RESISTANCE

Many of the women with whom we spoke implicitly recognised the complex and contradictory character of imprisonment and, in particular, its purpose of simultaneously disciplining and rehabilitating the individuals who are thereby constructed as 'criminals'. A striking number of inmates made insightful remarks about persisting influences of racism even within the context of an institution explicitly dedicated to its elimination. We were especially interested in how the women at County Jail #7 discussed control and surveillance, and whether they found ways of resisting the power of imprisonment.

Many of the women were acutely aware of the structural emphasis on developing qualities of passivity and obedience in the educational and vocational programs as evidence of individual rehabilitation. Female correctional philosophy has, in fact, focused sharply on transforming the female 'criminal' into a domesticated – i.e. passive and obedient – mother and wife. Jails aim to transform transgressive women – that is, to transform women so that they will acquire habits of passivity and obedience (Brenzel 1983). Considering the extent to which Black women are discursively represented as abnormally aggressive, this process often acquires racial implications. As Carol Smart (1976) notes, criminal behaviours are seen as masculine behaviours and, therefore, one of the objectives of women's incarceration is to make the women 'more feminine' by instilling in them passivity and obedience. However, as feminist criminologists have pointed out, passivity and obedience in the outside world are not qualities that assist women – and, we would add, especially for women of colour – to lead autonomous and productive lives once they have been released.

Women's bodies and minds are controlled via certain routines that are inherent to direct supervision jails. Women do resist such routines, though, and often successfully: laughter is an important weapon of resistance; devising collective means of protecting individual women from incursions of the guards and other expressions and acts of solidarity are another. Often individual strategies of respecting another woman's desire for privacy play an important role in affirming possibilities of resistance in this world where bodies, thoughts, and emotions are rendered public and subject to pervasive surveillance.

Although the prevailing academic and policy views deem custodialism and nurturance the two central organising principles for women's jails (Howe 1990), these views differ from those of the women inmates we interviewed. The women rarely described or discussed nurturant principles as institutional practice. Moreover, the concept of nurturance is replete with contradictions, particularly in relation to women's incarceration. That is, many have argued that women's prisons are designed to provide a 'pseudo-motherly' environment (Jackson 1989), which results in women inmates being treated like children.

SEXUALITY

Sexuality has always played a pivotal role in ideologies of female transgression. The Program Facility presents itself as a progressive institution, and explicitly attempts to promote an anti-racist, anti-sexist and anti-homophobic consciousness. All of the incoming women receive an orientation manual which states that:

> Racism, sexism, anti gay/lesbian remarks, or any other disrespect or devaluation of human beings are unacceptable in this facility. (Orientation Manual, p. 1)

Sanctions can be severe – one woman told us she had been transferred to a less desirable facility when allegations arose that she had made homophobic remarks about teachers and staff. In the education and counselling program, sexuality is invoked in a number of ways, both as a subject of study and as a locus of treatment. For example, there are workshops on sexual violence, AIDS, and non-heterosexual lifestyles. At the same time, sexuality – its expression and related behaviour – is strictly policed by the jail authorities.

For example, heterosexual contact is prohibited. Until recently, there were co-educational classes for the horticultural program; now, however, the majority of the classes are segregated according to sex, and there are strict rules about women even looking at – let alone talking to – inmates from the men's dormitories when they cross paths in the corridors of the jail. In other words, relations between women and men are *by definition* seen as sexual ones. Women are also forbidden to kiss any visitors on the mouth, for the authorities argue that drug smuggling may occur in this way. The Rules and Regulations of the Director of Corrections state:

> Inmates may not participate in illegal sexual acts. Inmates are specifically excluded in laws which remove legal restraints from acts between consenting adults. Inmates must avoid deliberately placing themselves in situations and behaving in a manner which is designed to encourage illegal sexual acts. (Title 15, Crime Prevention and Corrections, Article i, Section 3007 (Sexual Behavior))

Although the drug rehabilitation programs to which women are sometimes diverted as an alternative to jail or prison sentences are not under the jurisdiction of the Department of Corrections, these programs also require participants to refrain from sexual activity for long periods of time following their entry.

Many of the women pointed to the ideological legitimation of homo-sexuality – for example, that many of the deputies and teachers are openly lesbian or gay – and the simultaneous severe prohibition of homosexual expression on the part of inmates – 'homosecting', as it is called in prison parlance. The women feel homosexuality leads to more vigorous monitoring by jail authorities. Clearly, the constant threat of surveillance is an effective psychological weapon in the enforcement of rules that prohibit any behaviour that might be construed as sexual. If the prohibition of female–male physical contact tends to sexualise relations between women and men inmates, the rules against homosexuality have a similar effect on relationships between women. 'Visiting' is prohibited in the bed areas, despite the fact that beds are separated by less than two feet and each bed is surrounded by three other beds. No two inmates are allowed to sit on one bed at the same time.

The only other available seating is on metal stools that are anchored to the concrete floor around the metal tables at the front of the dorm. These often are within earshot of the deputy, so there is no place in the dorm where women are able to have ordinary physical contact. Women are expected to remain in their own space, even though space in the dorms is extremely tight. Thus, in these enclosed dormitories, space itself is sexualised, and sexuality in turn is criminalised.

CONCLUSION

This preliminary outline of our work begins to map some of the structures of incarceration. It also suggests points of collision and intersection between the women's concerns and official/public debates about women's imprisonment. We have not included in this chapter some issues that we know are central to women's incarceration in Britain and the United States – such as the ways in which therapeutic communities are used to perpetuate a mentality of punishment, in spite of their often initially radical origins. We also have not dealt in any depth with the profound difficulty many people have imagining a society without jails, with very different notions of criminality that are not constructed along racial and class lines, a society in which there would be a strategic emphasis on education as opposed to incarceration. The quote over the door of the first purpose-built women's prison, opened in 1645 in Amsterdam, said:

Fear not! I do not exact vengeance for evil, but compel you to be good. My hand is stern but my heart is kind. (cited in Dobash *et al.* (1986), p. 24)

This rationale for women's imprisonment may seem coercive for current sensibilities. However, discourse on prisons and incarceration has changed surprisingly little since the nineteenth century, and we would argue that only anti-penalty and abolitionist approaches provide viable possibilities for challenging the current ideological trend of 'Lock 'em up and throw away the key.' A focus on the structures of regulation in prison should be a concern of Marxists in psychology. In order to understand and change this carceral world, it is necessary for Marxists to understand different varieties of oppression, and the ways these are policed in class society.

Acknowledgements. The authors were assisted at various stages in the production of this chapter by Dana Collins and Stefanie Kelly. We conducted the research on which this chapter is based with the assistance of a resident fellowship from the University of California Humanities Research Institute at UC Irvine. We would like to thank the Institute's Director, Mark Rose, as well as the support staff (Sauni Hayes, Deborah Massey, Chris Aschan and Mia Larson), all of whom went beyond the call of duty to make our stay at the Institute as productive and as pleasant as possible.

REFERENCES

Arnold, R. (1990) 'Processes of Victimization and Criminalization of Black Women', *Social Justice*, **17**, 2.

Berkman, R. (1979) *Opening the Gates: The Rise of the Prisoner's Movement*, Toronto: D.C. Heath and Co.

Bloom, B. and Steinhart, D. (1993) *Why Punish the Children?* San Francisco: National Council on Crime and Delinquency.

Braithwaite, J. (1989) *Crime, Shame and Reintegration*, Cambridge: Cambridge University Press.

Brenzel, B. (1983) *Daughters of the State: A Social Portrait of The First Reform School for Girls in North America*, Cambridge, Mass.: MIT Press.

Burkhart, K. (1973) *Women in Prison*, New York: Doubleday and Co.

Carlen, P. (ed.) (1985) *Criminal Women*, Cambridge: Polity Press.

Carlen, P. (1988) *Women, Crime and Poverty*, Philadelphia: Open University Press.

Carlen, P. (1990) *Alternatives to Women's Imprisonment*, Milton Keynes: Open University Press.

Clark, J. and Boudin, K. (1990) 'Community of Women Organise Themselves to Cope with the AIDS Crisis: A Case Study from Bedford Hills Correctional Facility', *Social Justice*, **17**, 2, pp. 90–109.

Cookson, H. (1977) 'A Survey of Self-Injury in a Closed Prison for Women', *British Journal of Criminology*, **17**, 4, pp. 332–47.

Dobash, R., Dobash, P., Emerson, D. and Gutteridge, S. (1986) *The Imprisonment of Women*, Oxford: Blackwell.

Eaton, M. (1993) *Women After Prison*, Buckingham: Open University Press.

Fletcher, B.R., Shaver, L.D. and Moon, D.G. (1993) *Women Prisoners: A Forgotten Population*, Westport, CT: Praeger.

Foster, T.W. (1975) 'Make-Believe Families: A Response of Women and Girls to the Deprivations of Imprisonment', *International Journal of Criminology and Penology*, 3, pp. 71–8.

Foucault, M. (1977) *Discipline and Punish*, Harmondsworth: Penguin.

Giallambardo, R. (1966) *Society of Women*, New York: John Wiley and Sons.

Hancock, L. (1986) 'Economic Pragmatism and the Ideology of Sexism: Prison Policy and Women', *Women's Studies International Forum*, 9, 1, pp. 101–7.

Howe, A. (1990) 'Prologue to a History of Women's Imprisonment: In Search for a Feminist Perspective', *Social Justice*, 17, 2, pp. 4–22.

Jackson, K. (1989) 'Patriarchal Justice and the Control of Women', *New Studies on the Left*, Spring, pp. 153–71.

Jose Kampfner, C. (1990) 'Coming to Terms with Existential Death: An Analysis of Women's Adaptation to Life in Prison', *Social Justice*, 17, 2, pp. 11–125.

Kruttschnitt, C. (1983) 'Race Relations and the Female Inmate', *Crime and Delinquency*, October, pp. 588–9.

McDermott, K. and King, R. (1988) 'Mind Games: Where the Action is in Prisons', *British Journal of Criminology*, 28, 3, pp. 357–77.

Reiman, J. (1990) *The Rich get Richer and the Poor Get Prison*, 3rd edn New York: Macmillan.

Selke, W.L. (1993) *Prisons in Crisis*, Bloomington: Indiana University Press.

Smart, C. (1976) *Women, Crime and Criminology: A Feminist Critique*, London: Routledge and Kegan Paul.

Wilbanks, W. (1987) *The Myth of a Racist Criminal Justice System*, Monterey, CA: Brooks Cole.

14

THE REVOLUTIONARY PSYCHOLOGY OF LEV DAVIDOVICH BRONSTEIN

Ian Parker

Revolutionary psychology is not an academic system of knowledge. It is not a theory or set of theories, and it cannot be formalised, written, transmitted and learnt. Revolutionary analysis and theory, however, as political and economic critique can, of course, be developed and passed on as a corpus of knowledge and practice, and I take Marxism to be a case example of such a corpus. It is still, thankfully, not *only* an academic system, and when it is locked into the education system it will no longer be revolutionary. Marxism is an accumulating tradition of practical revolutionary knowledge that stretches in time from before Marx to our times. Its object now is the constellation of gendered, racialised forces and relations of production, including in culture the forces and relations of commonsense. Bourgeois psychology, in contrast to this, has as its object the individual abstracted from those forces and relations. Any variety of psychology, whether it be behaviourist or cognitive, psychoanalytic or Vygotskyan, can appear at one moment as a tool for empowerment, and twist at the next into part of the mechanisms of exploitation and oppression that comprise the psy-complex. A revolutionary psychology, then, can only be *lived*, and as a process of personal engagement, as political action.

A paradox starts to emerge here, for while examples of personal engagement and political action can be found embodied in the lives of individuals, it is not right to reduce things to the revolutionary psychology, the mind, of a person. Nevertheless, the object of psychology, the 'individual', does have some lived reality for us as the separate sentient centre that each human body feels to be their own. We can start to break from bourgeois psychology which abstracts individual minds from social context by understanding that object as it is expressed in the moral-political projects of personal life. Lev Davidovich Bronstein was one person whose life and work traced a trajectory of political and personal tragedy, and the development of revolutionary psychology.

The tensions and contradictions, the impossibility of confining any 'ensemble of social relations' within the body of one individual, mean that such psychology can only be understood in relation to the matrix of social and political circumstances that Bronstein, for example, lived within. The *relational matrix* is personal and political, and both the personal and the political are marked by various mechanisms of splitting and projection. In the personal realm there are splits and projections in the family matrix, here to a daughter (and not only the daughter) positioned as victim. In the political realm the splits and projections operate in a matrix in which the Soviet bureaucracy (and not only the bureaucracy) is positioned as persecutor. Already it will be clear that I am opting for psychoanalytic terminology to tell the story. This is no accident; not because psychoanalysis is true and the best system of explanation, but because it *became* true for historical reasons and so it provides an appropriate vocabulary for understanding this life in context. Psychoanalysis became true there and then, and it is still with us now. It is part of the cultural and psychic stuff of capitalist society that Marxists have to grapple with. It structures power and resistance in politics and personal relationships. In this chapter I want to explore each relational matrix in turn in this life before focusing on the connection between the two. This revolutionary psychology is formed in the connection between the two matrices, and it is Bronstein's revolutionary theory that allows us to comprehend that connection.

THE DAUGHTER

Zina was Lev Davidovich Bronstein's daughter by his first marriage. She was born in 1900 while Lev and Alexandra, his wife, were in Tsarist exile in Siberia. Zina, so the story goes, found the dummy her father left in his bed to fool the guards in 1902 when he escaped and fled to London (Deutscher 1954). He took a new name from one of his gaolers, the name by which he was to become better known.

Here are a number of exchanges and paradoxes ripe for psychoanalytic study, and they became embedded in the person of Zina who arrived for analysis thirty years later, in 1932, on Professor Kronfeld's couch in Berlin. Some of the personal twists and political issues are highlighted in Ken McMullen's film *Zina* (McMullen 1985). Because this is such a powerful film, and re-presents these issues to both politicised and yet-to-be-politicised audiences, I will refer to this film a number of times. As a general point, in addition, critical psychologists should be at least as concerned with the power of popular psychology as with its academic forms. The film focuses on the analysis, and shots of Zina on the couch are interspersed with flashbacks to her reunion with her father in Prinkipo (the Turkish island on which he spent early years of exile after being expelled from the Soviet Union) and meditations on the links between the personal and the political by Kronfeld.

The case of Zina (the 'case' Kronfeld was to call 'Fraulein B') raises a number of issues for revolutionary Marxists. Zina is crushed by Stalin's onslaught on the Left Opposition in the beleaguered Soviet republic, and in her fate there is a broken reflection of the bureaucracy's rise to power. Zina is caught in the practice of a theory of the mind which attracted so many of the Left, and Freud has touched Marxism many times since the 1930s. In the film we can see that Zina cannot live in the illusion of the passionate idealised relationship with her isolated father, a political hero.

Zina's case stands as an object lesson in political cruelty. Bronstein's supporters had tried to get her out of the Soviet Union and away from the pressures she had come under there. Her sister's death, her husband's deportation to Siberia, and her struggle to bring up her two children drove her near to breaking point. She also suffered from consumption. Eventually, in 1931, she was allowed to bring her five-year-old son, Seva, to her father at Prinkipo. Her daughter was left hostage in the Soviet Union with her mother Alexandra.

However, now she was a potential security risk to her father. He was in constant contact with the Left Opposition, and was busy writing (in the third person) his history of the Russian revolution. Zina felt rejected, and more distressed as the months went by. She moved to Berlin to seek psychoanalytic cure with Kronfeld. This was hopeless. Bronstein and his family were now deprived of Russian citizenship, and Seva was stuck in Prinkipo. Zina was refused permission to return to Russia, and she remained in Berlin to witness the rise of fascism.

The history of Zina's troubles in the Soviet Union are alluded to in the film, but the effects of the persecution are displayed only in her emotional reactions. One scene in an art gallery has her positioned as a neurotic Stalinophobe. We are invited to suspect that some blame for her condition might not actually lie in the situation in the Soviet Union, but in her treatment by her father (an interpretation eagerly canvassed in some reviews of the film when it first came out). The political economic context in Berlin is handled better, with the dominant symbol of the rise of fascism being the Mercedes star rather than the swastika.

Psychoanalysis appeared to be stupid to Zina (though for several months Kronfeld was convinced that the treatment was working). Her father had overcome her resistance to the 'talking cure' and persuaded her to go to Kronfeld. Her father himself was convinced that Freud's work was compatible with Marxism, and had spoken up in favour of psychoanalysis in the 1920s while Stalin's academic apparatchiks policed psychology and enthused about Pavlov's conditioning experiments as the basis for a materialist account of mental life.

As early as 1922 Bronstein wrote to Pavlov (who had not been at all sympathetic to Bolshevism before the revolution) and urged toleration of psychoanalytic research (Deutscher 1959). Against Pavlov, he felt some sympathy with what he took to be Freud's attempt to work down from the phenomena of dreams and imagination to physiology, and publically defended psychoanalysis:

The idealists tell us that the psyche is an independent entity, that the 'soul' is a bottomless well. Both Pavlov and Freud think that the bottom of the 'soul' is physiology. But Pavlov, like a diver, descends to the bottom and laboriously investigates the well from there upwards, while Freud stands over the well and with a penetrating gaze tries to pierce its evershifting and troubled waters and to make out or guess the shape of things down below (Trotsky 1926, p. 234).

As Bettelheim (1986) reminds us, Freud did, in the original German often refer to the *Seele*, or 'soul'.

The material dredged up in Zina's analysis in the film is fascinating. There are dream images which evoke the isolation of father and daughter. Kronfeld is given to much musing as to the relationship between Zina's premonitions about political developments in Germany and her unconscious interior. Here though, the viewer is also led from an exploration of the unconscious to a rather mystical account of Zina's 'instincts'. As we descend into Zina's dreamworld, we see her father descending the Eiffel Tower lift while we hear his description of Nazism as a regression of culture to the barbarities of the tenth and eleventh centuries. Maybe it is an open question as to whether the unconscious is the source of regressive destructive animal phantasies or is the fount of enlightenment and truth. It is certainly a question McMullen's film (perhaps deliberately) fudges.

The film picks up some of the threads of Zina's story and weaves them into a confusing mass of personal relationships, politics and Prinkipo (in colour), and psychoanalysis (in black and white). Some scenes have an hallucinatory quality, and we are led to believe that Zina has an 'instinctual' unconscious perception of the darker irrational side of German events which act as a counterpoint to her father's 'political reason'.

Most peculiar is the suggestion that Zina's instincts comprehend and resist 1930s Nazism. We are reminded of the courageous work in Germany of the Marxist psychoanalyst, Wilhelm Reich, whose writings on the mass psychology of fascism and on sexual liberation inspired not a few of the leftists who struggled to preserve the revolutionary Marxist tradition. Reich was expelled from the KPD, in part for his active support for sexual liberation and his refusal to support official Pavlovian psychology. Kronfeld was extremely sympathetic to Reich's work, and in 1927 he reviewed it and acclaimed it as being as important as Freud's.

On the other hand, the film is coy about the sexual aspect of psychoanalysis. The camera focuses on a photograph on Kronfeld's desk at one point. Beaming out is a squat figure who looks remarkably like Adler, an analyst who stressed the drive for power as being more important than sex, and who at the time opposed Freud from the left (even though his work ended up being linked to critiques of psychoanalysis from the right). Political and cultural contradictions are also played out in some of Trotsky's (1926, p. 234) embarrassing comments on Freud and sex:

This question has, of course, nothing in common with the cultivation of a sham Freudianism as an erotic indulgence or piece of 'naughtiness'. Such claptrap has nothing to do with science and merely expresses decadent moods; the center of gravity is shifted from the cortext to the spinal cord.

Was it the case, as Zina's mother charged, that Zina was being forced to talk about things best left unsaid? Zina did feel that this was the case. She wrote to her father: 'The Doctors have only confused me ... Do you know what sustained me? Faith in you.' Zina confessed her adoration of her father in another letter. Here she was with someone she worshipped, disappointed. 'This', she says, 'has been at the bottom of my illness.' The last we see of Kronfeld is a shot of him in the ruins of Stalingrad handing over the tapes containing his reflections on 'Fraulein B's' case, wanting them saved for posterity.

The attempt to trace the development of European history and politics in the mind of an individual subject risks reducing the committed viewer to despair, as the process did to Zina. The end of her life is not accurately depicted in the film, as if she died in a fall. In some senses, life outstripped the film in misery and irony. The eventual reconciliation with her son, Seva, in 1933 lasted barely a week. She blocked up her room and turned on the gas.

THE FATHER

Does one always identify with, internalise the prohibitions and beliefs of the father in order to develop the super-ego, foundation stone of morality, as bad psychology text books say Freud said? There is an issue running through the misfortunes of Zina, of political morality. It is an issue not only expressed in the treatment of her (and him) by others, but also in forms of moral life that enveloped them, envelop us all. As we turn to the father in this drama I also want to turn to the question of morality in revolutionary Marxism. Here, the gap between means and ends overlays the gap between the private and the public. I have wanted to make those connections in the form I have adopted here to talk about someone, Lev Davidovich Bronstein, who people *think* they know already when they hear the name he adopted, 'Trotsky'. I want to get a little distance from the image of the hard-line politico uninterested in personal and cultural life. But from now on in this chapter I will use Bronstein's 'proper' revolutionary name.

In an influential book on moral philosophy, *After Virtue*, Alisdair MacIntyre (1981) draws out some of the threads of the Western Enlightenment culture that nurtured both the modern projects of social reform to be found, for example, in Marx's work and the projects of individual self-understanding to be found, for example, in Freud's. I do not want to make a fetish of these two names 'Marx' and 'Freud'. These modern enlightenment projects borne along with culturally quite late-arriving beliefs in scientific and historical progress encompass all varieties of collective empowerment and individual therapy. MacIntyre argues that we have experienced a 'failure of the enlightenment project' (MacIntyre 1981, p. 58), and that we are suffering the effects in our experience of ourselves and others of the 'distinctively modern self ... the individual' (MacIntyre 1981, p. 59).

Although MacIntyre is no longer a Marxist (as he was once as a member of the state capitalist group 'International Socialists'), he does still balance his condemnation of Marxists in general for their collusion in the worst aspects of modernity with double-edged praise for one particular strand of that tradition. MacIntyre argues that Marxism 'embodies the ethos of the distinctively modern and modernising world' (MacIntyre 1981, p. viii), and that the 'moral impoverishment' of Marxism flows from its continual appeals to 'utility' and 'abstract moral principle': 'in their practice Marxists have exemplified precisely the kind of moral attitude which they condemn in others as ideological' (MacIntyre 1981, p. 243). The exception is Trotskyism, he says, but Trotskyism leads to a pessimism 'quite alien to the Marxist tradition' (MacIntyre 1981, p. 244).

The source of this pessimism lies in the analysis Trotsky (1936) gave before the Second World War in which he argued that the Stalinist bureaucracy was a temporary phenomenon and that when the workers in Western Europe overthrew capitalism they would then be able to aid the Soviet workers in an anti-bureaucratic political revolution. This did not, of course, happen, and the pessimism is compounded by Trotsky's (1939) prediction that in the absence of such a revolution the Marxist analysis of internal contradictions would have been falsified and the consolidation of the bureaucratic layer would eventually lead to the emergence of a new class. The role of those who had once called themselves Marxists would then be a hopeless *moral* one: 'a new "minimum" programme would be required – for the defence of the interests of the slaves of the totalitarian bureaucratic society' (Trotsky 1939, p. 9). It is this pessimism that MacIntyre takes to heart in his lament for humanity as it faces what he calls the 'new dark ages'.

The moral aspect of Trotsky's Marxism is highlighted here, and it was an aspect that came to the fore in the wake of the Moscow Show Trials, and the Commission of Inquiry into the frame-up of Trotsky which was headed by the pragmatist philosopher John Dewey. I want to mention two points about the role of morality in these events. The first is directly expressed in the debate between Trotsky and Dewey, in which both *seemed* to agree that the means justified the ends. In fact, and it is rather surprising in the face of the constant liberal chant that you must not separate the two (i.e. do anything with bad effects now, like have a strike, for longer-term ends), that Dewey (1938) was *more* insistent that means justify ends than was Trotsky. Trotsky argued that there was a dialectic in which means and ends switched places. It was precisely the commodity-fetishism of capitalist society that led liberals to think that each action comes ready labelled and priced with a quantum of moral value which could be used to bring about particular effects. It would be ridiculous, for example, he says, to equate 'A slaveholder who through cunning and violence shackles a slave in chains, and a slave who through cunning and violence breaks the chains' (Trotsky 1938a, p. 38).

The second point concerns Trotsky's writings on culture in the early years of the revolution in Russia. Some of the topics appear quaint, such as the piece entitled 'Leninism and library work', but it is important that the focus was on the *everyday*. One discussion was of the use of '*ty*' (familiar) and '*vy*' (polite) as old forms of address that needed to be combated in the Red Army (Trotsky 1922). The use of these terms violated 'civil and moral dignity', he said. (Boris Yeltsin, incidentally, now deliberately uses these old markers of status in speech.) Another discussion was on swearing and abusive language seen as a 'legacy of slavery' and as reproducing oppressive relations between men and women. In another discussion he expressed his scorn for the notion of 'progressive bureacracy', and he defended everyday discussion of problems and conflicts against patronising attempts by the party to 'present the proletariat with cultured conditions of life as with a sort of birthday gift' (Trotsky 1923, p. 57). Trotsky was well aware, years before Foucault, of the 'micro-political' aspects of revolutionary and counter-revolutionary action. This is one reason why he was concerned to defend the exploration of the 'soul' in psychoanalysis from politically correct Pavlovians.

CONNECTIONS

It is often said that Marxism is unable to theorise the inter-relationship between class oppression and other forms of oppression. The convoluted formulas adopted by the disintegrating 'Euro-communist' Stalinist parties in which they tried to say that all or no varieties of oppression are 'central' to an analysis of 'post-Fordism', 'new times' or 'postmodernity' are symptoms of this belief (cf. Mandel, 1978). Like an obsessional thought, for ex-Marxists (or, as they like to call themselves now in discourse circles 'post-Marxists'), the thought that Marxism cannot theorise the connections is ritualistically worried away at. The thought is then paranoically attributed to all who still call themselves Marxist, those who the obsessed new liberals like to call the 'hard left' (and they then like to hear the label as containing its own critique and magically dissolving the appeal of the enemy).

It is important that the denial of the problem should not be any more obsessive, and we need to find a continuity of the revolutionary tradition which takes connections between spheres of oppression seriously, and connections between the political and the personal, the public and the private, the vanguardistic and the therapeutic. The pessimism in Trotsky's analyses in the context of a public world whose collective forces were torn between Stalinism and fascism, and in the context of a private world whose objects had been torn apart by what appeared to be the death agony of capitalism in Europe, is understandable. In fact, we have to understand the predictions about the end of Marxism and the rise of a 'new class' in that context. Now we have moved beyond that context to a new incredible one in which the workers in the Soviet bloc have overthrown the bureaucracy (and may fail this time to construct real socialism from the rubble), and in which capitalism is gasping new breaths and a new lease of life in the markets of Eastern Europe. But the overall research programme and practice of Marxism is still vindicated if we look at the way the market, the bureaucracy and the progressive forces have continued to come into conflict in East and West (and still in North and South) in the last 10 years, the events in Chiapas being the most striking example at the time of writing this. It is also strengthened if we can hold to the moral aspect of Marxist critiques of oppression. Trotsky's contribution to the Marxist tradition is a *moral-political* system of analysis and theory. I will briefly take two aspects of that system to illustrate this point.

First, the theory of Permanent Revolution (Trotsky 1931) embodies an internationalist spirit that had been voiced by Marx and Engels (1848) [1965] p. 77): 'The proletarians have nothing to lose but their chains. They have a world to win. Working Men of All Countries, Unite!' But the theory is about more than what Trotsky called the 'uneven and combined development' of the world economy, the meshing in of formerly pre-capitalist regions into imperialism as a dependent and super-exploited 'Third World'. The theory is not a theory of simultaneous world revolution (as its liberal and Stalinist detractors try to pretend), but of the uneven and combined development, among other things, of the revolutionary movement. Instead of a stage model (in which nations, distinct from one another, must pass from feudalism to capitalism and only then to socialism), Permanent Revolution is about the dialectical linking and leaping of stages and the way the empowerment of one is potentially the empowerment of all. This does not mean to say that the revolution is always permanent and imminent, for that can play out in the individual as a sense of continual urgency which arrives eventually only at burn-out. What it does is to theorise the blocks on permanance and empowerment (including the appeal to interests of the nation, secret diplomacy or the defence of the 'workers state'). More than this, Permanent Revolution entails the interlinking of action and experience across continents, and the potential for resistance and empowerment in the *connection* between far away places and home. It is the moral imperative of internationalism as political practice and personal consciousness.

Secondly, *The Transitional Programme* (Trotsky 1938b) codifies the demands of the revolutionary movement coming to consciousness of itself and its powers in a series of slogans. Most of these, such as the call to open companies' books to public inspection or for the index-linking of wages to inflation, are still applicable. They are reasonable demands that take up the logic of playing fair that employers and governments pretend they adhere to, but they then reveal the unreasonable nature of current social and political arrangements when it becomes clear that they cannot be met without a radical systemic break. Transitional demands are desperately caricatured as a trick by opponents of Trotskyists, as being a simple ruse to 'expose' the employers and trade union bureaucrats who want to do deals. They do perform this unmasking work, of course, but, like Permanent Revolution, they are most concerned with action and experience, with self-activity and consciousness, with the connection between public and private life. Transitional demands are, to borrow a phrase from socialist feminism (Rowbotham *et al.* 1979), 'prefigurative' in that they voice human needs and anticipate forms of social relations that are not subordinated to profit. When transitional demands bridge the gulf between immediate goals and long-term desires for a better world, and insist that a compromise today which demobilises and disempowers is always a step away from socialism, they also bridge the gulf between the individual and the collective, the personal and political.

Trotsky maintained the continuity of the revolutionary tradition at a time when reaction (in Stalinist, fascist and then McCarthyite variants) was invading the inner spaces of all those who adhered to Marxism, and so he had to live the connection between the public and the private.

CONCLUSIONS

I will finish on three points. These return me to the preoccupations I voiced at the beginning. The first point is a disclaimer. I am not saying that Trotskyism as such is a revolutionary psychology. In fact, as a corpus of knowledge, a system of analysis, a theory of development and transformation it can mutate into something which is simultaneously revolutionary as a theory (or at least retrievable as such) and reactionary as a form of psychology. I am thinking here, of course, of the degeneration of many Trotskyist groups into sects which require members to display varieties of psychological function that are frankly pathological. One group based in Britain (the Workers' Revolutionary Party), for example, paid £2,000 for Trotsky's death-mask. When the group split and the leader (Gerry Healy) died, one faction employed a security firm to keep the other adoring faction away from the body at the funeral. Here too, not incidentally, is an example of the way in which activists make use of existing resources *and* wish for ideal models. During the 1970s the WRP used photos of an actor (Richard Burton) playing Trotsky rather than photos of Trotsky himself on their leaflets.

The second point is that it is Trotsky's actions, work, writings, beliefs and so on that constitute a revolutionary psychology. Against the parodies of Trotskyism that delight the tabloid press, we find in his work mistakes and reassessments of revolution, an engagement with issues of culture and education, and a sustained struggle with oppression. There is also a refusal to collude with the means–end thinking that mars other forms of Marxism. One of the important aspects of this is the engagement with what exists at a particular historical moment, rather than an attempt to wish it away. Trotsky lived through a series of crises and defeats, and the bureaucratic nightmare in the Soviet Union which claimed the lives of Trotsky and so many of his family, and so many others, has now twisted into an even bigger nightmare for socialism in the current crisis of Marxism.

Marxist psychologists too have to comprehend the nightmarish aspects of mental life using materials that are historically given rather than those they would wish for. Psychoanalytic notions are examples of such simultaneously useful and risky materials.

And the third point is that this embodiment in a revolutionary life brings us close to Marxist psychology. Maybe this also means that any worthwhile and progressive psychology must take the form of biography (cf. Young 1994). That we rediscover through example, through history, through past practice the forms of action that we might adopt. To take this line is to risk, of course, the resurrection of a cult of the personality (though here around Trotsky instead of around Stalin or Mao). It also risks lapsing into precisely the type of reductionism that plagues bourgeois psychology. What we need are transitional demands to bring us up against the limits of the discipline, and the interlinking of experience and resources from comrades working in and against different traditions, and political lives and examples outside the academe. This is the nearest we could get to a revolutionary psychology.

REFERENCES

Bettelheim, B. (1986) *Freud and Man's Soul*, Harmondsworth: Peregrine.

Deutscher, I. (1954) *The Prophet Armed, Trotsky: 1879–1921*, Oxford: Oxford University Press.

Deutscher, I. (1959) *The Prophet Unarmed, Trotsky: 1921–1929*, Oxford: Oxford University Press.

Dewey, J. (1938) 'Means and Ends', in D. Salner (ed.) (1973) *Their Morals and Ours: Marxist vs Liberal views on morality*, New York: Pathfinder Press.

MacIntyre, A. (1981) *After Virtue: A Study in Moral Theory*, Indiana: University of Notre Dame Press.

Mandel, E. (1978) *From Stalinism to Eurocommunism: The Bitter Fruits of 'Socialism in One Country'*, London: New Left Books.

Marx, K. and Engels, F. ([1848]/1965) *The Manifesto of the Communist Party*, Peking: Foreign Languages Press.

McMullen, K. (dir.) (1985) *Zina*, London: TSI Films Ltd.

Rowbotham, S., Segal, L. and Wainwright, H. (1979) *Beyond the Fragments: Feminism and the Making of Socialism*, Newcastle and London: NSC/ICP.

Trotsky, L.D. (1922) '"Thou" and "You" in the Red Army', in L.D.Trotsky (1973) *Problems of Everyday Life, and other writings on culture and science*, New York: Monad Press.

Trotsky, L.D. (1923) 'Against Bureaucracy, Progressive and Unprogressive', in L.D. Trotsky (1973) *Problems of Everyday Life, and other writings on culture and science*, New York: Monad Press.

Trotsky, L.D. (1926) 'Culture and Socialism', in L.D. Trotsky (1973) *Problems of Everyday Life, and other writings on culture and science*, New York: Monad Press.

Trotsky, L.D. ([1931]1970) *The Permanent Revolution, and Results and Prospects*, New York: Pathfinder Press.

Trotsky, L.D. ([1936]1973) *The Revolution Betrayed: What is the Soviet Union and Where is it Going?* London: New Park Publications.

Trotsky, L.D. (1938a) 'Their Morals and Ours', in D. Salner (ed.) (1973) *Their Morals and Ours: Marxist vs Liberal views on morality*, New York: Pathfinder Press.

Trotsky, L.D. (1938b) 'The Transitional Programme: The Death Agony of Capitalism and the Tasks of the Fourth International', in W. Reissner (ed.) (1973) *Documents of the Fourth International: The Formative Years (1933–40)*, New York: Pathfinder Press.

Trotsky, L.D. (1939) 'The USSR in War', in L.D. Trotsky (1973) *In Defense of Marxism*, New York: Pathfinder Press.

Young, R.M. (1994) *Mental Space*, London: Process Press.

PART FOUR:

PRACTICES OF EMPOWERMENT

The final four chapters consider the role of Marxist research in changing the world. Although such ambition is seen as impossible and grandiose by traditional psychology, there are many attempts to turn research into action. Mark Burton and Carolyn Kagan, in Chapter 15, review the contributions of Freire, Habermas and Gramsci to problems of power, but in the practical context of disability work. They argue for a focus on powerlessness, and a sustained challenge to that in the course of research. Questions of power and consciousness are also at the forefront of Jane Selby and Ben Bradley's exploration, in Chapter 16, of the way in which radical psychologists anticipate future possibilities for those in distress. Focusing again on a single case, they draw out the therapeutic potential in empowerment work. In Chapter 17, Bernardo Jiménez-Domínguez reviews the attempts to develop a thoroughly revolutionary form of action research in Latin America. While there are potentially progressive connections to be made between radical psychologists and liberation theology, Jiménez-Domínguez argues that this seemingly most Marxist of interventions in everyday life became mired in a liberal project obsessively suspicious of theory of any kind. Stephen Reicher, in Chapter 18, focuses on the other side of this problem, the toleration of radical theory in academic institutions, a fatal tolerance which bewitches Marxists into a comfortable co-existence with capitalist relations of production and reproduction of knowledge. The practice of empowerment in Marxist psychology will involve continual critical reflection on that co-existence, and an attention to the points of contradiction.

15

RETHINKING EMPOWERMENT: SHARED ACTION AGAINST POWERLESSNESS

Mark Burton and Carolyn Kagan

Socially responsible psychologists are aware of the problem of power in the interconnected domains of psychological practice, knowledge, theory and ideology. Doing something worthwhile about the problem requires more than a description of the experience of powerlessness. We need to know something about how power relations are constructed and maintained (produced and reproduced) – knowing that we can identify points for intervention, and the characteristics of viable strategies.

CONTEXT

We are both practical psychologists, involved in the provision and development of publicly funded services to people who are seriously disadvantaged through impairment and experience. Theory must therefore be applicable (cf. Argyris 1993).

Sheila is 42 years old. She lives with her elderly mother in an inner suburb of Manchester. Their house is owned by the City Council and, while structurally sound, it is expensive to heat. Across the road are some derelict flats, and the area has high unemployment, high crime, and few amenities or community-based organisations. Sheila has an intellectual disability, which in her case means that while she can wash, dress and feed herself, and she has the ability to hold a brief conversation, she finds it difficult to deal with novel situations and the unexpected. (We use the term 'intellectual disability' here since it is perhaps inoffensive (unlike the American 'Mental Retardation', or now obsolete British 'Mental Handicap'), but not misleading – like the current British term 'Learning Disability'.)

Sheila attends a day centre with about 40 other people with various intellectual disabilities. The staff treat her with civility, but the days are empty with little purposeful activity, little contact with identity-conferring social worlds, and Sheila has been going there for 26 years. Sheila's aspirations are for her own home, her own family, perhaps a job in a shop. Her likely prospects are for more of the same in the day, until her mother becomes unable to care for her, when after some delay and indecision, Sheila will move to a staffed group home (with three other people she doesn't like much) before being placed with a couple of about her age as a sort of 'honorary family member'. Occasionally she will meet outright hostility and discrimination, but more often the experience is one of a more subtle marginalisation. Sheila, then, has little power to influence what happens to her. While she has an intrinsic difficulty in identifying relevant aspects of the social situation to act on, a bigger problem is her almost total lack of access to power, that is to the means of influencing anything that has a bearing on her fate.

Other commentators have tried to characterise the problem facing people who both depend on others and who are seen as 'different'. The most systematic of these has been Wolfensberger (1992), who has argued that there is a universal dynamic of societal devaluation, whereby:

> entire classes of people are judged negatively by an entire collectivity, society, or majority thereof .... it creates and maintains societally devalued classes who systematically receive poor treatment at the hands of their fellows in society and at the hands of societal structures – including formal, organised human services (Wolfensberger 1992, p. 3).

Wolfensberger argues that this dynamic is universal across all societies, although the actual devalued class varies from society to society. Burton has argued (1994), that in addition to societal devaluation, there is a specific problem in modern Western societies whereby identity conferring social processes and structures (roughly coterminous with civil society) are subverted by the control mechanisms of both state and market. Moreover, the global reach of modern capitalism creates particular threats for marginalised persons as ecological and other traumatic destabilisations occur (Burton 1994).

A fundamental problem with accounts such as Wolfensberger's is that they get little further than a moral stance and a description of the phenomena. That description is grounded in the typical experiences of devalued people, but it fails to extend to the socio-historical origins of these phenomena (Burton, 1983). Without a multi-level analysis it is difficult to understand where devaluation comes from, and what should be done about it, psychologically or politically. We will show some of what happens when the problem of powerlessness is addressed without a multi-level societal analysis, and use work within the Marxist tradition – from Freire, Habermas and Gramsci – to construct an alternative approach.

SOME CURRENT RESPONSES

The first, and perhaps most traditionally psychological response is to treat lack of power as a characteristic of the individual, which is then tackled through therapy. The thinking seems to be that if, for example, the person has insufficient power, then they can be given more through additions to their behavioural repertoire. However, as we can see from the case of Sheila, powerlessness results from an interaction of personal, contextual and historical factors, and an intervention solely at the personal level is unlikely to create very much change, unless it is accompanied by more pervasive changes in her circumstances. This is not to disparage the idea of attempting to help people function more effectively in their social context, but to suggest that this is not the most immediate task if it is powerlessness that we wish to reverse. It should be noted that some writers on assertiveness recognise the contextual nature and hence the limitations of the approach (Trower 1982), or its growth at the point of transition from the political and social culture of the 1960s to the more introspective and private culture of the 1970s (Rakos 1991). Despite this, practice in the field is often far less sophisticated than the more thoughtful academic writers, and in some cases is functionally indistinguishable from the ideology of 'blaming the victim'.

A second response is the appeal to human rights, again in an untheorised way. As a typical example, a large welfare bureaucracy publishes a policy statement for its service provision to people with intellectual disability: the first section is a statement of the rights of these service users – for access to ordinary opportunities, to services that reflect individual need, for respect from staff, etc. Such statements often draw on the philosophy of normalisation/social role valorisation (Wolfensberger 1972, 1993; O'Brien 1987; O'Brien and Lyle, 1987), or on the United Nations Declaration of Human Rights. What comes next in the policy document is often in stark contradiction to the fine opening statements, for example, a financial framework and a service plan that involves most people living in four-person homes with staff rostered on a shift system, or assignment to day services on the basis of degree of disability. While service models have progressed considerably over the last 15 years (Towell 1988), we are still a long way from real inclusiveness of our most disabled citizens. While we can discount the mismatch between the rhetoric and practice of bureaucratic organisations, a similar phenomena can be found in the rhetoric and practice of individual service providers, including psychologists. Here there may be advocacy of a person's individual rights, but while this may be quite effective in preventing bad things from happening, and in some cases can improve access to various entitlements, it seldom leads to any transformation in the power relations that operate, and can paradoxically increase the reliance of the impaired person on formal services, so perpetuating powerlessness. Rights, like other concepts from the liberal tradition, can be useful in identifying the problems of a society based on social domination, but as guides to action they are of limited usefulness.

Thirdly, an emphasis on empowerment has become popular in social welfare circles since the early 1980s. As Gomm (1993) points out, it is usually vaguely defined, and like 'community' it has a generalised meaning of being a 'good thing', but specifically contradictory meanings to those of different political persuasions. There is much rhetoric about empowerment, but little real giving or sharing of power with marginalised people. While acting as a healthy critique of the power of welfare professionals (cf. Illich *et al.* 1977), the notion of empowerment can easily disguise unchanged social relations.

In these times, with socialism in retreat and the market seen as the bringer of all good things, the tendency is increasingly to identify empowerment with consumer choice in a commodity market. While there may be some gains from the curbing of monopoly power, the question remains: *how might being a consumer of services fundamentally change Sheila's experience of powerlessness?* She might have a little more clout in terms of the service system supports she requires in order to construct an identity and life that meets her various needs (see Doyal and Gough 1991), but her involvement in the social processes available to others (deformed as they are by capitalism) will still be limited by the dead weight of societal construction of her attributes, roles, relationships, and hence place. Moreover, we can, with Habermas (1987, see also Ray 1993), see the recourse to markets as the outcome of crises in the legitimation and in the steering mechanisms of the modern state, rather than any kind of a rational choice of a more effective model of meeting people's needs.

The above 'solutions' to the problem of powerlessness share a common ideological basis, 'individualism', that sees social reality in terms of the behaviour, beliefs, values, etc. of individuals. This way of seeing the world, far from being inevitable, emerged only with the emergence of the labour market, and was only labelled in the nineteenth century (Williams 1976). A consequence in psychological work has been the emphasis on power relations in the dyad, where person A exerts influence over person B, rather than on the effects of power wielded by social institutions, for example on interactions between A and B. The latter kind of multi-level set of relationships is more difficult to analyse, especially within the dominant paradigm of social psychology, where models which are both reductionistic and individualistic have been developed, some of which are fine as far as they go (e.g. French and Raven 1968), but which still fail to consider how power is produced and reproduced in an isolate-self-producing society. It has been left to non-psychologists (e.g. Lukes 1974; Wrong 1979), to analyse power more adequately.

MARXISM AND POWERLESSNESS:
POINTERS TO PSYCHOLOGICAL PRACTICE

We now want to show (all too briefly) some of the ways in which Marxist analysis can help us understand the production and reproduction of powerlessness, and suggest ways forward.

We will begin with Marx and his classical analysis of exploitation. In its full articulation (Marx [1865]1968, [1867]1976) this account has the following characteristics (we are less concerned with its accuracy as social theory than with its style of analysis):

1 It identifies the difference in power (control of the means of production versus sale of labour power) between those with different interests (classes).

2 It describes the historical development of these particular social relations.

3 It provides an account of why this exploitative relationship is not usually seen for what it is (commodity fetishism, individual contracts between property owner and labourer).

4 It describes and accounts for some of the psychological phenomena experienced by the oppressed (alienation, but also the development of consciousness as a result of 'the contradiction between the 'forces of production' and the social 'relations of production' – people work together collectively and learn new skills).

5 It makes some statements about what has to happen for these relationships to be transformed (proletarian revolution).

The above characteristics might be a reasonable set of criteria for assessing the adequacy of a theoretical approach to power and liberation. Now let us move on to more specific applications and elaborations of this framework.

Freire (1972a, b) writes on the basis of practical work with non-literate people in North Eastern Brazil. His is an explicitly liberatory educational practice that he contrasts with what he calls the 'banking' model of education, where neutral knowledge is put into passive recipients, by those who know better. Instead, for Freire, education is a 'dialogic' practice, whereby the learner assumes the role of knowing subject in dialogue with the educator, so reality is 'demythologised', as those who had been 'submerged' in oppressive social relations begin to understand these relations and the ideology that hides them, so recasting their social role with critical awareness. Freire articulates this approach against the 'culture of silence', where oppressed people are prevented from what Doyal and Gough (1984, 1991) called 'critical autonomy', the opportunity for participation in the political process. Without this, Freire suggests, people are not allowed 'to be'.

Freire (1972a, pp. 42–44) is clear that such transformations go hand in hand with changes in social relations, using the example of agrarian reform in Chile: he quotes one peasant who explains that he had not learned to read and write previously because 'I didn't even think. Neither did my friends. ... Because it wasn't possible. We lived under orders. We only had to carry out orders. We had nothing to say' (Freire 1972a, p. 43).

The process of 'conscientisation', as Freire calls the deepening awareness of both social relations and the possibility of their transformation is, then, not a magical power, or a technique, but a fundamental kind of reflection in action which underpins the work of principled social change agents.

The situation for people like Sheila is not so very different from that of the Chilean quoted earlier, and it is possible to witness a kind of conscientisation as people come to simultaneously understand their social situation and find a voice to begin altering it, for example, and in an albeit constrained way, in the self-advocacy groups and movement of people with intellectual disabilities (e.g. Williams and Shoultz 1982; Shearer 1986). Although Freire's work analyses the oppression of class and of North–South expropriation, he argues (Freire and Macedo 1993) that the other sources of oppression (race, gender) work in the same general way. While ultimately schematic and suggestive rather than providing an analysis and action orientation which we can 'lift off the shelf' and use in our context (others have developed this line of work, however, see for example McLaren and Leonard 1993) Freire develops the subjective element in Marx and Engels' classic analysis, always keeping it connected with the historical determinants of the context in which we find ourselves. We can take these ideas further by connecting them with the work of Habermas.

Habermas (e.g. 1987) is associated with the Frankfurt School of Critical Theory, another home of the subjective side of Marxism. However, Habermas combines a variety of frameworks from Western social theory, phenomenological and linguistic philosophy, and psychology (G.H. Mead and Piaget) in a 'reconstruction' of Marxist theory of society and its contradictions (see Dews 1992; Pusey 1987; Ray 1993; White 1988). While Habermas is chiefly regarded as an academic writer, he has also intervened in politics in Germany (see Holub 1991). Like Marx, Habermas starts from 'first principles' to build his social theory. He identifies three kinds of rationality, or types of references that could be made in justifying a statement:

1   To a world of events or facts, (teleological, strategic, rational choice, cognitive, or means–ends rationality – 'truth').

2   To the world of others and hence of social norms, (contextual, normative, or inter-subjective rationality – 'moral rightness').

3   To the world of personal subjectivity – and that of others – (dramaturgical or aesthetic rationality – 'authenticity').

Habermas argues that the competent human actor and speaker has access to all three of these sources of rationality, simultaneously, and that we have the capacity to select the most appropriate for interpreting a given situation. He argues that we therefore have a shared basis for intelligible communication. It is this recourse to a shared basis for the assessment of rationality that makes social interaction possible, because participants enter with two implicit expectations: that the other person's actions are intentional and that she could, if called upon, justify any claims made in interaction. Habermas postulates an *ideal speech situation* wherein coordinative speech acts are subject to such an open and equal process of justification.

Habermas connects this formal analysis of communicative pragmatics to the phenomenological concept of the shared 'lifeworld'. The lifeworld is both the social world in which we learn to become social beings, and the stored work of preceding generations. The lifeworld as a totality is not apprehended, but aspects of it are subject to critical reflection, and as that happens they become no longer part of the lifeworld as such, but part of critical consciousness. Habermas counterposes to the lifeworld, the idea of the *system*, examples of which include the capitalist economy or a bureaucratic organisation. These systems employ *steering media* – money and power, which substitute for the implicit or communicatively attained agreement among actors, in order to coordinate social activity. Under 'late-capitalism' the steering media of market and bureaucratic organisation have grown without control, increasingly governing (commodifying and bureaucratising) activities within the lifeworld which would otherwise be intrinsically bound to communicative action: this is the thesis of *colonisation of the lifeworld*.

Habermas is pointing both to contradictions in modern societies and to social pathologies resulting from them – analogous to 'alienation' (Dews 1992). Coordination of action through implicit or explicit agreement is essential for the everyday transmission of culture, social integration and the socialisation of individuals, but when such social relations become instead coordinated (colonised) by the steering media of a modern capitalist society, with their bias to strategic rationality, they become distorted, leading to a variety of individual and collective social pathologies. More specifically, Habermas reviews the trajectory of late capitalist society: Advanced capitalism defused class conflict in the sphere of production, and at the same time the public sphere has been neutralised as a site for authentic public participation. So while the social roles of employee and citizen have been delimited and curtailed, compensations have flowed via the roles of consumer and client.

Habermas has been criticised (e.g. Alvesson and Willmott 1992; Flood 1990) for having little to say about power. Yet his whole analysis is concerned with the ways in which open and democratic coordination of human action is subverted by media of power and money. His concern

with the erosion of the public sphere, although in the context of a different society from that of Freire, is also a radical concern with the preven-
tion of vast numbers of people from gaining access to the political process.
His analysis of the effects of welfare bureaucracies is also of great relevance
to the situation of people like Sheila whose already impoverished lifeworld
is further colonised and objectified by the formal and technical surrogates
for human solidarity. Both Marx and Freire wrote in social contexts very
different from our own. Habermas lives in a society much more similar to
ours, but while providing us with a comprehensive and sophisticated 'definition of the problem', he offers little in the way of an action orientation.
To address this issue we need to turn to Gramsci.

Gramsci was both a revolutionary activist and a social theorist, and he
was explicitly concerned with problems of political action and the organisation of power in a society which showed at least some of the features of
the Western democracies.

Some Marxist approaches to ideology have tended to stress the base/
superstructure metaphor, false consciousness, and conspiracy. This gives a
rather dualistic notion of ideology, seeing it as *ideas* that – while reflecting
basic class divisions – are somewhat disconnected from the fundamental
social relations, as it were standing above them as non-functional epiphenomena. Gramsci developed an alternative and more integrated approach to ideology in his *Prison Notebooks* (1971). They are not the
easiest of writing, but Williams (1973), Sassoon (1980), and Simon (1982),
among others, provide accessible discussions. Elsewhere we discuss Gramsci in relation to the radical behaviourist concept of the 'verbal community' (Burton and Kagan 1994). While in the nineteenth century order was
maintained mainly by force (the threat of starvation or violence) in modern
capitalist societies it is maintained on a day-to-day basis (although the
threat of force is always there) by the organisation of consent. Gramsci
uses the concept of *ideological hegemony* to explain how this is done. His
understanding of hegemony is not just about beliefs and ideas, but concerns the whole of society, 'saturating' it as Williams (1973, 1980) puts it,
and even defining the nature and limit of common sense. In the Gramscian view, ideology is not simply a set of ideas that can be 'read off' from
an economic base. Nor is it a world view imposed by a conspiracy master-
minded by the ruling class. Both these formulations are one-sided, and
both imply a split between the world of ideas, of beliefs, of world views, or
of subjectivity, and that of production, of practice, action, objectivity. As
Raymond Williams puts it:

> ... hegemony is not to be understood at the level of mere opinion or
> mere manipulation. It is a whole body of practices and expectations;
> our assignments of energy, ... It is a set of meanings and values which
> as they are experienced as practices appear reciprocally confirming
> (Williams 1980, p. 38).

For Gramsci, ideology acts as a kind of 'social cement', unifying a bloc of varied social groups and interests. In this, a hegemonic social group exercises leadership and power, not through crude ideological domination, but rather through the combination of key elements from the ideologies of those social groups that form an alliance or social bloc with it. Thus the Thatcher government was able to appeal to the anti-egalitarian sentiments of the skilled working class, as well as to the more traditional ideologies of middle England.

While Gramsci's analysis was constructed for explaining this kind of phenomenon, we can also use it to examine the maintenance of power relations in other social and organisational contexts. Moreover, the point of Gramsci's work is to use the theoretical understanding of domination to construct an action orientation that leads to a transformation in social relations.

A limited example of this can be seen in the widespread adoption of normalisation/social role valorisation, as formulated by Wolfensberger, O'Brien, and others, in the intellectual disability field. Much of this can be attributed to the work of activists inside and outside the formal human service system, including groups such as Values into Action CMHERA. Training workshops for human service workers have been a large part of this work, but because it has been possible to interpret developments in service provision (dispersed, small scale, ordinary housing based residential provision, for example) as exemplars, the endeavour has been articulated with other social forces (progressive aspects of social policy changes) and with a changing reality on the ground. As a result, although we do not want to overplay the robustness and sustainability of these gains, there is a new received common sense about people like Sheila, and what she might reasonably expect from life (see Burton 1989, for a detailed example of a Gramscian analysis of social and service system change). Normalisation can also be seen as a candidate for hegemonic status since it combines a variety of other ideological currents, for example those of civil rights activists, service users, professionals, families of service users, and those concerned with the cost of hospital provision, and it covers several areas of content including social inclusion and equal rights, autonomy and self-determination, and human development and educational/clinical technology.

Gramsci, then, shows us how the exercise of power suffuses civil society, so even if people are not silenced, their understanding of social reality may reflect the ideology of the hegemonic coalition. However, none of this is fixed, and because we all take part in reproducing power and ideology, we have numerous points at which we can subvert it, and join with others to construct counter-hegemonic alliances. In the case of Sheila and people in similar positions, such alliances and their ideologies must incorporate at least a majority of those individuals, groups and interests that impinge on her day-to-day experience, including family, workers including professionals and managers in a variety of organisations, and so on. The tasks of constructing such alliances for principled change are extremely complex, requiring a broad horizon and the opportunity for critical reflection as well as principled action.

IMPLICATIONS

We have considered naive attempts to tackle the problem of powerlessness, and reviewed a sample of Marxist approaches to the problem. These approaches have differences of emphasis, each has its gaps, but they are all helpful in different ways. In attempting to do something about the powerlessness of others we might try to keep the following principles in mind:

1 Power is a relative attribute: some have more than others.

2 However, power is primarily systemic in nature, tied to material relations between groups of people with irreconcilable interest.

3 Power is all around us, in our everyday practices and speech, and in our understanding of the world, and as such its exercise is greatly hidden.

4 Power decays – it has to be continually regenerated through social interaction.

5 Power is not in our gift, although we can alter social relations on a small scale to catalyse the winning of more power.

6 Power can be acquired by joining with others – the more diverse the social movement, the more powerful, but the more prone to fragmentation, and this involves sharing power.

7 Power to change things rests on a vision of what things could be like, and a criticism of the world as it is.

8 While power exists on a societal level, it (or its absence) also exists in the consciousness of individuals, and this self-perception of power can, within limits, become a self-fulfilling prophecy.

We can not prescribe a course of action: that would be bad psychology and bad Marxism, but socially responsible psychologists can use a multi-level analysis such as that sketched above to identify the most important power relations and to decide where to intervene. Beware the twin traps of individualism and social determinism: power is both systemic in nature and exercised by people (see Bhaskar 1989, p. 36), so while it can be challenged and won, and social relations transformed, this will never be done outside a broad alliance that can be mobilised for sustainable change.

REFERENCES

Alvesson, M. and Willmott, H. (1992) 'On the idea of emancipation in management and organization studies', *Academy of Management Review* 17, pp. 432–64.

Argyris, C. (1993) 'On the nature of actionable knowledge', *The Psychologist* **6** (1), pp. 29–32.

Bhaskar, R. (1989) *The Possibility of Naturalism: A Philosophical Critique of the Contemporary Human Sciences*, Hemel Hempstead: Harvester Press.

Burton, M. (1983) 'Understanding mental health services: theory and practice', *Critical Social Policy* **7**, pp. 54–74.

Burton, M. (1989) *Australian Intellectual Disability Services: Experiments in Social Change*. Working Papers in Building Community Strategies, No. 1, London: The King's Fund College.

Burton, M. (1994) 'Towards an alternative basis for policy and practice in Community Care, with particular reference to people with learning disabilities', *Care in Place: International Journal of Network and Community* **1** (2), pp. 158–74.

Burton, M. and Kagan, C. (1994) 'The Verbal Community and the Societal Construction of Consciousness', *Behavior and Social Issues* **4** (1/2), pp. 1–10.

Dews, P. (ed.) (1992) *Autonomy and Solidarity: Interviews with Jürgen Habermas*, London: Verso.

Doyal, L. and Gough, I. (1984) 'A Theory of Human Needs', *Critical Social Policy* **4**, pp. 6–38.

Doyal, L. and Gough, I. (1991) *A Theory of Human Need*, Basingstoke: Macmillan.

Flood, R.L. (1990) *Liberating Systems Theory*, New York: Plenum.

Freire, P. (1972a) *Cultural Action for Freedom*, Harmondsworth: Penguin.

Freire, P. (1972b) *Pedagogy of the Oppressed*, Harmondsworth: Penguin.

Freire, P. and Macedo, D. (1993). 'A dialogue with Paulo Freire', in McLaren, P. and Leonard, P. (eds) *Paulo Freire: A Critical Encounter* London: Routledge.

French, J.R.P. and Raven, B. (1968) 'The bases of social power', in D. Cartwright (ed.) *Studies in Social Power*, Ann Arbor: Institute for Social Research.

Gomm, R. (1993) 'Issues of power in health and welfare', in Walmsley, J., Reynolds, J., Shakespeare, P. and Woolfe, R. (eds) *Health, Welfare and Practice: Reflecting on roles and relationships*, London: Sage.

Gramsci, A. (1971) *Selections from the Prison Notebooks*, London: Lawrence and Wishart.

Habermas, J. (1987) *The Theory of Communicative Action. Volume 1: Reason and the Rationalisation of Society; Volume 2: The Critique of Functionalist Reason*, Cambridge: Polity Press.

Holub, R.C. (1991) *Jürgen Habermas: Critic in the Public Sphere*, London: Routledge.

Illich, I., Zola, I.K., McKnight, J., Caplan, J. and Shanken, H. (1977) *Disabling Professions*, London: Marion Boyars.

Lukes, S. (1974) *Power: A Radical View*, London: Macmillan.

McLaren, P. and Leonard, P. (1993) *Paulo Freire: A Critical Encounter*, London: Routledge.

Marx, K. ([1865]1976) *Wages, Price and Profit*. Reprinted in K. Marx and F. Engels, *Selected Works*, London: Lawrence and Wishart, 1968.

Marx, K. ([1867]1976) *Capital*, Harmondsworth: Penguin.

O'Brien, J. (1987) 'A guide to personal futures planning', in G.T. Bellamy and B. Wilcox (eds) *The Activities Catalogue: A Community Programming Guide for Youths and Adults with Severe Disabilities*, Baltimore: Brookes-Cole.

O'Brien, J. and Lyle, C. (1987) *Framework for Accomplishment*, Decatur, Georgia: Responsive Systems Associates.

Pusey, M. (1987) *Jürgen Habermas*, London: Tavistock.

Rakos, R.F. (1991) *Assertive Behaviour: Theory, Research, and Training*, London: Routledge.

Ray, L.J. (1993) *Rethinking Critical Theory: Emancipation in the Age of Global Social Movements*, London: Sage.

Sassoon, A.S. (1980) *Gramsci's Politics*, London: Croom Helm.

Shearer, A. (1986) *Building Community: with people with mental handicaps, their families and friends*, London: Campaign for People with Mental Handicaps and King's Fund.

Simon, R. (1982) *Gramsci's Political Thought – An Introduction*, London: Lawrence and Wishart.

Towell D. (ed.) (1988) *An Ordinary Life in Practice*, London: King Edward's Hospital Fund for London.

Trower, P. (1982) 'Toward a generative model of social skills: A critique and synthesis', in J. Curran and P. Monti (eds) *Social Skills Training: A practical handbook for assessment and treatment*, New York: Guilford Press.

White, S.K. (1988) *The Recent Work of Jürgen Habermas: Reason, Justice and Modernity*, Cambridge: Cambridge University Press.

Williams, P. and Shoultz, B. (1982) *We can speak for ourselves!* London: Souvenir Press.

Williams, R. (1973) 'Base and superstructure in Marxist cultural theory', *New Left Review* **82**, pp. 3–16.

Williams, R. (1976) *Keywords: A Vocabulary of Culture and Society*, Glasgow: Collins.

Williams, R. (1980) *Problems in Materialism and Culture*, London: Verso Editions and New Left Books.

Wolfensberger, W. (1972) *The Principle of Normalisation in Human Services*, Toronto: National Institute on Mental Retardation.

Wolfensberger, W. (1992) *A Brief Introduction to Social Role Valorization as a High-Order Concept for Structuring Human Services*, Syracuse, New York: Training Institute for Human Service Planning, Leadership and Change Agency, Syracuse University.

Wrong, D.H. (1979) *Power: Its Forms, Bases and Uses*, Oxford: Blackwell.

16

THERAPY, CONSCIOUSNESS RAISING, AND REVOLUTION

Ben Bradley and Jane Selby

Psychologists have distinctive contributions to make in the struggle for social revolution. Our aim here is to set out the practical grounds for those contributions. As such, we stand in a long tradition of people who have aimed to devise a psychology of social design (Cahan and White 1992). To date, a crucial problem has been with the subject-position taken by the designers, one which assumes solutions can be imposed from above – as in Skinner's (1946) *Walden II*. Drawing our illustrations from psychotherapy, we derive a subject position for the social designer by way of a new psychological *poetic* of change (Bradley 1994b). To define a poetic is to define a form of language that images forth reality in a distinctive way. The poetic we describe takes as central the relational quality of psychological knowledge, interpretive uncertainty and the future-determined understanding of temporal relations in mental life. This is quite at odds with the past-determined understandings now orthodox in the discipline. Only in such a form of discourse can the psychological questions raised by the push for radical social change in social theory and political debate find their appropriate practical basis. The revolutionary is not so much someone who knows what is coming next. The revolutionary is someone who knows how not to be sure what is coming next.

PSYCHOLOGY AND REVOLUTION

Roszak (1979, p. xxviii) writes:

> We live in a time when the very private experience of having a personal identity to discover, a personal destiny to fulfil, has become a subversive political force of major proportions.

Giddens (1991, p. 209ff) retorts:

> It is not the reflexive project of the self as such which is subversive; rather, the ethos of self-growth signals major social transitions in late modernity as a whole.

This is the classic stand-off between the psychologist and the social theorist, the social theorist attempting to move our attention away from the individual's personal projects to large-scale currents in society at large. Yet it is clear that in any sensibly integrated social science these two authors are accentuating two crucial but challengingly different aspects of social structure. This is particularly true for those of us who seek social change.

Social theorists certainly make progress by re-theorising one side of the internal/external divide. But in the job of reconstructing what we might also call subject/object splitting, the innovating psychologist must be given, at least provisionally, equal say. To continue to take Giddens' (1991, 1992) work as an example, we may observe how, during the 1990s, social theorists have increasingly come to dwell on topics that classically fall within the psychological domain: trust, faith, separation, uncertainty, identity, the self, reflexivity, intimacy, sexuality, the effects of childhood experience in later life and incidents from psychotherapy. But, due to his impatience with the psychological, Giddens is forced to bolster his arguments with unreconstructed theoretical ideas drawn from Erikson, Freud and Winnicott, without any apparent awareness of the efforts by psychologists critically to rethink these ideas.

In fact, the critical movement in psychology has gone much further than the reconceptualisation of old theoretical ideas. It has called into question the very image of a grand-theory expounding, fact-finding discipline, an image which still defines most versions of social theory. It is this clash which means there can be no easy melding of these neighbouring areas of work.

For us, the main upshot of the critical tradition has been to cast into stark relief a dominant and dominating way of holding forth about subjective reality in the psychology which takes the natural sciences as its model. This form of talk is epitomised by the transformation of language achieved by Charles Darwin in his mature work. Not for nothing do most walks of psychological science hail Darwin as their forefather. Darwin forged from Victorian science a way of talking about the mind which apparently did away with the interpretive ambiguities, the allegories, the self-confessedly philosophical speculation, the overt moral judgments of his predecessors in the discussion of human origins (Bradley 1994a). Darwin pioneered a subject-position which set the scientists of the mind above their subject-matter, at the same time reducing the otherness of the observed to raw material, grist for universalising explanations that made of them value-free, God-like, law-making scientists. See for example the proto-behaviouristic way in which passion is reduced to dispositions of muscular contraction in Darwin's (1872) book on emotions. There is a parallel here to Wordsworth's creation of the so-called egotistical sublime – in which the reader is invited to share in a vision of Nature otherwise only available to the all-seeing eyes of genius (Bradley 1993, in prep.).

Scholars have shown that Darwin's appropriation of evolutionary theory stood against a tradition in which evolutionary ideas were explicitly, if allegorically, linked to the push for social revolution (Desmond and Moore 1991; Bradley 1994a). Behind Darwin stretches a long-suppressed poetic of radical thought about femininity, psychology, social change and the mind. This is the tradition of psychology in which we understand Marx and his colleagues, at least in their *Theses on Feuerbach*, to have written. Viewed in the round, it is a tradition where psychological terms jostle unashamedly with a politics which grapples to explain and change what Kierkegaard in particular, but also Blake, Wollstonecraft, Swift and Freud, called the 'repetitions' of human experience:

> Every man's [sic] life is an imperfect sort of circle, which he repeats and runs over every day; he has a set of thoughts, desires and inclinations, which return upon him in their proper time and order, and will very hardly be laid aside, to make room for anything new and uncommon (Swift 1745; quoted in Bradley 1989, p. 46).

Insofar as the revolutionary tradition has been unsuccessful, this imperfect circle of repetitions has subverted the social changes being fought for – repetitions of self-oppression in the face of new material opportunities. To persist with a poetic of social science consonant with Darwin's is to court just this kind of subversion. The social scientist will then just perpetuate the imperfect cycle of relations between power and knowledge typical of their day. What is needed instead is a poetic which recognises the social construction, the provisionality, the uncertainty of knowledge about social circumstances, a poetic that makes room for what Swift calls the new and the uncommon. Such a poetic is instanced by the therapist-researcher's use of the counter-transference.

THE UNCERTAINTY OF INTERPRETATION

The practical problems inhering in the model of psychology as a branch of Darwinian biology – the psychologist having a direct, unmediated and objective way of seeing Nature which reduces the pluralistic universe of otherness to a flattened explicandum – had to be thoroughly worked out by those who most intensively face the problems of interpreting others as others, namely, psychologists who talk with the mentally ill.

In this section we show how the psychological or egotistical sublime epitomised by Darwin must collapse when the therapist/psychiatrist who is (mis)taken for 'the one who is supposed to know' understands their role in the therapeutic process as part of what psychoanalysts call 'the counter-transference'. An understanding of counter-transference allows us to emphasise the need in psychology to emphasise the plethora of future possibilities which makes us unable alone to direct or judge particular individual fates or feelings. Other- or client-centred discourses provide a practical basis for the inspiration of social and political endeavour where the individual is not expertly judged or knowledgeably imposed upon.

Rather, possibilities of understanding are opened up through which individuals may together find themselves.

There are two ways of viewing counter-transference: one negative, one positive. Freud ([1910]1957) defined counter-transference as what 'arises in [the analyst] as a result of the patient's influence on his [sic] unconscious feelings'. He claimed that the most notable amongst these feelings were the analyst's 'own complexes and internal resistances'. In fact, Freud only discussed counter-transference in the negative – as a problem, a source of error, as feelings causing the doctor's professional 'neutrality' and 'authority' to waver toward treating the patient's 'fond feelings' and fantasies about the analyst as for real, for example, by returning them in kind, by physically gratifying the patient's 'craving for love'.

Alternatively it has been urged that counter-transference 'not only does not inhibit, but, on the contrary, actually facilitates analytic work' (Hann-Kende in Devereux 1953, p. 167). Thus Laplanche and Pontalis (1973, p. 92) define the counter-transference as 'the whole of the analyst's unconscious reactions to the individual analysand (especially to the analysand's own transference)'. Seen thus, the counter-transference gives the most important basis for any interpretation the analyst offers, for any finding she or he makes about analysands, whether working with individuals or groups. Interpreters are inevitably directed by their feelings. Thus we find Bion (1961) hypothesising that groups often unwittingly adopt a primitive phantasy that they depend for their achievements on a leader because Bion found he felt uncomfortable in certain group-situations when he did not act as a leader; for example, when he tried to remain silent.

How are these two conflicting views to be reconciled? Relke (1993) argues that the term is being used to embrace two different processes. The first is a form of distortion resulting from the analyst's personal rigidities, theoretical or emotional. The second process is what Relke calls 'intersubjectivity', 'intuition' or 'empathy' – as when Hann-Kende (in Devereux 1953, p.164) speaks of counter-transference as 'the prompt correspondence between the analyst's and the patient's unconscious'.

Now, however they define their terms, *all* psychoanalysts recognise *both* these processes. Freud ([1910]1957) may have talked in a negative way of counter-transference, as something that 'holds back from his consciousness what has been perceived by his unconscious'. But, as this quote implies, he also recognised another (unnamed) process with which the counter-transference interferes. This is a fundamental form of unconscious communication, a form of communication which necessarily occurs when all goes as it should – with the patient free-associating and with the doctor's 'free-floating attention' following what Freud called the main rule for psychoanalysts, viz:

> To put it in a formula: [the analyst] must turn his [sic] own unconscious like a receptive organ towards the transmitting unconscious of the patient. He must adjust himself to the patient as a telephone receiver is adjusted to the transmitting microphone. Just as the receiver

converts back into sound-waves the electric oscillations in the telephone line which were set up by sound-waves, so the doctor's unconscious is able, from the derivatives of the unconscious which are communicated to him, to reconstruct that unconscious, which has determined the patient's free associations ([1912]1957, pp. 115–16).

We are talking here of metaphors and attempts to describe and understand how we come to think we understand someone else. Contrary to Freud, Moeller (1977) defines the negative process that Freud called countertransference as the analyst's *transference*, reserving the word counter-transference for 'an undistorted, appropriate (i.e. non-neurotic) response to transference' – a synonym for the empathy or 'sympathetic understanding' (Relke 1993, p. 95) which Freud saw as founding therapy. In the view typified by Moeller (whose terminology we will now adopt) the analyst's transference is an intra-psychic process, whilst counter-transference is inter-psychic or inter-personal. Both analyst and patient may experience both transference and counter-transference. In fact, pioneers Hann-Kende and Deutsch both illustrated the existence of counter-transference by describing incidents from therapy in which *patients* demonstrated accurate knowledge *of their analysts* that could only have been acquired non-rationally, mystically even, by what Deutsch called an occult process and Hann-Kende called telepathy (in Devereux 1953). (Freud had earlier given similar examples which he had described as 'telepathy' or 'unconscious thought-transfer'; see Devereux 1953.)

The key question for the practice of therapy and consciousness-raising is whether what Moeller called the analyst's transference is always distinguishable from their 'counter-transference'. Are these genuinely independent processes? And can they always be told apart? Freud's attitude to training assumed that they could. The trained analyst would be able to tell the pathological part (transference) from the healthy part (the counter-transference) of their own, initially unconscious, emotional response to the client.

Others disagree. For instance, Little (1951, p. 33) said that, 'every transference and every counter-transference is different from every other'. A therapist may sometimes be helped in identifying the false component of their reaction to clients by their previous experiences, self-analysis and, if they are psychoanalytically trained, their own didactic analysis. But only an impossibly omniscient analyst-researcher could be expected *always* to be pre-aware of her or his blind spots and unconscious quirks. Furthermore, as an incident described by Heimann (1960, pp. 13–14) suggests, what the analyst's own self-examination may see as an emotional reaction which does not relate to the client's therapy (i.e. as the analyst's transference) may nevertheless, if revealed to the client, function as a productive therapeutic intervention, that is, as counter-transference!

Immediately before a session with a young analysand, I learnt of the death of an analyst and was profoundly affected. I considered whether I should cancel the session, but it was too late. The analysand began her session as usual. Twice I could not follow her and asked what she had said. When this happened the second time, she apologised, and said she must be very unclear today and something must be wrong with her. I then said that the fault was mine, and mentioned that I had just heard of the analyst's death. The young analysand, who had not had any personal contact with him, expressed her regrets, adding that she knew how much this must mean to me. The analysis which followed dealt with the theme of my mourning, which had specific and high relevance in view of the patient's history ... As I later examined the situation, I saw possibilities of dealing with the situation without making such a personal communication as I did make. I acted as I did because I was disturbed.

Relke remarks that Heimann had no need to be apologetic about her 'deviation from sound analytic procedure' because her self-disclosure functioned as a 'highly successful intervention'. Yet what Heimann disclosed was not by any mark identifiable to her at that time as being of inter-personal origin. Certainly Heimann herself viewed it as personal business, irrelevant to the therapy, that is, as what we have been calling her transference. It was to do with her own libidinal attachment to the dead analyst, her own form of mourning, her personal priorities. Her inattention was not counter-transference, as defined by Moeller and Relke. It was apparently of intra-psychic origin. Yet in retrospect we must define it as counter-transference because of its success as an intervention.

Of course, because of its success, we may wonder whether Heimann's feelings did have some inter-personal components. Perhaps, for example, her feelings of mourning, and her wish to disclose them, were heightened by the (unconscious) knowledge that her analysand was someone for whom maternal mourning was important. But this does not detract from the two points of the illustration: first, what appeared to the analyst to be her own personal preoccupation, her transference, may nonetheless function productively as counter-transference when communicated to the client; second, the only sure sign that an analyst's feelings are counter-transference is their subsequent therapeutic success.

To us, everything the analyst says must be based at first on transference, however well the transference is sifted:

> Any analyst who believes that he [sic] perceives *directly* his patient's unconscious, rather than his own, is deluding himself ... It is the analysis of *his* unconscious which he presents to her [sic] as an analysis of *her* unconscious ... (Devereux 1968, pp. 304 –5).

There is no firm way to know beforehand which interpretation is going to be on target and which wide of the mark. The definition of what is true or false about an interpretation can only be determined after the client has reacted to it (sometimes decades after, as Freud [1937]1957, argued). What

Relke and co. call the counter-transference is simply a way of registering that interpretations, which are inevitably based on the analyst's self-analysis of his or her own feelings and thoughts about the client-subject, sometimes work. Put in Relke's language, the analyst's intra-psychic reactions to the client (transference) sometimes have inter-personal validity. But the analyst-researcher *cannot know in advance* of any particular interpretation when or whether this will be the case (Selby 1990).

We find in therapy, therefore, an attitude on behalf of the practitioner that stands in marked contrast to the universalising, law-giving, quasi-divine aspirations of authors who take as their model *On the Origin of Species*. For the analyst/therapist/psychologist may set as a goal or contract with the client/analysand to work together to understand the client's psyche, but the achievement of this goal is never inevitable, no matter how experienced and well trained the therapist. The psychologist's work must always be tentative, its significance being subject to later developments. Far from being determined by events in the past, the significance of what happens in the present of therapy will be determined by events yet to unfold in the future. If it is true, in consciousness-raising and psychotherapy, that 'individuals are likely to reskill themselves in greater depth where consequential transitions in their lives are concerned or fateful decisions are to be made' (Giddens 1991, p. 7), then it is only the subsequent fate of our work as psychologists that will determine where and when consequential transitions have been made.

ANN

What do we hear in therapy? We hear of babes in the wood. We hear of Cinderella, the girl whose parents died when she was small and who was brought up by an evil stepmother. We hear about the revenges of a baby prince whose father had him nailed to a hillside and left to die. We hear about children at the mercy of merciless parents. And of magical solutions. We hear of Ann, 22, who sought help for bulimia, for which sin she had twice been put in hospital. She binged, puked, was chronically constipated. This was endangering her life as well as her career.

A crisis in her therapy occurred when she remembered having been sexually abused by her father. She had always 'known' in some superficial way that something had happened in childhood, at five, but had made almost unknown what her father had done to her. Then it was as if the floodgates were opened, and Ann would rapidly make links between her physical symptoms and the past. In a session typical of these discoveries, she talked of how in vomiting she had just come to realise that it was 'because of oral sex with Father from five years, vomiting part of trying to get it all out, the gagging'.

But she had always been close to her father. Until her flashbacks started she was on the phone to him every week. Now she saw that this closeness had been closely nurtured. He had always told her she was 'bad',

that everyone, including her mother, hated her, and now she knew the
only way that *he* would not hate her was for her to do these things in the
night with him. In a later session, she said, whilst it was important to
talk, she was terrified. When asked what of: 'All the pain, I'm frightened
that I can't cope with all the pain.' And rather than reassure her in some
way and stop the experience of not coping, the therapist took the uncertain route of risking the uncopable, the disintegration, without knowing
what would happen. Ann was eventually enabled to draw into herself,
crying, very sad, just saying things occasionally for the rest of the session,
a curled up five-year-old, seeing her father's face, experiencing her father's
body, a man now seen as a monster, now as the person she loves most in
the world.

Here we meet someone at a turning-point in their life. This kind of
moment is significant, less for what was remembered than for what
enables that memory and for what becomes possible. Ann's 'memory',
whether one views it as veridical or constructed with her therapist, is part
and parcel of a new and profoundly felt uncertainty about how to go
forward in her life. That which manifests itself most obviously as a new
memory, is simultaneously a moment when language and understanding
cease to be yoked solely to the repetition of a status quo and becomes
reorganised in the light of the possibility of living in a different and
yet-to-be-defined way. Ann not only lives the 'something that happened
when she was five' in a much different way than hitherto, but while she
painfully experiences this 'something', the more articulate *meaning* of her
realisation will ultimately be determined in her future by the way in which
she does or does not try to change her life, by the way she manages and
fails in bringing the monster and lover together into one discourse, without self-destruction, without overwhelming pain. What kind of turning-
point will this turn out to have been?

Further, if we now 'zoom out' and talk of historical 'moments' (such as
the 'moment' of *Capital*), Ann stands not just at a personal turning-point.
She stands at a turning-point for her culture. And here too, we must ask:
what kind of turning-point will this turn out to have been? And what role
will psychologists have played in bringing about whatever state of affairs
will have occurred today from the vantage-point of posterity? Will our age
turn out to have been merely more of the same, or will it be the harbinger
of a social-subjective reorganisation that will have cast in a new and more
comprehending light the plight of Ann and the multitude like her, of a
society in which the endemic sexual and emotional abuse of children has
begun to become a thing of the past? Can psychology only be an onlooker
in the processes of social transformation, or might it help to ring the bells
of change?

Our answer to these questions is that we psychologists must seek a
change as much in the form our language of mind as in its immediate
content. If we are to break the cycle of repetition, in our teaching, our
research, our writing, our domestic/political lives, we must make room in our
speech for the uncertainty whose sense is not fixed by fiat but yet-to-be-

determined, a space open to a future that may be 'new and uncommon'. Our critiques can quickly become a too-rigid and apparently all-knowing denouncement of the status quo in defence against the anxiety of an unease that knows something is wrong, but does not know what. Likewise, Ann had 'known' all along that 'something had happened in childhood, at age five'. She may even have remembered that it had something to do with her parents. She may even have mentioned it to friends. But there was something wrong with the way she remembered and spoke about it. Her pre-flashback 'memories' formed part of a false series. What was true about her past was to be determined by the light of events which were still in a future where she would feel things and see things which had previously been locked off by the oblivious compulsion of self-abuse. The key to the lock was the 'negative' capability of a therapeutic situation that could hold her ignorance, her pain and uncertainty, without an irritable grasping after quick solutions or soothing denials.

CONCLUSION

Rosa Luxemburg once said that a lasting revolution will not be won with bayonets and barricades: it will come from small and subtle changes in our everyday lives. The changes we have tried to suggest for psychology may be subtle, perhaps, but are also central designs for revolution. Just as the therapeutic situation creates circumstances where uncertainty can surface and be oriented toward a changed future, so can psychology become that discursive space which frees up social process for transformation. For psychology to be enabled to create such a space requires that psychologists, whether critical or scientific, should in all the occasions of their practice, entirely alter the poetic – the way of imaging forth reality – that has dominated our work. We need to learn how to constitute between subjects a situation where psychologists play in discourse, whether of teaching, therapy, research or informal conversation, the role of a not-knowing, holding attentiveness – as in a kind of negative theology of knowledge – quite at odds with the universalising positive theology pioneered by Darwin. And we need to act so that this way of being can be resumed by our others with their others.

To this end we have outlined a synthesis of debates between us and within the fora of critical and feminist psychology. We point out how social theory needs psychological language. The reduction of subjectivity to social structures which themselves implicate psychological processes is as arbitrary as reducing social structure to subjectivity. In either case psychological discourses are needed and must be appraised. We argue that a psychology based in the practice of therapy and consciousness-raising must explore understanding in communication as an uncertain procedure that can point to possibilities and futures, but not dictate them. Only in this form of discourse can the psychological questions raised by the push for radical social change in social theory and political debate find their appropriate practical foundation.

REFERENCES

Bion, W.R. (1961) *Experiences in Groups*, London: Methuen.
Bradley, B.S. (1989) *Visions of Infancy: A Critical Introduction to Child Psychology*, Cambridge: Polity Press.
Bradley, B.S. (1993) 'A Serpent's Guide to Children's "Theories of Mind"', *Theory and Psychology* 3, pp. 497–521.
Bradley, B.S. (1994a) 'Darwin's Intertextual Baby: Erasmus Darwin as Precursor in Child Psychology', *Human Development*, 37(2), pp. 86–102.
Bradley, B.S. (1994b) 'Why Revolutionaries Need a New Psychological Poetic: Reply to Valsiner', *Theory and Psychology* 4(1), pp. 151–4.
Bradley, B.S. (in prep.) *The New Psychology: Poetics for a New Vision of Mental Life*.
Cahan, E. and White, S. (1992) 'Proposals for a Second Psychology', *American Psychologist* 47(2), pp. 224–35.
Darwin, C.R. (1872) *The Expression of the Emotions in Man and Animals*, London: Murray.
Desmond, A.J. and Moore, A.J. (1991) *Darwin*, London: Michael Joseph.
Devereux, G. (ed.) (1953) *Psychoanalysis and the Occult*, New York: International Universities Press.
Devereux, G. (1968) *From Anxiety to Method in the Behavioural Sciences*, The Hague: Mouton.
Freud, S. ([1910]1957) 'The Future Prospects of Psycho-Analytic Therapy', in J. Strachey (ed.) *The Standard Edition of the Writings of Sigmund Freud, vol. x*, London: Hogarth.
Freud, S. ([1912]1957) 'Recommendations to Physicians Practising Psycho-Analysis', in J. Strachey (ed.) *The Standard Edition of the Writings of Sigmund Freud, vol. xi*, London: Hogarth.
Freud, S. ([1937]1957) 'Constructions in Analysis', in J. Strachey (ed.) *The Standard Edition of the Writings of Sigmund Freud, vol. xxiii*, London: Hogarth.
Giddens, A.J. (1991) *Modernity and Self-Identity*, Cambridge: Polity Press.
Giddens, A.J. (1992) *The Transformation of Intimacy*, Cambridge: Polity Press.
Heimann, P. (1960) 'Counter-Transference', *British Journal of Medical Psychology*, 33, pp. 9–15.
Laplanche, J. and Pontalis, J.-B. ([1973]1967) *The Language of Psycho-Analysis* (trans. D. Nicholson-Smith) London: Hogarth Press.
Little, M. (1951) 'Counter-Transference and the Patient's Response to it', *International Journal of Psychoanalysis, 32*, pp. 32–40.
Moeller, M.L. 1977) 'Self and Object in Countertransference', *International Journal of Psychoanalysis*, 58, pp. 365–74.
Relke, D.M.A. (1993) 'Foremothers Who Cared: Paula Heimann, Margaret Little and the Female Tradition in Psychoanalysis', *Feminism and Psychology*, 3, pp. 89–109.

Roszak, T. (1979) *Person-Planet*, London: Gollancz.
Selby, J.M. (1990) 'Uncertainty in Counselling and Psychology', in *Proceedings of the Third National Conference of the Alcohol and Drug Foundation*, Brisbane: Drug and Alcohol Foundation.
Skinner, B.F. (1946) *Walden II*, New York: Macmillan.

17

PARTICIPANT ACTION RESEARCH: MYTHS AND FALLACIES

Bernardo Jiménez-Domínguez

How might critical psychology work in practice? Does action research provide the basis for both understanding and changing the world? This chapter explores one of the most radical forms of action research – a form developed in Latin America to deal with problems posed to psychologists by difficult political circumstances – and argues that there are a number of enduring problems in this framework which critical psychologists must take into account.

In the 1980s, Participant Action Research (PAR) became the preferred methodology proposed by the 'new social psychology' in Latin America as a way of solving questions over the role of socio-political commitments made by researchers in community interventions. The new approach which used PAR was termed 'community social psychology', and was designed to be a radical community psychology which would go beyond the criticisms of Anglo-Saxon versions of psychology and integrate, in theory and practice, the fields of environmental and political psychology (see Quintanilla 1980; Marín 1980–83; Sanguinetti 1981; Montero 1983; Jiménez 1983; Carvajal 1984; Grupo Acción Psicología Social 1984).

In a previous paper (Jiménez 1991) I have described how we developed the concept of Participant Action Research from the militant sociology of the 1970s, but without adding almost anything from a social psychological perspective bar some critical recognition of its origins in the work of Kurt Lewin. I will review some of the criticisms which were presented in the 'World Symposium on Active Research and Scientific Analysis' in Cartagena in 1977, and developed after that symposium during the 1980s.

POPULAR SCIENCE APPROACH

In Participant Action Research, theory is substituted by an ethics of action and commitment, which undoubtedly can produce activism but does not necessarily produce knowledge. The method then comes to replace theory and, regardless of the ethics of commitment (which pretends to go beyond positivism), it cannot avoid falling back into a populist empiricism, albeit with a militant liberation discourse which covers its conceptual emptiness. According to Parra, in his book describing the evolution of the PAR Group 'La Rosca' (1983) in Colombia, 'Active research does not pretend to provide a theoretical construction alone, but grasps objective reality for human and social liberation.' Liberation rhetoric here excuses them from any serious theoretical reflection. This was an issue which was included in their self-criticisms when they recognised that an intellectual attempting to become a political cadre overlooked the reflection which was necessary to the Participant Action Research process in practice. The recognition that this practice must entail *some* theoretical reflection led them to a hasty adoption of Marxism, but so hasty that it showed that any other convenient or fashionable theoretical approach could have been adopted a posteriori. Because in Participant Action Research we are specifically referring to a kind of 'technique' not to a method, a mere technique of inquiry, as Briones (1978) says, in which commitment is seen as a bridge for solving theory–practice relations, theoretical production is replaced with idealisations. Such is the case in the adoption of a simplistic solidarity ideology with the working classes emphasising politics as an explanatory variable, treating it as equivalent to the economic structure and avoiding the fundamental fact of exploitation. In this moral version of Marxism, which neglects an understanding of economic structure, ideology and false consciousness, instead of classes there are merely 'oppressed groups'. Knowledge is thereby reduced to Utopian-humanistic objectives, and history is transformed from a materialist account into a teleological orientation in search of justice, liberty and human development (Molano 1978).

Kalmanovitz's critique (1983) of Dependency Theory, which is very close to Participant Action Research in its teleological 'ethical finalist' aspects, correctly points to the static logic of the 'dependentists' for whom the world economy is seen as a sort of 'superior will' and imperialism an 'overdetermined demiurge'. Understanding the world in terms of a moral imperative in this way leads the researcher to prejudge any empirical investigation. An analysis which focuses on the evils of the system (because it must be so, theologically speaking) is insufficient for understanding *why* it is that way. Kalmanovitz's critique applies both to the dependentists and to Participant Action Research. He argues that a normative view (derived from commitment) replaces an account of the causal process of development, and this view then contributes very little to an analysis of relations and contradictions of the social formation. History, in these cases, is reduced to the researcher's own goals, for otherwise, once either of these frameworks has been adopted, there is no place for causality or rationality. The problem is that history does not follow *our* individual final rational goals and, in order to change history more than 'moral' imperatives are needed. As Kalmanovitz points out, workers' liberation is not a simple matter of social justice or human redemption.

It has been said that the most typical negative outcome of Participant Action Research is atheoretical *activism*, a political and ideological stance which ends up working to the detriment of knowledge. This can then lead, because of frustrations on the part of the researcher working without an adequate theoretical framework, to the trivialisation of research. Demo (1985) sees the evil 'conspirator capitalism' vision of Participant Action Research as excessively moralist. Social transformation is possible and, from a dialectical perspective, is a necessary part of history, but for sure it is not produced by pure enthusiasm.

Now, in this new socio-political context which afflicts us all, Participant Action Research needs to take account of the specific characteristics of the present conjuncture in order to avoid the replacement of theory with idealisations. The idealisation of 'unstable concepts' (Pereda 1990) such as 'the masses', 'proletariat', 'the people', and so on, also facilitates ideological manipulation. This idealisation pretends to give them a reality, but it is one which is infused with illusions about their ideal potential. This idealisation stabilises social categories and reduces reality and possibilities to their present and autonomous existence. As Baudrillard (1978) stresses, this existence is one of silence, the 'silent majorities' that refuse to accept the imposed meanings and keep themselves in sheer inertia. Instead of political consciousness and engagement, the masses today resist through a stubborn refusal to participate. Abstentionism and inertia can become a form of resistance, floating between passivity and spontaneity, irreducible to any conventional theory and practice. The political language of the 1970s in Participant Action Research does not fit with this present moment of what Pipitone (1991) calls 'the third conservative wave'. Now we need to develop a critical but renewed approach. This is not only because of the novelty of this new political situation that we are faced with, but also because words tend to lose their meaning with ritualistic and excessive repetition. Moreover, the old words are associated with wasted projects in a moment of disenchantment when neoliberalism is presented as the only way out from the difficulties of reorganising the world in these times of disorientation and crisis.

It should be pointed out that, although this 'new-liberal' perspective works as an aspirin, problems are of such magnitude that everything points against neoliberal assertions. We are being driven towards more and not less organisation of everyday and institutional life, at the level of international relations, in the economy, and, above all, in ecology. This brings onto the present agenda the action of specific, democratic, self-managed social movements, because contemporary disenchantment is also with the traditional forms of doing politics.

PARTICIPANT ACTION RESEARCH METHOD

Participant Action Research method is the response of a group of intellectuals to the need for linking research into social reality with social transformation, which means doing militant research. This is the case for one of the more important and recognised groups, 'La Rosca' (see Parra 1983), whose best known and most often quoted author by social psychologists in Latin America is Orlando Fals-Borda (see Martín-Baró 1989; Montero 1990).

It is commonly accepted that Participant Action Research comes from action research as it was known in Sociology and Anthropology and in the Social Psychology of Kurt Lewin. But if we go back in time, we find that it was an English public official serving as Commissioner for Indian Affairs in the 1930s who was the first to use the expression 'action research' to emphasise the importance of research in social planning, and the need for involvement not only by civil servants but also by citizens creatively contributing to the decisions derived from that planning (Pareek 1978). We have to recognise the Anglo-Saxon origin of Participant Action Research, as well as its relationship with Protestant methods of indoctrination and its derived community participation in the local solution of its own problems which follow the American tradition. This tradition then has been all too easily extrapolated to the present day when the poorest and most powerless communities are the focus of action. We find once more, the construction of a social space for 'charity' and humanitarian 'compassion'.

In this context, Community Psychology and Psychiatry appeared in 1963 in the United States through the Community Mental Health Center Act during the Kennedy Government, deinstitutionalising the mental health problem and, in the process, institutionalising the social problems from which these originated *in* the community. This is the best form of therapy, for the government, for relieving all kind of problems, by developing optimism, promoting solidarity links, and encouraging trust in the government agencies. Apart from this, the word 'community' itself has a clear ideological function thanks to the multiplicity of meanings it has; when talking, for example, about 'community participation' as meaning collaboration with government, and when a geographical area is defined on the basis of poverty and lack of services and is labelled as a 'community' to make it appear to be an isolated phenomenon with its own dynamics and dependent on external help if it is to be integrated in the world of progress. 'Community' could be any number of things – animal community, Indian community, European community, academic community, town, village, nation, parish. And maybe this last sense, the sense of parish, is the dominant meaning in the light of its Protestant roots and kinship (Jiménez 1983).

According to Fals-Borda (1973), the difference between traditional action research and Participant Action Research is that the former was considered to be insufficient to link a liberating theory with a corresponding practice. He created the concept of 'insertion' ('*inserción*') to mean that the scientist must be an active agent in the investigative process, like a militant in a movement with explicit political goals. He acknowledges having been influenced by Mao and Giap, influences which are easily traced in the concept of 'militant-observation' and which led this methodological alternative to be criticised as populist, and its members to be seen as 'barefoot theorists' (Molano 1978). Nowadays, nobody would present this as a model to follow after the tragicomedy of the Chinese Cultural Revolution.

We could ask what the difference is between political activism and
Participant Action Research, given that 'La Rosca' recognised that the
former dominated the latter, and argued that the real achievements were
basically produced in the field of education and political consciousness. As
Demo (1985) stresses, although Participant Action Research begins with a
critique of the deficiencies of traditional research in order to then go
beyond them, it is sometimes difficult to see what the specific *research*
component is in Participant Action Research, because what we really find
is a process of learning which merely transmits and reproduces existing
commonsense knowledge, rather than creates theoretically illuminating
knowledge. In that sense, Participant Action Research is not much different from consciousness-raising in active education.

Fals-Borda *et al.* (1972) counterposes his 'insertion' version of Participant Action Research to unfocused interventions in which official groups
may use PAR to manipulate communities, and political groups with an
inadequate approach will then fall prey to such propaganda. This supposes
that his notion of 'insertion' is so well focused that the militant researcher
will be neither manipulative nor propagandistic. However, even if this were
true and the researcher really 'ascends to the people', as Fals-Borda and 'La
Rosca' claim, it is still quite possible that they will mystify popular knowledge by confusing collective memory and historical truth. In this sense
Participant Action Research confirms its empiricist background by looking
for the 'truth' in communities, rather like playing hide-and-seek, and then
gives it back to them, once it has been systematised. This is an old trick
in psychology. It is important to point out once again that a researcher
does not 'discover' history in a direct way, even though they may appear to
by virtue of the power granted by their specialised knowledge. It is this
power that makes all the difference, and which allows an all the more
sophisticated manipulation, in which the researcher, covered by the discourse of community 'participation', makes the objects of inquiry *believe*
that they are subjects.

It can also happen, of course, that the community manipulates the
researcher in turn because it is convenient, and lets the researcher lead the
process. The researcher with a fundamentally political interest can then
end up talking on behalf of the community due to a very strong feeling of
identification derived from what they think is their 'successful' community
insertion. This situation can easily lead to the political authoritarianism
which is so close to militantism in Latin America. Fals-Borda's notion of
'insertion' is thus derived from a militant conception, but is carried out by
a research group with an idealised view of political commitment with
popular organisations. 'La Rosca' thus ended up substituting itself for
popular organisations and even discussed the possibility of becoming a
political movement (a process described by Parra 1983). At this moment
the differences between researcher and their object are wished away, and
Participant Action Research becomes pure activism, giving total priority to
practice over theory. At this point, according to Pareek (1978), criticisms
from the Left and the University are inevitable; the Left demands stronger

action and the University want more rigorous research. It is in this circuit of desire and power that Participant Action Research can end up being trapped.

PAR IN PSYCHOLOGY

Returning to psychology, where Participant Action Research developments are really vague, we can find well known authors including it in their psychology of liberation projects, albeit with some criticisms. In the case of Martín-Baró calling for political psychology in Latin America (1988), he said

> I myself defended and still maintain the value of PAR as an alternative to positivism ... although I have to accept that I know very few relevant cases in which this methodology has been applied, and it often has been less than ideal. My own experience also leads me to recognise that until now a coherent integration between the instruments used by the neopositivism (undoubtedly useful, but which has not necessarily been linked with its principles), and the epistemological principles in which PAR is based has not been achieved, something which creates additional problems for the validity of the products which have been obtained.

Martín-Baró also insisted that we should take seriously the difference between the partiality of commitment and the objectivity of knowledge.

Maritza Montero (1991) warns about the confusions generated by Participant Action Research in the forms recently rediscovered by some writers. Some attribute PAR to Kurt Lewin, others to Martín-Baró, and Montero argues that its muddled diffusion, adoption and practice could be explained by way of the following points:

1   The required commitment is so intense that even with the best will it can hardly be accomplished.

2   It is not applicable indiscriminately to any psychosocial problem and it is not useful for each and every situation.

3   Many people still do not understand what it really is and so they actually often end up using traditional methods.

It is clear that both Martín-Baró and Montero share a common methodological interest when they question the possible validity of the products of Participant Action Research, and they reject a wholesale Manichean schism between methods. Regarding this point it is relevant to quote the sharp critique by Cano (1988), who makes a distinction between method, technique and *mode* of research. Mode is more linked to the technical aspects of methodology, but it is not so much a procedure (or quality of the technique), as a means for contrasting data with theory. The mode guides the logic of research while the method guides the logic of the proof. In this view Participant Action Research could be seen as more a mode than a method. Participant Action Research is presented as qualitative in nature, and this has led practitioners of the approach to neglect the form in which the effects and conditions of change act, because the active researcher makes do with an intersubjective *agreement* of the process. There is no assessment, qualitative or otherwise, of the *level* of agreement. The different roles played by the active researcher as counsellor, animator, educator and concept-builder, also makes project evaluation difficult. The specificity of the meanings of Participant Action Research must be articulated in relation to some theoretical framework, and its usefulness for producing new knowledge identified. In that way a reflection on the specifics of the practice of research can be made. As Cano stresses, the modes and techniques must be subordinated to the research problem and not the problem to the modes of research. It is not possible to adopt a particular methodology in an abstract way regardless of the nature of the problem to be addressed. These remarks point to the pragmatic character which Participant Action Research could eventually have.

TOWARD PARTICIPANT ACTION RESEARCH ACTUALISATION

Participant Action Research and Lewin's action research are not different things. If we take the militant clothes off the first and the scientific ones off the other, they are basically similar projects. If we take this similarity to heart, we must then critically revalue Lewin's proposal in social psychology. In the same way, 'participatory research', or 'militant-action research', or 'intervention-research', or 'action in research', or Participant Action Research must not be overvalued at the methodological level, nor transformed as an alternative panacea, but must be taken as it is, as a limited and sometimes useful tool. It is a mode of intervention into social problems focused on small populations, with the premise of self-managed participation of the community with the collaboration and assessment of social science professionals. Action research in general in psychology is still fairly vague, as is also the problem of its links with alternative theoretical paradigms.

What we should discard from any variety of action research are oversimple notions of activism and so-called 'deprofessionalisation'. First, political activism is valid in itself and desirable for psychologists but does not need to be called social psychology or action research. If the terms are muddled in that way they can end up being mutually invalidated. Secondly, what has been ambiguously labelled as 'deprofessionalisation' often amounts to little more than the Maoist claim that it is possible to give 'science to the people'. This supposes that the knowledge coming from psychological theories is relevant and useful for solving problems of the poor, and that giving it to them is a progressive act, without thinking that it could be the opposite; a way of causing indigestion, even poisoning and, for sure, fooling them with ideologically contaminated and theoretically irrelevant products.

It cannot be denied that, independently of training and orientation, a conscious and experienced professional or intellectual with experience and understanding of a problem, can contribute creative and innovative concepts and methods. What is needed is what Foucault has called a 'specific intellectual', one who fights in terms of their own intellectual experience based on their own effective professional work. This allows them to be a *transformative* intellectual, as has been proposed in the field of radical education. Foucault, in his dialogue with Fontana, makes it clear that it is not possible any more to talk of an intellectual as being committed to universal values, rather they should be thought of as someone with a specific position linked to the general functions of the regimes of truth in capitalist societies (Jiménez 1988). This proposal is in line with a disenchantment with holistic currents and objectivist reductionisms (Zamora 1990), and it has forced an emphasis on subjectivity and everyday life as a field of study, an emphasis which presupposes an implicit critique. The psychosocial study of everyday life must create a wider and more dynamic framework for going beyond dichotomies between social structure and quantitative methods on the one hand, and everyday life and qualitative approaches on the other, for analysing action and the social reality of what Zamora (1990) calls, a 'social tridimensionality', that is, subjects in their subjectivity and singularity, in particular social contexts and in structured institutions.

The current multidisciplinary interest in everyday life, in its vagueness and conceptual indefinition, can be explained, as Lechner (1990) argues, by disenchantment with everyday life itself and with traditional ways of doing politics. In this sense, a new multidisciplinary or 'socially tridimensional' approach must operate as a critique of quotidian life but also of non-quotidian life. Lechner proposes that we should see quotidian life like a bridge space for the social sciences, and as the crossroads of two relations; the relation between macro and micro processes, and the relation between the quotidian life of persons and their actual life conditions.

Studies of everyday life understood in this way, and linked to an alternative social psychology, call for a general attitude of critique (Jiménez 1983–88), a questioning of present knowledge which rearticulates it at the methodological and theoretical level for producing specific explanations. It is in *this* framework that Participant Action Research coming from militant sociology, and even the action research coming from Lewinian social psychology, can be reinterpreted and used to validate and refine knowledge, and to turn it into social action.

CONCLUSIONS

Participant Action Research has been identified as an alternative methodology by Latin-American social communitarian psychology projects since the beginning of the 1980s, and in new social psychological critiques towards the end of the decade. Despite this, its theoretical development and its complex articulation as an alternative practice in social psychology has been insuffi-

cient, and substituted by general proposals based on a teleological and politically moral fundamentalism. It must be acknowledged that the experiences,
contributions, difficulties, contradictions and critical evaluations of Participant Action Research in the 1970s are not well known, and the proposals are
taken from general and secondary sources. This is a problem, however, which
afflicts all those attempting to take up its proposals. In addition, experiences
in community social psychology are very scarce, not well elaborated, and
almost unknown. Participant Action Research must be critically reworked,
and this re-evaluation must take into consideration the new situations in
which we are living at the end of the millennium, the new forms of conceiving science and politics, the disenchantment with authoritarian fundamentalism and objectivist holism in both fields, and also the opening to new
concepts and a language free of rigid models and self-censorship. In social
psychology the study of quotidian life permits us to incorporate a critical and
constructionist vision on the socialisation process, as a microsocial expression of elaborated macrosocial processes or, as Lechner says, quotidian practices produce the objective life conditions. That could be the redefined field
for a progressive Participant Action Research which would complement
Marxist theory and practice.

Acknowledgement. This chapter, which is adapted from work published in
M. Montero (ed.) (in press) *Psicología Social Comunitaria: Teoría, Practica
y Experiencias Latinoamericanas* (University of Guadalajara), was translated in collaboration with Dr Joan Pujol, Universitat Autonoma de
Barcelona and Ian Parker.

REFERENCES

Baudrillard, J. (1978) *A la Sombra de las Mayorías Silenciosas*, Barcelona:
    Kairós.
Briones, G. (1978) 'Sobre Cuestiones de Objeto y Método en la Investi-
    gación Militante', in *Simposio Mundial de Cartagena, Crítica y Política
    en Ciencias Sociales, vol. I*, Bogotá: Punta de Lanza.
Cano, F. (1988) 'La Subjetividad como Objeto de la Psicología y los modos
    de Investigación', *Cuadernos de Psicología* 9, p. 2.
Carvajal, C. (1984) 'La Psicología Social Comunitaria: una discusión abi-
    erta'. (Unpublished.)
Demo, P. (1985) *Investigación Participante. Mito y Realidad*, Buenos Aires:
    Kapelusz.
Fals-Borda, O., Bonilla, V., Castillo, G. and Libreros, A. (1972) *Causa
    Popular, Ciencia Popular*, Bogotá: Publicaciones de la Rosca.
Fals-Borda, O. (1973) 'Reflexiones sobre la aplicación del método de Estu-
    dio-Acción en Colombia', *Revista Mexicana de Sociología* 35, p. 1.
Giroux, H. and McLaren, O. (1986) 'Teacher Education and Politics of
    engagement: the case for democratic schooling', *Harvard Educational
    Review* 56, p. 5.
Grupo Acción Psicologia Social (n.d.) mimeo, Iztapalapa: UAM.

Jiménez, B. (1983) *Evaluación Crítica y Alternativa en Psicología Social Comunitaria*, Bogotá: II Seminario de Psicología Comunitaria.

Jiménez, B. (1988) *La Enseñanza de la Psicología como Historia y como Política Cultural*, Guadalajara: Universidad de Guadalajara.

Jiménez, B. (1991) 'Investigación Acción Participante: una dimensión desconocida', Simposio Construcción y Crítica de la Psicología Social, XXIII Congreso de la SIP. San José (Costa Rica), 7–12 July.

Kalmanovitz, S. (1983) *El Desarrollo Tardío del Capitalismo. Un enfoque crítico de la Teoría de la Dependencia*, Bogotá: Siglo XXI.

Lechner, N. (1990) *Los Patios interiores de la Democracia: Subjetividad y Política*, Santiago de Chile: Fondo de Cultura Económico.

Marín, G. (1983) 'The Latin American Experience in Applying Social Psychology to Community Change', in F. Blackler (ed.) *Social Psychology and Developing Countries*, New York: John Wiley & Sons.

Martín-Baró, I. (1988) 'Hacia una Psicología Política Latinoamericana', in B. Jiménez and G. Pacheco (eds) (1990) *Ignacio Martín-Baró (1942–1989) Psicología de la Liberación para América Latina*, Guadalajara: University of Guadalajara and ITESO.

Martín-Baró, I. (1989) 'Retos y Perspectivas de la Psicología Latinoamericana', in B. Jiménez and G. Pachecho (eds) (1990) *Ignacio Martín-Baró (1942–1989) Psicología de la Liberación para América Latina*, Guadalajara: University of Guadalajara and ITESO.

Molano, A. (1978) 'Anotaciones acerca del papel de la Política en la investigación social', in *Simposio Mundial de Cartagena, Crítica y Política en Ciencias Sociales, vol. I*, Bogotá: Punta de Lanza.

Montero, M. (1983) *La Psicología Comunitaria y el Cambio Social. En Búsqueda de una Teoría*, Bogotá: Taller-Seminario sobre Psicología Comunitaria.

Montero, M. (1990) 'Psicología de la Liberación. Propuesta para una Teoría Psicosociológica', Simposio sobre Cultura y Situación Psicosocial en America Latina, Hamburgo.

Montero, M. (1991) personal communication.

Pareek, U. (1978) 'El Papel de la Investigación-Acción en la elaboración de sistemas autorenovadores', in *Simposio Mundial de Cartagena, Crítica y Política en Ciencias Sociales, vol. II*, Bogotá: Punta de Lanza.

Parra, E. (1983) *La Investigación-Acción en la Costa Atlántica*, California: FUNCOP.

Pereda, L. (1990) 'Conceptos inestables', *Sociológica* 5, pp. 14–24.

Pipitone, U. (1991) 'La Tercera Oleada', *La Jornada*, no 2423.

Quintanilla, L. (1980) 'La Psicología Social Aplicada en una comunidad marginada a partir de su propio autodiagnóstico', in *I Seminario Interamericano sobre Psicología de la Comunidad*, Havana: Cuba.

Sanguinetti, Y. (1981) 'La investigación en los procesos de desarrollo en América Latina', *Revista de la ALAPSO*, vol. II.

Zamora, A. (1990) 'Aproximaciones para el estudio de la Acción social: De los reduccionismos objetivistas y subjetivistas a propuestas globalizadoras', *Sociológica* 5, no. 14. UNAM-Azcapotzalco.

18

THE REACTIONARY PRACTICE OF RADICAL PSYCHOLOGY: REVOKING THE FAUSTIAN CONTRACT

Stephen Reicher

'I CAN SAY WHAT I LIKE ...'

As an academic, I can say what I like. Were I tempted to deny it, the very existence of this chapter could be used against me. In addition, the time I spend in writing, the word-processor with which I write, even the postage stamp I use, are all paid for through government expenditure. Of course it can easily be countered that, as with all formal rights that exist in a capitalist social formation, such an assertion ignores the structural limitations upon my ability to act. What are the conditions under which psychology becomes constituted as an academic discipline? What criteria must I satisfy in order to be accepted into the discipline? Who provides funding for me to do research and how is that funding constrained? What sort of writing is considered is to be of value, what sort of outlets are deemed to have status and who are the gatekeepers to these outlets? Thus a chapter in a book on psychology and Marxism may be tolerated as a sort of eccentric pastime amongst my other work. However it is unlikely to be held up to the greater glory of myself or my institution. Were I to produce nothing but, the tolerance may become strained.

What is more, even the space which exists for critical work becomes squeezed under conditions of crisis. This is clearly illustrated by developments in the British University system in parallel with Conservative attempts to restructure the economy over the last decade or so. There has been an interlocking set of changes. First, the so-called system of 'dual support' whereby every department received both teaching and research money as of right has been replaced by one where an increasing proportion of research money goes to research councils to which one makes competitive bids. Secondly, the research councils devote increasing proportions of their money to central initiatives which address 'socially relevant' issues (which, naturally, means the concerns of state). Thirdly, the remaining amount of research money allocated directly to departments depends upon their research rating. Like a hotel guide, this is a five-star system which depends, in large part, upon a central panel's assessment of our publications. Of particular value are articles in the high status traditional journals. The upshot of all this is that survival depends upon fitting to the concerns of government, of industry and the traditional mainstream of the discipline. Those who wish to dissent damage not only themselves but also those with whom they live and work day by day. If not simple self-interest, a sense of collective responsibility and collective pressure act as powerful disincentives.

However, important as it is to identify the constraints upon our freedom of expression and to analyse the conditions under which these constraints wax and wane, it remains undeniable that they are not prohibitions. Pockets of critical work are apparent throughout psychology: in the area of race, in research into the social antecedents of mental distress and, perhaps most notably, in the flowering of work into gender and sexuality. We can and do regularly thumb our noses at our paylords. The reason why I wish to stress this freedom is not out of some empiricist belief in the predominance of autonomy over constraint, but rather because of the role it plays. Constraint is not the point. Even if enquiry were completely free, it would still be an abstract freedom and a practical sham. My argument is that the permission we have to produce knowledge does not extend to giving that knowledge effect. In fact, our right to research is bought at the cost of accepting a divorce between ideas of practice. The consequences of this are far more powerful in maintaining hegemony than any attempt to muzzle us.

'... IF I DO AS I'M TOLD'

At the height of the anti-apartheid upsurge in the mid-1980s one of the leaders of the National Education Crisis Committee (NECC) addressed a meeting in London. He drew a distinction between three classes of academic in South Africa: those who support apartheid, those who oppose it but are happy to benefit from it and, finally, those who are actively engaged in the liberation struggle. His point was that those passive opponents of apartheid are more dangerous than its proponents, since it was they who were most likely to bring about a breach of the boycott and thereby legitimise apartheid's educational institutions. However, his point was also that such people give a misleading idea of the role of the academy. There may be many who carped at apartheid, there are few who opposed it.

Lest this be thought melodramatic, it is worth recalling that when psychologists were recruited to the Nazi eugenic and extermination programs, not only did some provide the intellectual justification and some participate in the process of selection at the rate of 5 pfennigs per life, but not one single member of the profession actively raised a voice in protest

(Muller-Hill 1988). Given such wilful acquiescence, the direct application of constraint is relatively uncommon. Nevertheless, in those cases where critical ideas are matched by critical practice, the reaction becomes apparent on a number of institutional levels. I recall, a number of years ago a postgraduate student being warned that it was inappropriate for her to combine her research on unemployment with her work at an unemployed people's centre. I also remember being part of a series of workshops funded by the Social Science Research Council (SSRC) on 'race' and intergroup relations. At the end, we discussed the possibilities for future research with an attendant SSRC representative. As each successive topic was raised, the response was that it would be eligible for funding. No question, however critical, fell outside these limits – until the issue of practice was raised. In the context of addressing how to research the dynamics of anti-racist movements (no problem so far) it was pointed out that such work would be both impractical and unjustifiable unless one shared a commitment to the development of such movements. This was the sticking point. As the representative made clear, the SSRC might give us free rein to find out all about anti-racism as long as we didn't thereby support anti-racism.

If these prohibitions are informal and unwritten, the British Psychological Society (BPS) has gone further in explicitly dividing ideas from practice as part of defining what it means to be a professional. While the BPS allows that practitioners (who now need to go through scrutiny in order to qualify for the title 'chartered psychologist') may provide a service for their 'clients', researchers are debarred from providing any such services. To do so undermines the acceptability of the researcher and the 'objectivity' of the research. Thus, even if we managed to find alternative funds in order to do research with (rather than on) an anti-racist movement, the institution of psychology would certainly not applaud us, it would not even condone us: it would disown us. Were psychologists inclined to become activists, academic institutions, professional institutions and state institutions would all be ranged against them. Freedom of enquiry is only half of the story. Its presence depends upon the knowledge remaining abstracted. I can say what I like, but only if I do as I'm told.

THE PERILS OF PASSIVITY

Obviously, the fact that we are discouraged from intervening in the usage of our research does not mean that it is not used. It simply means that there is no counter-weight to its use by those who are sufficiently rich enough and organised to fund or to monitor research. Exploration has always been linked to processes of control. This is true literally, whether one refers to the Belgian funding of Stanley's travels down the Congo, linked to Belgian colonial ambitions in Africa (Levering-Lewis 1988); to the British funding of explorers along the North-West frontier of the Indian empire, linked to British fears of Russian imperial advances (Keay 1993) or, more recently, to the Americans placing a man on the moon, where the 'giant leap for mankind' was, more parochially, to be a manoeuvre against Soviet domination of space.

In the case of psychology, explorations of the psyche have more to do with what Rose (1989) calls 'governing the soul'. However they differ from physical exploration in that they not only 'discover' aspects of psychology that facilitate domination, they also create forms of subjectivity which are necessary to the social order. One of the clearest examples of this concerns the development of social psychology in the United States (Paichler 1988). One of the greatest problems for the producers of the time lay in the creation of a mass market. Fordism in production would be of little use unless supply was met by demand on a similar scale. How then could a society composed of immigrants from all over the world be turned into a unified set of consumers? As Paichler puts it: 'these immigrants posed "social" problems. They needed to be employed, educated and integrated, in a word *Americanised*' (emphasis in the original) (1988, p. 65). Social psychology eagerly lent itself to participating in this task. In April 1921, when the *Journal of Abnormal Psychology* renamed itself the *Journal of Abnormal and Social Psychology* it marked the transition with an editorial which outlined the practical applications of the new discipline:

The most important of these is the problem of socialisation, the fitting of the behaviour to the social order. Socialisation involves likewise a reconstruction or reorganisation of the social order so that it shall be better fitted to the individual (quoted in Paichler 1988, p.71).

This symbiotic relationship between psychology and the social order is not only a matter of the discipline itself, it is also a matter of wider institutional constraints. In the late 1980s, for instance, the then British Department of Education proposed a scheme whereby all university courses contain an 'enterprise' element which relates the discipline to its usage in the community. Institutions were invited to bid for funds to develop the scheme. However the term 'community' was in practice extremely one sided. It meant working with employers and with state institutions. It did not mean forming relationships with trades unions, tenants, organisations and the like. It certainly excluded links with activist campaigns of any sort. Increased 'community' involvement in the University Funding Council actually meant the appointment of business magnates to control universities. No clearer example could be given of the apparent neutrality of academia in practice denoting service in the cause of capital. Similarly, the adoption of a neutral stance with regard to the usage of academic work in practice means colluding with the cause of capital.

However, there is more to it than that. Such passivity not only provides a technical service for the existing order, it also serves a key ideological role. In pre-capitalist social formations, the juridical subordination of some people to others was plain for all to see and therefore had to be justified by the notion of an unalterable human hierachy. Such a justifica-

tion was found in the transcendental sphere of religion which thereby lay
at the heart of ideological practices (Engels, in Marx and Engels 1970). In
contrast, capitalism itself involves juridically free subjects who are equally
at liberty to enter into systems of exchange. For Marx, the market is 'a
very Eden of the innate rights of man. There alone rule Freedom, Equality,
Property and Bentham' (Marx 1974, p. 172). Of course, such rights to buy
and sell ignore the difference in the sphere of production between those
who own the means of production and those who have to sell their labour
power in order to survive. Nevertheless, the ideological emphasis on liberty
and equality marks out our era from its forerunners.

The question which arises from this is how the illusion of universal
freedom is maintained. This is, clearly, a source of enduring controversy.
Recently, much stress has been laid upon the way in which ideas about
social relations stem from the limitations upon how people can relate to
each other in practice. Thus, as Larrain (1983) argues, if ideology is a
matter of ideas which express practice inadequately 'the reason for this is
not a faulty cognitive process but the limitations of practice itself' (1983,
p. 23). The implication of this is that one should look for a theory of
ideology in Marx's most extended analysis of the capitalist social formation – that is in the volumes of *Capital* (e.g. Mepham and Ruben, 1979).
However important this might be for substantiating bourgeois ideology, it
is also important to consider those institutions which serve to promulgate
and legitimate this ideology.

Different theorists have identified different candidates. Gramsci (1971),
for instance, stresses the central role of parliamentary democracy itself in
establishing all subjects as free to select who they will to rule them.
Althusser (1984) on the other hand, explicitly denies this and asserts that
'the ideological State apparatus which has been installed in the *dominant*
position in mature capitalist social formations ... is the *educational ideological apparatus'* (emphasis in the original) (1984, p. 26). For Althusser,
educational institutions work by drumming into students a certain amount
of 'know-how' wrapped in the ruling ideology, by serving up the ruling
ideology in its pure state and by ejecting differing cohorts of youth each
equiped with the appropriate ideology to serve their role in class society.
For professional ideologists, into which category we probably fall, this consists of the 'ability to treat consciousnesses with the respect i.e. with the
contempt, blackmail and demagogy they deserve, adapted to the accents of
Morality, of Virtue, of "Transcendence", of the Nation ... etc.' (p. 30).

I do not wish to deny that such craven compliance exists, I only wish
to add that the apparent freedom of opposition reinforces rather than
undermines the ideological role of the academy. By dissenting, and by
doing so on public funds, we serve further to reinforce the idea of liberty.
The fact that we can speak threatens to be far louder than anything we
might say. A few troublesome academics play a valuable role for Vice-
Chancellors and Ministers who can point to them and then ask, quite
compellingly, 'how can you say we don't live in a free society?' Through
this, higher education not only inculcates the idea, it also (like parliamen-

tary democracy) illustrates the practice of bourgeois freedom – and hence reinforces Althusser's insistence on the ideological centrality of education. It is also this which makes the radical academic such a pathetic figure and such a figure of fun (Malcolm Bradbury's 'History Man' being a case in point). The more we criticise the system, the more we give it credibility. The more we struggle to get out of the web the more we become entangled in it. Our very existence threatens to negate everything we believe in. Once again, then, passivity becomes the opposite of neutrality. Our ideas can be held up as demonstrating the benevolence of the system. If these are not sufficient grounds for action, there is a further danger that the separation of ideas from action may distort our very object of study as psychologists.

A FAUSTIAN CONTRACT

If the separation between ideas and practice is ultimately a political constraint, its maintenance depends upon a series of epistemologies, methodologies and theories which shape the nature of psychology. The predominant ideal of psychology as science has us serenely observing, describing, analysing and measuring a world which is 'out there'. Occasionally the psychologist may slip from this Olympian detachment and influence that which he or she is studying. However this is poor design, sloppiness or error to be described in such terms as 'experimenter bias' or 'demand effects'. They are signs of methodological weakness rather than inherent problems.

Such an ideal assumes that the outcome of research is independent of the process of research, that is to say, we are involved in discovering inherent truths about the 'real world'. It further assumes that we are studying phenomena which occur independently of us. Even outside our gaze, they would continue unperturbed. Finally, it is assumed that our measures extract and scale given characteristics of the phenomenon under study.

Such assumptions give considerable autonomy to the researcher for, if we are only searching for what already exists we do not need to ask about the effects of our interventions – except insofar as they cause actual distress. Ethics committees tend to be concerned with individual experience rather than ideological effects. Thus we can ask white children whether they believe black children to be stupid without considering whether asking the question leads them to consider their peers in racialised terms. Similarly, we may render gender identities salient in our studies on the grounds that these are identities to which people already subscribe, but without asking whether such procedures reinforce or else perpetuate ideologies of inequality. Being freed from responsibility for reproducing existing social relations, virtually no limits are placed upon what may be researched. Such uncomfortable considerations can be set aside in the quest for knowledge and career advancement.

Maintaining the myth of independence is therefore dependent on occluding the role of the experimenter and discarding any instances where that role comes into view. This is well illustrated by Sherif's famous 'boys' camp' studies which have so influenced the psychology of intergroup relations (Sherif 1967). These studies have always been represented as examining the interactions between two groups of boys; how they become hostile when put in competition and how this hostility is attenuated when they combine to attain mutually valued goals. One of the most famous incidents occurs when Sherif takes the two groups and tells them that there will be a reconciliation banquet which will allow the competing groups to overcome their hostility, but where the food has been deliberately spoilt. What is particularly interesting is that the well known studies are in 1949 and 1954 when the boys construe their social relations as Sherif desires. However there was a third study in 1953 when the boys realised that they were being set against each other and did turn against the staff. Having exposed the role of the experimenter, the study was abandoned and was never fully written up.

This instance is particularly powerful since resistance to the experimenters exposes their role and requires a deliberate act of suppression. However, the disappearance of the researcher from the process of research is not limited to such dramatic examples, it is endemic within psychology. Consider the whole enterprise of psychometrics where the isolated individual is given some scale designed to measure some internal construct – whether it be personality, intelligence, attitudes or whatever. The assumption is that the scale is a tool of extraction: it allows the expression of that which exists inside the head. The fact that filling in a scale is an act of communication is ignored. The possibility that responses may depend upon who subjects think they are communicating with, what they think of these people and what they want to say to them is likewise ignored. If, say, black youth view an IQ test as an act of oppression and refuse to take it seriously, this is read as inability to respond in the terms the experimenter requires. The inter-personal and more general politics of communication cannot be taken into account as long as the experimenter is removed from the interaction (Reicher 1993).

Likewise, the classic cognition paradigm involves an individual alone in front of a tachistoscope or, latterly, a computer screen and responding to the stimuli presented. Here again it is assumed that this can assess mental functioning in its pure form. However the fact that computerisation has removed the subject from direct contact with the experimenter does not render the relationship irrelevant. In the first place, the use of a computer involves an indirect interaction with the programmer. In the second place the subject's performance will still be determined by their assumptions about the nature of the task, the requirements of the researcher and their willingness to fulfil those requirements (Stapel et al. 1994).

This great disappearing trick has three consequences for the nature of psychological theory. First, the fact that the role of the researcher in constructing the context and the terms in which subjects respond means that these constructions are taken for granted. Existent social relations are reified, the processes through which they are constructed are characteristically ignored. Secondly, the importance of power relations in structuring human action is likewise ignored. Indeed, it might be said that power is the great missing term in psychology. Thirdly, insofar as the behaviour of the subject is abstracted from the process of interaction with the researcher, it is characteristically represented as deriving from determining internal processes. This gives rise to an image of the subject as essentially passive, as acting out rules and principles which are controlling rather than controlled. It is a subject without agency.

The ultimate irony is that we have bought our own autonomy as academics at the cost of denying autonomy to those that we study. To risk a poetic allusion: we have bought our own freedom at the cost of everyone else's soul – a truly Faustian contract. Such limiting concepts of the discipline are not only intellectually impoverishing, they also have direct political consequences. As Billig (1987) argues, the proliferation of psychologies which deny agency is part and parcel of constructing both a passive subjectivity and pacifying social practices. In Foucauldian terms it is a technique of governance. From a Marxist perspective it is important to add that it is governance in opposition to social change.

PRACTICE MAKES PERFECT

The aim of this chapter has been to show that critical ideas in the absence of a critical practice do more to sustain than to undermine the social order: the reactionary uses of psychological technologies goes on undisturbed, the illusion of bourgeois democracy is reinforced and our own passivity is translated into a general notion of subjectivity. Gramsci remarked that the process of abstract thought is 'one typical of pure intellectuals (or pure asses)' (quoted in Merrington 1977, p. 149). How, then, is it possible to overcome the breach between ideas and practice, and thereby to rescue the radical psychologist from assininity?

In order to address this question is is worth looking at Gramsci's analysis in more detail (Gramsci 1971, 1985). For Gramsci, there is no independent class of intellectuals, but rather every social group has its own stratum, or else tends to form one. Moreover a distinction can be made between 'traditional' intellectuals whose work continues without reference to even the most profound changes in political/social forms, and 'organic' intellectuals whose work is intimately related to the activities of social classes. The task of the revolutionary movement is to win over the traditional intellectual and, above all, to develop its stratum of organic intellectuals. These will develop 'directly out of the masses, but remain in contact with them' (1971, p. 340). Their task is to make coherent 'the principles and the problems raised by the masses in their practical activity, thus constituting a cultural and social bloc' (1971, p. 330).

As Merrington (1977) notes, this concept of the intellectual involves breaking down the distinction between mental and manual labour. All workers are intellectuals insofar as they participate in a world-conception, all intellectuals should be actively involved in practical life. This need not necessarily imply the destruction of the academy. However, it does imply an integral link between the academy and working-class movements. In Gramsci's time, with an unstable state, with mass state education in its infancy, and prior to the commercialisation of leisure, it was possible for such movements to develop their own institutions affecting all spheres of life. However in developed capitalist societies at the end of the twentieth century these conditions no longer apply. The notion of the Trades Union movement, the women's movement or other movements of the exploited and oppressed having their own academies is simply not on the agenda in the short term (although reforming the agenda is an important task). Most psychologists work in universities or in the health services. The question becomes, can we address the 'principles and problems raised by the masses' from our position within ideological state apparatuses and, if so, how?

I will finish by suggesting three areas of activity in which radical psychologists should be involved if we are to move nearer to becoming 'organic intellectuals'. The first issue is access. Universities are peopled by an overwhelming disproportion of the middle classes. If future psychologists are to come from the masses and address the problems raised by their activity, the academic of today cannot abstain from the fight to ensure entry for students who have traditionally been denied a university education.

Secondly, it is necessary to legitimate the problems of the masses, and the way in which psychology relates to these problems, as acceptable subjects of study. This is not simply a matter of addressing the syllabus, it also means ensuring that, once qualified, those who enquire into such issues can maintain their positions. It means creating all those structures by which traditional academics sustain and promote themselves: books, journals, conferences, summer schools and so on. Quite apart from providing the citations which are necessary to survive in the academy, such structures will help to bring together and empower radical psychologists who otherwise may feel isolated and undermined in their individual institutions.

Thirdly, entry to and survival in our institutions will be futile unless our work does directly arise out of the experiences of those to whom we orientate politically and serves to advance their causes. It is not for us to decide what the problems of working-class people, of women, black people etc. might be, but rather for us to respond to the issues as experienced by such groups themselves. In other words we need to place ourselves in relation to the organisations of exploited and oppressed people. Such a task cannot be undertaken individually, it requires the organisation of radical psychologists. Over many years and in many different organisations, radical psychologists have organised. However, they have predominantly limited themselves to an intellectual critique of the reactionary nature of psychology (Reicher and Parker 1993). In July 1994, a new organisation of psychologists and non-psychologists entitled 'Psychology Politics Resistance' (PPR) was formed with the following aims:

- To expose the oppressive consequences of current psychological ideas, practices and institutions and to contest them wherever they appear.

- To promote the development and dissemination of emancipatory psychologies in opposition to oppressive practices of all kinds.

- To support those individuals and organisations who seek help in challenging the contribution of psychology to their oppression or exploitation.

- To contest the oppressive and exploitative usage of psychological ideas in public debate.

- To persuade both individual psychologists and organisations of psychologists to adopt an active opposition to exploitation and oppression as a central aspect of their work and, in particular, to encourage such considerations as a key element in the education of all psychologists.

Whatever the fate of PPR itself, it points, especially in the third aim, towards the minimum conditions for giving substance to the term 'radical psychologist'. Clearly, this is not the same as a Marxist psychological practice – which must involve a political analysis of those forces and those struggles with which we should be involved on the basis of a commitment to transcend, rather than to humanise, the existing social order. However, it is a minimum condition for creating the context out of which Marxist psychology could be born.

REFERENCES

Althusser, L. (1984) *Essays on Ideology*, London: Verso.
Billig, M. (1987) *Arguing and Thinking*, Cambridge: Cambridge University Press.
Chomsky, N. (1972) *Problems of Knowledge and Freedom*, London: Fontana.
Gramsci, A. (1971) *Selections from the Prison Notebooks*, London: Lawrence & Wishart.
Gramsci, A. (1985) *Selections from Cultural Writings*, London: Lawrence & Wishart.
Keay, J. (1993) *The Gilgit Game*, Karachi: Oxford University Press Pakistan.
Larrain, J. (1983) *Marxism and Ideology*, London: Macmillan.
Levering-Lewis, D. (1988) *The Road to Fashoda*, London: Bloomsbury,
Marx, K. (1974) *Capital. Vol. 1*, London: Lawrence & Wishart.
Marx, K. and Engels, F. (1970) *Selected Works in One Volume*, London: Lawrence & Wishart.
Mepham, J. and Ruben, D.-H. (1979) *Issues in Marxist Philosophy (3 vols)*, Brighton, Harvester Press.

Merrington, J. (1977) 'Theory and Practice in Gramsci's Marxis', in New Left Review (ed.) *Western Marxism: A Critical Reader*, London: New Left Books.

Muller-Hill, B. (1988) *Murderous Science*, Oxford: Oxford University Press.

Ng, S.H. (1980) *The Social Psychology of Power*, London: Academic Press.

Paichler, G. (1988) *The Psychology of Social Influence*, Cambridge: Cambridge University Press and Paris: Maison des Sciences de l'Homme.

Reicher, S.D. (1993) 'Policing normality and pathologising protest', *Changes* **11**, pp. 121–6.

Reicher, S. and Levine, M. (1994a) 'Deindividuation, power relations between groups and the expression of social identity: the effects of visibility to the out-group', *British Journal of Social Psychology* **33**, pp. 145–63.

Reicher, S. and Parker, I. (1993) 'Psychology, Politics, Resistance: the birth of a new organisation', *Journal of Community and Applied Social Psychology* **3**, pp. 77–80.

Rose, N. (1989) *Governing the Soul*, London: Routledge.

Sherif, M. (1967) *Group Conflict and Cooperation: Their Social Psychology*, London: Routledge & Kegan Paul.

Stapel, D., Reicher, S.D. and Spears, R. (1994) 'Some contextual modifiers of the availability heuristic', *European Journal of Social Psychology*.

INDEX

Index by Linda English